A READER'S PRAYER

Charles Lamb once said he felt more like saying grace before a good book than before meat. H.H. Barstow, receiving his suggestion from Dr. Henry Van Dyke's "Writer's Prayer," in "The Ruling Passion," gives us a suggestive "Reader's Prayer."

Lord, let me never slight the meaning nor the moral of anything I read. Make me respect my mind so much that I dare not read what has no meaning nor moral. Help me choose with equal care my friends and my books, because they are both for life. Show me that as in a river, so in reading, the depths hold more strength and beauty than the shallows. Teach me to value art without being blind to thought. Keep me from caring more for much reading than for careful reading: for books than the Book. Give me an ideal that will let me read only the best, and when that is done, stop me. Repay me with power to teach others, and then help me to say from a disciplined mind a grateful Amen.

The People
You Meet
&
The Books
You Read

Books by Charles E. Jones

Life Is Tremendous
Humor is Tremendous
Wit and Wisdom
The Books You Read—Business Edition
The Books You Read—Professional Edition
The Books You Read—Devotional Edition
The Books You Read—Historical Edition
The Books You Read—Classical Edition—1992
The Books You Read—International Edition—1993

You are the same today
as you will be five years from now
except for two things—

The
People You Meet and
THE BOOKS
You Read

edited by
Charles E. Jones

Foreword by
James Newton

Published by
Executive Books
P.O. Box 1044, Harrisburg, PA 17108

THANK YOU

Willard Neisen

Mike Kubiatowicz

Ernie Reisenger

For LOVING and SHARING BOOKS

THE WORLD OF BOOKS

...is the most remarkable creation of man. Nothing else that he builds ever lasts. Monuments fall ... nations perish ... civilizations grow old and die out. After an era of darkness people build new nations. But in the world of books there are volumes that live on, still as young and fresh as the day they were written ... still telling men's thoughts of generations long past.

—Clarence Day

Foreword

by James Newton

Many years ago I had the immense good fortune to spend a great deal of time with the industrialists Henry Ford, Harvey Firestone, the unparalleled inventor, Thomas Edison, Charles Lindbergh, aviator, scientist and thinker, and Nobel Prize winner Dr. Alexis Carrel. The wisdom that these men passed along to me, when I was finding my way as a young man, became a guide in developing my God-given potential, as well as the basis for my book *Uncommon Friends* (HBJ 1987). In his monumental collection of wisdom from the great thinkers and achievers of history, Charlie Jones has enabled us to read what shaped the lives of those who were history makers. You are in for quite a personal adventure.

This book has brought back a flood of warm memories of the times I've spent with Thomas Edison observing his humor and hunger for reading. His mother taught him to read because his teacher had given up on him. She said his mind was "addled." His mother not only taught him to read but challenged him later with difficult books to expand his thinking—a habit he never gave up.

I've seen him, after dinner parties at his home, sit off in the corner with a stack of books, and because of his almost total deafness, read one of them through while we talked of other things. He, like Lincoln, had read every good book he could get his hands on by the time he was fifteen years of age.

When Mr. Edison ran into a particularly difficult problem, he took his constantly expanding knowledge, a pole, line and hook (no bait) down to his dock and "fished." In this way, neither man nor fish bothered him.

His escalating knowledge and experience lifted him to a profound awareness of his Creator. He held up a glass of milk one day and said, "The Almighty is the best chemist after all." He went on to say, "The deeper I get into these things (science) the more I know there has to be Captain on the bridge." His last words on this earth were, "It's very beautiful over there."

My friend, Charles Lindbergh, had an expanding spiritual side to him also. The only book he took with him to the South Pacific in World War II, when he flew fifty combat missions as a civilian and upped the range of our fighters immensely, was the New Testament. He said to me, "This wouldn't have been my choice ten years ago." He carried that book with him the rest of his life.

In countless conversations with these special friends, I saw what their self-built storehouse of history meant to them. A consistent habit they all shared was their learning from others. As Sir Isaac Newton said when asked how he was able to write the *Principia*, "I stood on the shoulders of giants."

In addition to the library I gathered myself, a lot of my reading came from great books sent to me by friends, especially Charles and Anne Morrow Lindbergh. Those books were always relevant to my life and our times--as you will find this one that you hold. To this day I have the autographed red letter Bible and *McGuffy Readers* from Henry Ford. I treasure receiving books from young and old friends across the world and sharing those I have discovered.

Thanks to Charlie Jones we, too, can now stand "on the shoulders of giants."

The future is brightly lit with the light of the great minds shining from these pages. And standing at the control switch with a twinkle in his eye and an impish grin, ready to go "fishing", is the Wizard of Menlo Park.

So take your pole, line, hook (no bait) and meet Thomas Edison on the dock.

Contents

Great Thoughts on History

The Books That Shaped
the History Makers

Edward Everett Hale & Books   110

A School Teacher Makes a President   120-121
Herbert Hoover

Presidents of the United States   130-131
James Buchanan-Zachary Taylor-Andrew Johnson

Advice to Law Students   132-133
Thomas Jefferson

The Book

Read Good American Biographies 195
William Lyon Phelps

You must know History—George S. Patton 198-199

The Making of a President—James Polk 207

Serious Books Produce Serious Men—John Randolph 213

On Reading Lenin—Will Rogers 217

Great Thoughts on Reading

HISTORY IS BIOGRAPHY

The important part of **history is biography.**

Men epitomize periods. If you fully comprehend the man's life, you will understand the forces that shaped his character and the influence of his personality upon the time.

If you understand the life of Abraham Lincoln, you know the history of America's frontier days and of her Civil War.

If you know Robert Clive and his career in the Orient, you grasp the kernel of knowledge of England's conquest of India.

If you appreciate all of the life of the Little Corsican, Napoleon, you piece the soul of the history of the times that enveloped him.

They focus the essential historical elements into a small space.

Dates and dry-as-dust facts are of slender importance for the future. Motives, ideas and reactions are of primary significance.

One focuses the attention upon the dead phase of history, the other upon the loving phase which helps illuminate the road of history that is in the making.

Not only is biography an aid to correct understanding of any age, but it is the most fascinating avenue of approach.

First and last we are interested in men.

Personalities rather than ideas hold our attention.

Biography is history in its most assimilable form.

—Dr. Frank Crane

In books you can read the minds of the best men.
—Alfred A. Montapert

GREAT THOUGHTS ON HISTORY

The best service a book can render you is, not to impart truth, but to make you think it out for yourself.
—Elbert G. Hubbard

A Tribute to the Power
of the Printing Press

By Robert H. Davis, 1869-1942
Editor, Playwright;
Columnist for the New York Sun

"I am the printing press, born of the mother earth. My heart is of steel, my limbs are of iron, my fingers are of brass. I sing the songs of the world, the oratories of history, the symphonies of all time. I am the voice of today, the herald of tomorrow. I weave into the warp of the past the woof of the future. I tell the stories of peace and war alike. I make the human heart beat with passion or tenderness. I stir the pulse of nations, and make brave men do braver deeds, and soldiers die. I inspire the midnight toiler, weary at his loom, to life his head again and gaze, with fearlessness, into the vast beyond, seeking the consolation of a hope eternal.

"When I speak, a myriad people listen to my voice. All comprehend me. I am the tireless clarion of the news. I cry your joys and your sorrows every hour...I am light, knowledge, power. I epitomize the conquest of mind over matter. I am the record of all things mankind has achieved. My offspring comes to you in the candle's glow, amid the dim lamps of poverty, the splendor of riches; at sunrise, at high noon, and in the waning evening. I am the laughter and tears of the world, and I shall never die until all things return to the immutable dust. I am the printing press."

Fellow-Citizens, we cannot escape history. We...will be remembered in spite of ourselves. No personal significance can spare one or another of us. The fiery trial through which we pass will light us down in honor or dishonor, to the latest generation.

—Abraham Lincoln

Jefferson & the Bookburners

A Letter Written to Congress, September 21, 1814

On the night of August 24-25, 1814, General Robert Ross burned Washington. Most, though not all, of the infant congressional library went up in flames.

"I learn from the newspapers that the vandalism of our enemy has triumphed at Washington over science as well as the arts by the destruction of the public library with the noble edifice in which it was deposited... I presume it will be among the early objects of Congress to recommence their collection. This will be difficult while the war continues, and intercourse with Europe is attended with so much risk. You know my collection, its condition and extent...It is long since I have thought it ought not to continue private property, and had provided that at my death, Congress should have the refusal of it at their own price. The loss they have now incurred, makes the present the proper moment for their accommodation, without regard to the small remnant of time and barren use of my enjoying it. I ask of your friendship, therefore, to make for me the tender of it to the Library Committee of Congress...

I have been fifty years making it. ...While residing in Paris, I devoted every afternoon I was disengaged, for a summer or two, in examining all the principal bookstores, turning over every book with my own hand, and putting by everything which related to America...Besides this, I had standing orders during the whole time I was in Europe, on its principal book-marts, for such works relating to America as could not be found in Paris. So that, in that department particularly, such a collection was made as probably can never again be effected, because it is hardly probable that the same opportunities, the same industry, perseverance and expense, with the same knowledge of the bibliography of the subject, would again happen to be in concurrence."

Fiction Can Forecast History

By Brander Matthews, 1852-1929; Educator; Author, "The Development of the Drama"

When Mrs. Stowe visited the White House, Lincoln bent over her, saying, "And is this the little woman who made this big war?" A few years later the Tsar told Turgenef that the freeing of the serfs was the result of thoughts aroused in the autocrat of Russia by the reading of the novelist's story.

Consider how the chief qualities of a people are unconsciously disclosed in its novels. Robinson Crusoe is as typically English in his sturdiness and in his religious feeling as the sorrowful Werther is typically German or the light-hearted Manon Lescaut is typically French. Any one who chanced to be familiar with the serious fiction of Spain and America might have forecast the conduct of the recent war between the two countries and foretold the result. Perhaps the salient inconsistency of the Spanish character, the immense chasm between its poetic side and its prosaic, could be seized by the mastery of a single volume, one of the world's greatest books, *Don Quixote*.

The modern novel, wisely studied, is an instrument of great subtlety for the acquiring of a knowledge of ourselves and of our fellow men. It broadens our sympathy, by telling us how the other half lives, and it also sharpens our insight into humanity at large. It helps us to take a large and liberal view of life; it enlightens, it sustains, and it cheers. What Mr. John Morley once said of literature as a whole is even more accurate when applied to fiction alone: its purpose is "to bring sunshine into our hearts and to drive moonshine out of our heads."

The supreme purpose of history is a better world.
—Herbert Hoover

Historical Insight

By Albert Schweitzer, 1875-1965
Medical missionary, Nobel Peace Prize winner

We have not yet arrived at any reconciliation between history and modern thought—only between halfway history and halfway thought. What the ultimate goal towards which we are moving will be, what this something is which shall bring new life and new regulative principles to coming centuries, we do not know. We can only dimly divine that it will be the mighty deed of some mighty original genius, whose truth and rightness will be proved by the fact that we, working at our poor half thing, will oppose him might and main—we who imagine we long for nothing more eagerly than a genius powerful enough to open up with authority a new path for the world, seeing that we cannot succeed in moving it forward along the track which we have so laboriously prepared.

There are some who are historians by the grace of God, who from their mother's womb have an instinctive feeling for the real. They follow through all the intricacy and confusion of reported fact the pathway of reality, like a stream which, despite the rocks that encumber its inevitably to the sea. No erudition can supply the place of this historical instinct, but erudition sometimes serves a useful purpose, inasmuch as it produces in its possessors the pleasing belief that they are historians, and thus secures their services for the cause of history. In truth they are at best merely doing the preliminary spadework of history, collecting for a future historian the dry bones of face, from which, with the aid of his natural gift, he can recall the past to life.

The history of the world is in the record of man in quest of his daily bread and butter.

—Van Loon

The Value Of Reading History

By Helen Keller, 1880-1968
Blind lecturer; Author, "Out of the Dark"

Next to poetry I love history. I have read every historical work that I have been able to lay my hands on, from a catalogue of dry facts and dryer dates to Green's impartial, picturesque *History of the English People*, from Freeman's *History of Europe* to Emerton's *Middle Ages*. The first book that gave me any real sense of the value of history was Swinton's *World History*, which I received on my thirteenth birthday. Though I believe it is no longer considered valid, yet I have kept it ever since as one of my treasures. From it I learned how the races of men spread from land to land and built great cities, how a few great rulers, earthly Titans, put everything under their feet, and with a decisive word opened the gates of happiness for millions and closed upon millions more: how different nations pioneered in art and knowledge and broke ground for the mightier growths of coming ages; how civilization underwent, as it were, the holocaust of a degenerate age, and rose again, like a Phoenix, among the nobler sons of the North; and how by liberty, tolerance and education the great and wise have opened the way for the salvation of the whole world.

"All that Mankind has done, thought, gained or been is lying as in magic preservation in the pages of Books. They are the chosen possession of men."

—Carlyle

The men who make history have not the time to write it.

—Metternich

Thucydides: The Greatest Historian,
c. 460- c. 400 B.C.

Read by Thomas Macaulay, 1800-1859
Author, "History of England"

This day I finished Thucydides, after reading him with inexpressible interest and admiration. He is the greatest historian that ever lived. -February 27th, 1835.

I am still of the same mind. -May 30th, 1836.

The perfect historian is he in whose work the character and spirit of an age is exhibited in miniature. He relates no fact, he attributes no expression to his characters, which is not authenticated by sufficient testimony. By judicious selection, rejection and arrangement, he gives to truth those attractions which have been usurped by fiction. In his narrative a due subordination is observed: some transactions are prominent; others retire. But the scale on which he represents them is increased or diminished not according to the dignity of the persons concerned in them, but according to the degree in which they elucidate the condition of society and the nature of man. He shows us the court, the camp and the senate. But he shows us also the nation. He considers no anecdote, no peculiarity of manner, no familiar saying, as too significant for his notice which is not too insignificant to illustrate the operation of laws, of religion, and of education, and to mark the progress of the human mind. Men will not merely be described, but will be made intimately known to us.

Francis Parkman:
An Heroic Historian, 1823-93

By Lovell Thompson,
Writer, Saturday Review & Atlantic Monthly

One hundred years ago there was born in Boston a man who became, as we believe, the greatest of American historians and one of the five or six great historical writers of the world. No American who has not read the eight volumes in which Francis Parkman told the story of the struggle of France and England in the New World has any true notion of the dimensions or of the significance of the struggle, out of which issued two great nations—Canada and the United States; nor has he any idea of the vigor and charm that a great historian can impart to an historical narrative. Romance is implicit in the words of the French and English pioneers with each other and with the Indians; but it is romance that many a dry-as-dust historian successfully keeps from his pages. Parkman's distinction is that he produced a work both scholarly and delightful. Everything is carefully documented, as a result of painful and thorough research. The thing is so accurate and so complete that it left little for succeeding scholars to do; yet the books are as fascinating and as full of movement and color as a novel. Parkman's achievement is a remarkable triumph of the intellect and the imagination united—a work of genius.

It was a triumph too over obstacles and discouragements that would have broken the spirit of almost any other man. Delicate in health from his birth, he had hardly begun the task that he had set himself when his nerves and eyes gave out together. For years he was virtually blind and could open his eyes only in a darkened room. But he had books and documents read aloud to him, and he invented a contrivance that enabled him to write and make notes legibly with his eyes closed.

A Key to History: Biography

By Dr. George C. Lorimer, 1868-1937
Editor, Saturday Evening Post, 1899-1937

There is no real rivalry between philosophy and poetry. They are allies, not enemies, and their mission is to coordinate, not antagonistic; and it is the peculiar merit of Browning that in his words we behold the two in actual fellowship. The great charm of this wonderful author is that he enshrines philosophy in poetry, and offers poetry as a precious sacrifice on the altar of philosophy. As he has united them in his productions we ought not to divorce them in our reading. Ovid, Virgil, Horace, Edmund Spenser, Dryden, Tennyson, Longfellow, Bryant, Schiller and Racine, in addition to poets already named, ought to keep company with Socrates, Aristotle, Spinoza, Cousin, Hamilton, Hegel, Coleridge, and Emerson. This is a goodly fellowship and, like all true fellowships, mutually helpful.

But independent of its value as a key to history, biography has a worth all its own as an exposition of human nature and as an inspiration to the highest achievements. Who can forget the impression made on his mind by the reading of Plutarch's *Lives,* a book of the most stimulating qualities? It not only deals with ancient heroes, but it has made heroes. No doubt other volumes of a similar kind have been the real parents of many of the noblest characters that have appeared on the stage of time. It is impossible to compute the influence of Carlyle's *Oliver Cromwell,* or even Boswell's *Johnson,* a very different book indeed and with a very different hero. Such works place us on terms of fellowship with giant minds and gentle hearts, and at once humble and exalt us. They humble by making sadly apparent our own deficiencies, and they exalt by reminding us that we belong to the race which is continually producing men of glorious genius.

Gallery of Imagination

There is a certain art in reading. Passive reading is of very little use. We must try to realize what we read. Everybody thinks they know how to read and write; whereas very few people write well, or really know how to read. It is not enough to run our eye listlessly or mechanically along the lines and turn over the leaves; we must endeavor to realize the scenes described, and the persons who are mentioned, to picture them in the "Gallery of the Imagination."

—John Lubbock

Books are lighthouses erected in the great sea of time.
—E.P. Whipple

THE BOOKS THAT SHAPED THE HISTORY MAKERS

In old days books were rare and dear. Our ancestors had a difficulty in procuring them. Our difficulty now is what to select.
—John Lubbock

Book Of Knowledge

Read by Morris Abram, 1918-
President, Brandeis University; Representative, United Nations Commission on Human Rights

Even as a child I insisted on setting the record straight, a course that would later lead me to Rome and a frank talk with Pope Paul VI.

But this habit of contradicting established myth did not endear me to my schoolmates, nor did my noticeable abstention from the refrains of "Onward Christian Soldiers," which was a lot easier to sing than the National Anthem.

I was further estranged by my almost obsessive desire for learning. When I won the approval of good teachers, I found myself envied by my peers, whose paths I crossed on the way home, no longer protected by the discipline of the classroom.

As the separation grew between me and other children, I retreated increasingly into my world of books. When I was eight, mother bought the twenty-volume *Book of Knowledge*, and I set out to devour one subject after another; the *Book of Wonder*, about science; the *Book of Famous Men and Women*, about history. I provoked an intense quarrel with some of my classmates by bragging that "my parents had bought me a book that knew everything." Of course, my adversaries were correct—even the *Book of Knowledge* had its gaps—but it was painful to learn my error from the fists of those who had not even seen a single precious volume.

From the fifth grade on, that *Book of Knowledge* provided the source material for additions to class discussions on every subject. Mrs. Mathis, a fierce redheaded disciplinarian would have preferred, I suspect, to teach only me and a few others rather than a bored mass of thirty.

In the Heart of the Sierras

Author- James M. Hutchings
Read by Ansel Adams, 1902-1984
Photographer, Naturalist

In April 1916, I was in bed again, this time with a cold. Aunt Mary gave me her copy of *In the Heart of the Sierras*. I became hopelessly enthralled with the descriptions and illustrations of Yosemite and the romance and adventure of the cowboys and Indians. The text is florid, commonplace, and not too accurate, but I did not know that—I devoured every word and poured over the pages many times. The following quote from *In the Heart of the Sierras* was written by Dr. Lafayette Bunnell in 1851, who was a member of the first expedition of "white men" to "discover" Yosemite.

"None but those who have visited this most wonderful valley, can even imagine the feelings with which I looked upon the view that was there presented. The grandeur of the scene was but softened by the haze that hung over the valley—light as gossamer—and by the clouds which partially dimmed the higher cliffs and mountains.

"To obtain a more distinct and quiet view, I had left the trail and my horse and wallowed through the snow alone to a projecting granite rock. So interested was I in the scene before me, that I did not observe that my comrades had all moved on, and that I would soon be left indeed alone. My situation attracted the attention of Major Savage, who hailed me from the trail below with, 'You had better wake up from that dream up there, or you may lose your hair; I have no faith in Ten-ie-ya's statement that there are no Indians about here.' I hurriedly joined the Major on the descent, and as other views presented themselves, I said with some enthusiasm: 'If my hair is now required, I can depart in peace, for I have here seen the power and glory of a Supreme Being.'"

Great Women and Books

ABIGAIL ADAMS, 1744-1818
Wife of President John Adams; Noted Letter Writer

So the Quincy's fireside became Abby's second home; the large collection of books in their house, hers to enjoy—always remembering that of all the volumes both there and at her own home, the Bible was the most important, a familiar book to live by, to quote from, to pray from and to gain courage from.

In other books in both houses she read famous histories of England, and something of the younger history of these British colonies; for Massachusetts was a colony of King George II, and proud of it. Abigail prayed every day for the King and the royal family. She took patriotic pride in the works of William Shakespeare and of Alexander Pope; and when her grandmother introduced her to a British periodical of the early 1700's composed of essays full of wit and style and known as the *Spectator*, she made it at once and forever her literary model. —Dorthee Bobbe

MARY WALKER, 1832-1919
Pioneer

Mary's diary reflects the busy routine of the pioneer home. She refers to dipping candles, making soap, washing, baking, milking, and caring for little Cyrus. During the first months of 1840 she has the following entries about her reading: (Feb. 2) "Finished reading Baxter's life"; (Mar. 1) "Reading life of Brainerd"; (Mar. 8) "Have been reading Reinhard's Memoirs"; (June 7) "Have been reading Mrs. Trollopes Domestic Manual." Most of the references to her reading appear in her entries for a Sunday and indicate the way in which she spent the day. On November 22, 1840, she mentions giving "the Encyclopedia" to Cyrus in order that he might amuse himself by looking at the pictures.
—Clifford Drury

Great Women and Books

JANE ADDAMS, 1860-1935
Settlement Worker, Sociologist, Author

When Jane Addams was seventeen she went to Rockford Seminary, Illinois, which soon after became a college. Here she concentrated upon studying Greek and mathematics. "My genuine interest was history," she says, "partly because of a superior teacher, and partly because my father had always insisted upon a certain amount of historical reading ever since he had paid me, as a little girl, five cents a *Life* for each *Plutarch* hero I could intelligently report to him, and twenty-five cents for every volume of Irving's *Life of Washington*." —Sarah Bolton

LILLIAN MOLLER GILBRETH, 1878-1972
Engineer, Industrial Psychologist

When Lillian finally entered the Oakland public schools, she easily mastered the educational requirements. But the social hurdles were something else. Having constantly been unfavorably compared to her pretty little sister, she felt she was unattractive. "I ... decided very young, that since I couldn't be pretty, I had to be smart," Lillian later recalled.

Smart she was. Lillian became the teachers' pet, though her classmates were less than thrilled by her familiarity with the works of Emerson, Thoreau, Irving, Cooper, Louisa May Alcott, Longfellow, Whittier, and Lowell. In high school, Lillian was an honor student and an amateur poet and musician. She showed so much promise in music that her parents engaged composer John Metcalfe to give her lessons. Lillian wrote the lyrics for one of Metcalfe's songs, "Sunrise." But the composer refused to continue the lessons when Lillian decided to go to college. She must choose—music or books. For Lillian it was simple—she chose books. —Joan Marlow

Albert Gallatin, 1761-1849

"The Father of American Ethnology"
Read by Henry Adams, 1838-1918
Author, "History of the United States"

Adams studied American personalities because in America individuals typified the evolution of the race. "The interest in such a subject exceeded that of any other branch of science," for, as he ominously remarked, "it brought mankind within sight of its own end." Biographical ventures preceded the *History*. He assessed Federalist leaders in the *Documents Relating to New England Federalism*, he struggled with the erratic Virginian, John Randolph, and he drew the portrait of Albert Gallatin with sympathetic understanding.

Albert Gallatin, not Jefferson or Madison, was the hero of the *History*. "After long study of the prominent figures of our history, I am more than ever convinced that for combination of ability, integrity, knowledge, unselfishness, and social fitness, Mr. Gallatin has no equal. He was the most fully and most perfectly equipped statesman we can show. Other men, as I take hold of them, are soft in some spots and rough in others. Gallatin never gave way in my hand or seemed unfinished. That he made mistakes I can see, but even in his blunders he was respectable."

When Adams left Harvard in 1877 further to pursue his education, he was dissatisfied with the way history was taught and written. "A teacher," he wrote "must either treat history as a catalogue, a record, a romance, or an evolution; and whether he affirms or denies evolution, he falls into all the burning faggots of the pit. He makes of his scholars either priests or atheists, plutocrats or socialists, judges or anarchists, almost in spite of himself. In essence incoherent and immoral, history had either to be taught as such—or falsified."

—Bert James Loewenberg

Plato, 427-347 B.C.

Read by John Adams, 1735-1826
2nd President of the United States

from a Letter to Thomas Jefferson, 1814:

I am very glad you have seriously read Plato, and still more rejoiced to find that your reflections upon him so perfectly harmonize with mine. Some thirty years ago, I took upon me the severe task of going through all his works. With the help of two Latin translations and one English and one French translation, and comparing some of the most remarkable passages with the Greek, I labored through the tedious toil. My disappointment was very great, my astonishment was greater, and my disgust was shocking. Two things only did I learn from him. First, that Franklin's ideas of exempting husbandmen and mariners, &c., from the depredations of war, were borrowed from him; and second, that sneezing is a cure for the hiccoughs. Accordingly, I have cured myself and all my friends of that provoking disorder, for thirty years, with a pinch of snuff.

Some parts of some of his dialogues are entertaining, like the writings of Rousseau; but his *Laws* and his *Republic*, from which I expected most, disappointed me most. I could scarcely exclude the suspicion that he intended the latter as a bitter satire upon all republican governments. In a late letter to the learned and ingenious Mr. Taylor, of Hazelwood, I suggested to him the project of writing a novel in which the hero should be sent on his travels through Plato's republic, and all his adventures, with his observations on the principles and opinions, the arts and sciences, the manners, customs, and habits of the citizens, should be recorded. Nothing can be conceived more destructive of human happiness, more infallibly contrived to transform men and women into brutes, yahoos, or demons, than a community of wives and property.

Horace, 65-8 B.C.

Read by John Quincy Adams, 1767-1848
6th President of the United States

From the Diary of John Quincy Adams:

February 12: I am exceedingly pleased with what I have done in Horace; and have come across many very noble Sentiments. One of those in the 9th Ode, which I read this morning, comes, very near to one, that proceeded from the Saviour of the World. Matthew VI. 34. Take therefore no thought for the things of itself. Sufficient unto the day is the evil thereof. Horace Ode IX. 13. The writer, that has ideas, so correspondent to those uttered by the mouth of god, and that without the real inspiration, must very justly hold his rank among the greatest authors.

February 15: In the Evening I read the 5th Book of our Poem. This too seems to be entirely Episodic; and has no tendency to advance the Action, of the Poem; but it is in itself charming, and perhaps, if a Poem, is moral, instructive and entertaining it is not necessary that it should be confined to the severe rules of a phlegmatic, cold-blooded Critic. The Character and history of Irad appears to be an Imitation of that of Pallas, in Virgil, and the additional Circumstance of his being in Love, is not amiss. The Reflections upon the first fall, are noble, and pleasing, the different effects that the intention of Irad to join in the war, has upon Hezron, and Selima, are proper and natural. The Sentiment of Irad

But doom'd to fall, should Heaven my life demand
And death betide me from a heathen's hand,
I fall in Virtue's cause. Far happier doom,
In that bless's path, to find a speedy tomb!
Than, lost in sports, or sunk in shameful ease,
To drag a worthless life, and swell inglorious days.

...ought to be that of every youth, who wishes for the applause of his Country, and the Esteem of mankind.

Casa Guidi Windows

Author- Elizabeth Barrett Browning, 1806-1861
Read by Susan B. Anthony, 1820-1906
Founder, National Woman Suffrage Assoc.

To satisfy her longing for a better understanding of people and events, she turned to books, first to Elizabeth Barrett Browning's *Casa Guidi Windows*, which she called "a grand poem, so fitting to our terrible struggle," then to her *Sonnets from the Portuguese*, and George Eliot's popular *Adam Bede*, recently published. More serious reading also absorbed her, for she wanted to keep abreast of the most advanced thought of the day. "Am reading Buckle's *History of Civilization* and Darwin's *Descent of Man*," she wrote in her diary. "Have finished *Origin of the Species*. Pillsbury has just given me Emerson's poems."

She read, one after another, Carlyle's *Sartor Resartus*, George Sand's *Consuelo*, Madame de Stael's *Corinne*, then Frances Wright's *A Few Days in Athens* and Mrs. Gaskell's *Life of Charlotte Bronte*, making notes in her diary (1855) of passages she particularly liked. She discussed current events with her cousin Seth on long drives in the country, finding him a delightful companion, well-read, understanding, and interested in people and causes.

—Alma Lutz

"Cautious, careful people, always casting about to preserve their reputation and social standing, never can bring about a reform. Those who are really in earnest must be willing to be anything or nothing in the world's estimation."

—Susan B. Anthony

Up From Slavery

Author- Booker T. Washington, 1859-1915
Frank Willis Barnett, Journalist
Literary Digest, June 1922

Let any man, it makes no difference his race, color or creed, read the story and he will have to confess that it is a human document in a class by itself, and of tremendous significance not merely from the standpoint of personal endeavor, but from the impersonal consequences which flowed from one life into the lives of a people. This gives it its status as one of the great autobiographies of all time.

Truth is stranger than fiction, is a trite old adage, and yet it can never grow stale if used in connection with the story of such a one as "The Moses of His Race." The character could not have been invented even by a Shakespeare, "the myriad-minded," and if it had the critics would have written it down as being wholly beyond the bounds of human possibility. It staggers even the credulity of those who lived close to the man or followed the simple facts of the unknown slave boy from obscurity until he touched in a personal way the lives of millions of his race and stood in the presence of presidents and kings.

Born on a slave plantation in Virginia, near a crossroads post office named Hale's Ford, he is not sure of the place of his birth, but first saw the light in a typical cabin, about 14 by 16 feet square, where he lived with his mother and a brother and sister until after the Civil War, when they were all declared free. The day, the month or the year of his birth was unknown, though he thought it was some time in the year of 1858 or 1859. The great fact, however, is that he came into the world.

The man who was to receive an honorary degree from Harvard University says that the first thing he ever learned in a book was the number "18," which was the number alloted to his stepfather who worked in a salt factory, it being painted on the barrel under his charge. But it was a great day when his mother procured for him an old copy of Webster's "blue-back" spelling-book, and gave him a chance to wrestle with the alphabet without help from any one, as none of his race could read. Freedom set a race eager to master the art of reading, none were too young or too old to make the attempt. The great ambition of the older ones being to learn enough to read the Bible.

It was by chance that "Booker," while at work in a coal mine, happened to overhear the miners talking about a great school for colored-people somewhere in Virginia, and the story of how then and there he made up his mind to go to it and the terrible journey is one of the romances of education. Starting with a "blue-back" speller he gradually began to collect a "library." It was housed in a dry-goods box, knocked out on the sides and arranged with shelves in which were stored a few precious volumes. John helped him, and others gave him from a nickel to a quarter, and the great day came when he started from Malden, West Va., to Hampton, Va., about 500 miles away.

It was a trip as full of hardships for him as was the cross-country voyage of the '49er, who went to California in search of gold, with this difference, the lure before them were the golden sands, while the lone star which drew "Booker" was the chance to get an education. Money gone, he walked the streets of Richmond hungry, while at night he crawled beneath a board walk, and with his satchel for a pillow slept, on an empty stomach.

After getting work he continued to use his soft spot on the ground in order to save enough to get to his destination.

The Oxford Self-Pronouncing Bible
Read by Clarence W. Barron, 1855-1928
Publisher, Wall Street Journal

Clarence W. Barron—"CW" as I called him—publisher of the *Wall Street Journal*, always kept a volume of the Bible on his bedside table and read it first thing on arising in the morning and before retiring at night. He gave me what he considered the most useful edition of the Bible, *"The Oxford Self-Pronouncing Bible—Sunday School Teacher's Edition,"* printed on extremely thin paper, with many excellent maps and elaborate Cyclopedic Concordance. He often quoted the Bible to make a point in the letters he wrote me from his travels and on his return would question me as to what I thought of the relevance of the quotes. His letters meant so much to me that I pasted them into a special scrapbook. And I am still amazed at the way in which he was able to write to a girl fifty years younger than he was in a way that meant so very much her at the time.

CW urged me to keep a line-a-day diary. And he persuaded me to learn to type and to set up my own files of subjects for articles and stories.

He'd send me packages of books on every imaginable subject with no rhyme or reason in their selection. And he'd enclose a note asking me to write him what I thought of the books after I'd read them. He took all my ideas seriously and spent time, either arguing with me or questioning me as to why I felt as I did.

I have never known anyone more alive than CW. Even today when I think about him, as I do so often, I cannot help smiling to myself and feeling the same warmth I always felt in his presence. He made the world seem a glittering, exciting and very worthwhile place to be and that it was a privilege merely to be alive.

Everything by Henry & William James
Read by Ethel Barrymore, 1879-1959
American Actress

There were so many books that I loved, by such quite unlike authors—everything of Henry James—I loved his sentences that lasted for three pages—and, more exciting to me then and since, everything of his brother William's, too. I had a terrific "thing" about William James; I remember going to his house in Cambridge long after his death and sitting in his chair, a queer sort of rocking chair, and having a strange feeling of his presence in the room.

And at the same time I was reading Henry and William James, I was loving *The Story of an African Farm*, by Olive Schreiner, and *Friendship* and *Under Two Flags*, by Ouida, and those delightfully imaginative Ruritania books, The *Prisoner of Zenda*, and *Rupert of Hentzau*, by Anthony who invented the whole idea of an imaginary modern European kingdom that so many later writers have imitated. I have always resented those imitations. Anthony also invented another fiction form in *The Dolly Dialogues*, which he wrote when he was quite young.

I had begun to worship Mark Twain, and since I have been writing this book I have often thought of what he once wrote—"I find that the farther I go back the better I remember things, whether they happened or not."

It was some time after those days and nights at Mrs. Wilson's and on tour that I began to read and love poetry, but I never stopped reading it and loving it. I am an absolute lunatic about William Blake. I have a special love for Keats and Shelley, for some of Francis Thompson, for some of John Donne, for all Walt Whitman, for all of Shakespeare, not only the plays but the sonnets.

Caesar, Napoleon & Emerson

Read by Bruce Barton, 1886-1967
U. S. Congressman; Business Executive,
Author, "The Man Nobody Knows"

The other night my friend Ferrero and I spent a few years with Julius Caesar in ancient Rome.

We went with him on his campaigns in Gaul. Those were wonderful battles—wonderful fighters.

From a hill-top we could watch the whole battle—thousands of men driving at each other with their swords, hurling their javelins at short range. No smoke, no trenches; just primitive, hand-to-hand conflict.

We came back to Rome. The city was in a turmoil. Our great chariots thundered through the streets in triumph; our captives, our spoils, our banners made a magnificent procession. The crowds cheered wildly.

Another evening my friend Green and I had a great time together in ancient Britain.

We went down to Runnymede with a group of English nobles. They were powerful men, each a petty king in his own section; but every one of them took his life in his hand on that expedition. And there we gathered around King John, and forced him, against his will, to put his name to the Magna Charta, the Great Charter which is the foundation of English liberties—and our own.

I had a fine time with Napoleon a few nights before.

I met him when he landed in France, after the escape from Elba. Up through the southern provinces he came, gathering a few troops there, winning over by the force of his eloquence the regiments sent to capture him.

We arrived in Paris. Hurriedly, but with supreme confidence that the Little Corporal could never fail, we got together a makeshift army and set out to strike the winning blow at Waterloo.

That battle—I shall never forget it.

Another day I went over to old Concord, and spent the

whole afternoon with Emerson. We talked about Representative Men.

Well, well, you say, what foolishness is this? What do you mean by saying you lived with Caesar and Napoleon and Emerson—all centuries apart, all long since dead?

If you do not know what I mean, then I pity you.

Have you never come home tired from your office, and with a book transported your foolish little mind clear out of the present day? Have you never learned the joy of surrendering yourself to the companionship of the great men of the past?

Have you never sat in the little London Club and heard Sam Johnson thunder his philosophy of life? Have you never sailed up and down the American coast with Captain John Smith, dodging the Indians and opening up a new continent? Are you one of the wretched, poverty-stricken souls who have never learned to escape from yourself through the blessed magic of good books?

Have you contented yourself all your life with the companionship of good pinochle-players, when you might have been a familiar friend of Socrates and Milton and Napoleon and Cromwell and Washington and Columbus and Shakespeare and Lincoln and Rousseau?

If so, cut out this paragraph from a great and paste it in your hat: "I would rather be a beggar, and dwell in a garret, than a king who did not love books."

There are some marvelous experiences coming to you.

You can in the evenings to come jar yourself out of the petty rut where circumstance has placed you, and become a familiar of the immortals.

You may learn to face the world with a new confidence, a new poise, a new self-respect, because you have made yourself a citizen of the ages.

Do some real reading. Do it for the joy it will give you: do it for the good it will do you.

"Show me a family of readers," said Napoleon, "and I will show you the people who rule the world."

Abraham Lincoln

Read by William E. Barton, 1861-1930
Clergyman, Editor, Educator, Father of Bruce Barton

I first became dissatisfied with books and pamphlets concerning Lincoln's religion. It seemed to me that most of them attempted to prove that Lincoln held to the same general system of faith which the authors of these books professed. I noticed the laborious manner in which most of these books endeavored to prove that the skepticism which some of the authors admitted to have characterized Lincoln's youth, gave place to a practically complete acceptance of the orthodox religion. I was not convinced by the reasoning of these writers.

Furthermore, I did not find evidence that Lincoln was ever as skeptical as he sometimes was thought to have been. I knew, perhaps better than any biographer of Lincoln, just what kind of theology Lincoln heard preached in his boyhood, and if he revolted against it and was thought to have been an infidel, or even thought himself to have been one, I was in a fair position to judge of the extent and the quality of his supposed infidelity.

I owned a few of the standard Lives of Lincoln, but I had no Lincoln collection. I set about procuring every book that dealt in any important way with Lincoln's religion. I determined not to become a purchaser of rare and expensive Lincoln books. In the first place I did not need them, and in the next place I could not afford them. It was rather a momentous day for me when I paid thirty-five dollars for a first edition of Herndon's *Lincoln*. It seemed to me a very large price. However, I needed the book, and I bought it. I started to write what I thought would be a pamphlet on the religion of Lincoln. The plan enlarged, and the pamphlet became a small book, and the small book became a large one. By the time I finished it, I owned a very respectable Lincoln collection.

History & Liberty

Ethan Allen, 1738-1789
Revolutionary War Hero &
Commander of "The Green Mountain Boys"

Ever since I arrived at the state of manhood, and acquainted myself with the general history of mankind, I have felt a sincere passion for liberty. The history of nations, doomed to perpetual slavery, in consequence of yielding up to tyrants their natural-born liberties, I read with a sort of philosophical horror; so that the first systematical and bloody attempt, at Lexington, to enslave America, thoroughly electrified my mind, and fully determined me to take part with my country. And, while I was wishing for an opportunity to signalize myself in its behalf, directions were privately sent to me from the then colony, (now state) of Connecticut, to raise the Green-Mountain Boys, and, if possible, with them to surprise and take the fortress of Ticonderoga.

*   *   *   *   *   *

Ethan was educated from an early age by his mother and his father, then by the preacher and the scholarly people of the community. When Ethan was in his teens, his father made the big decision that the boy would be spared from farm duties so that he might go away to school.

So in the middle of the 1750's young Ethan rode to Salisbury and was duly brought to the Reverend Mr. Lee's house to board and undertake his studies. Since his previous education had consisted mostly of listening to his elders and reading the *Bible and Plutarch's Lives*, there was a great deal of learning to be done. Ethan's mind was retentive, though, and his spirit contemplative. He did well in his new environment.

—Edwin Hoyt

A Message to Garcia

Author- Elbert Hubbard, 1856-1915
Read by James Beckman, his secretary

The thing that brought fame to Elbert Hubbard almost overnight and which is still popular was the *A Message to Garcia*. It was written without any appreciation of its greatness on the part of its author. Speaking of it, Elbert Hubbard said:

"This article, covering only fifteen hundred words, was written one evening after supper in a single hour. The thing leaped hot from my heart, written after a rather trying day. The immediate suggestion came from a little argument when my son Bert suggested that Rowan was the real hero in the Cuban war. Rowan had gone alone and done the thing—carried the message to Garcia.

"It came to me like a flash! Yes, the boy is right, the hero is the man who does the thing—does his work— carries the message. I got up from the table and wrote *A Message to Garcia*. I thought so little of it that we ran it without a heading. The edition went out, and soon orders began to come for extra March *Philistines*. When the American News Company ordered a thousand, I asked one of my helpers which article it was that had stirred things up.

"It's that stuff about Garcia," he said.

"The next day a telegram came from George H. Daniels of the New York Central Railroad: 'Give price on one hundred thousand Rowan articles in pamphlet form—Empire State Express advertisement on back— also state how soon can ship.'

"A hundred thousand pamphlets looked like a huge undertaking. The result was that I gave Mr. Daniels permission to reprint the article in his own way. Two or three half-million lots have been sent out by Mr. Daniels, and in addition the article has been reprinted in over two hundred magazines and newspapers."

Hamlet, MacBeth, Julius Caesar

Author- William Shakespeare, 1564-1616
Read by Alexander Graham Bell, 1847-1922

Merely to spend a year in the company of an old man would have affected a boy in his middle teens. But Grandfather Bell's influence on Aleck was more positive than that. "We became companions and friends," Aleck later remembered. The companionship of such a man did much to steady and inspire the boy.

Together they read through several of Shakespeare's plays, and Aleck learned speeches from *Hamlet, Macbeth, Julius Caesar,* and others. His grandfather saw to it that he put aside light reading and applied himself to serious studies. Aleck at last tried the toughness of his mind and found exhilaration in the trial. His mind raced to catch up with his years, and he looked beyond to a university education.

Aleck must have absorbed something of his grandfather's outlook on men and affairs. Manuscripts of the grandfather's lectures reveal much about those ideas. Grandfather Bell believed, that individual worth was not determined by class or heredity, that education would disclose ability as often in the humblest-born as in the highest. He scoffed at the notion that education might make the poor unruly. "The poor have eyes," he said. Education, on the contrary, would enable the poor to raise themselves by creating wealth rather than by despoiling others. Education might be a ladder out of even lower depths than poverty. "Our criminals, with few exceptions, are the neglected portion of the Community. . . our brethren, God's creatures," the products of "man's neglect, and not innate viciousness." Conversely, he held merit to be no more subject to bequest than was villainy, and so he felt that to reward achievements with hereditary titles was nonsense.

—Robert Bruce

Walden

Author- Henry David Thoreau, 1817-1862
Read by James O. Bennett, 1870-1940
Essayist, Chicago Tribune

Walden! When the lover of that book writes its title he would like to make the word a joyful shout, a kind of hail to good people who know not the book.

Of Thoreau's masterpiece two wonderful things are true: No man having attentively read it is ever the same man again. And nobody ever wrote a book in our tongue like it—not even Thoreau, although his *Week on the Concord and Merrimack Rivers* is highly authentic Thoreau.

Why does *Walden* take such a hold of men as it does? Because it is such an honest book that there is no gainsaying it. When I say that a man having read it is never the same man again I do not mean that he forthwith begins living very differently. He may not, but he will ever earnestly regret that he does not. That is at least a step in grace.

Thoreau died untimely from exposure while counting the rings of a tree amid December snow, but he died at peace. One of those bedside comforters who add a new terror to death asked, "Henry, have you made your peace with God?" The friend of birds and field mice and all helpless beings, the lover of truth to the ultimate, smiled and answered, "I have never quarreled with him."

He is the bonniest, gravest, honestest spirit in our literature, and his great book has the sunshine, the crisp snow, the bird notes, the morning light and the morning fragrance of Walden pond bound in with every one of its nearly 400 steadying, exhilarating, comforting pages. It lives and sings.

The Making of a Statesmen

Thomas Hart Benton, 1782-1858
U.S. Senator, 1821-1857
Author, "Thirty Years' View"

Young Benton was always fond of reading. He began his studies at home, and continued them at a grammar school taught by a young New Englander of good ability, a very large proportion of the school-teachers of the country then coming from New England; indeed, school-teachers and peddlers were, on the whole, the chief contributions made by the Northeast to the personnel of the new Southwest. Benton then began a course at Chapel Hill, the University of North Carolina, but broke off before completing it, as his mother decided to move her family westward to the almost unbroken wilderness near Nashville, Tennessee, where his father had left them a large tract of land. But he was such an insatiable student and reader that he rapidly acquired a very extensive knowledge, not only of law, but of history and even of Latin and English literature, and thus became a well-read and cultivated, indeed a learned, man; though his frequent displays of learning and knowledge were sometimes marked by a trace of that self-complacent, amassing pedantry so apt to characterize a really well-educated man who lives in a community in which he believes, and with which he has thoroughly identified himself, but whose members are for the most part below the average in mental cultivation.
—Theodore Roosevelt

"This new page opened in the book of our public expenditures, and this new departure taken, leads into the bottomless gulf of civil pensions and family gratuities." —Senate speech by Benton against a grant to Pres. Harrison's widow

United States Constitution

Read by Hugo Black, 1886-1971
Supreme Court Justice for 34 Years

"Where's my Constitution?" Justice Black asked, ruffling through his pockets and spreading out the papers on his desk.

"I always keep my Constitution in my coat pocket. What could have happened to it? Have you got one on you?" he asked of a visitor a few years ago.

"You ought to keep one on you all the time," he said, buzzing for his secretary. "Where's my Constitution?"

The woman searched his desk drawers and scanned the library shelves in the spacious Supreme Court chambers, but found no Constitution.

"I like to read what it says, I like to read the words of the Constitution," Justice Black said in a slight Southern drawl, after dispatching the secretary to fetch one. "I'm a literalist, I admit it. It's a bad word these days. I know, but that's what I am."

Shortly, the Constitution was delivered. Hugo Lafayette Black, then 81 years old and completing his 30th year on the United States Supreme Court, laid it tenderly on his lap and opened it to the Bill of Rights.

"Now," he said with a warm smile, "now let's see what it says."

Perhaps no other man in history of the Court so revered the Constitution as a source of the free and good life. Few articulated so lucidly, simply and forcefully a philosophy of the 18th-century document. Less than a handful had the impact on constitutional law and the quality of the nation as this self-described "backward country fellow" from Clay County, Alabama.

New York Times obituary, Sept. 26, 1971

The Making of a Statesman

James G. Blaine, 1830-1893
U. S. Senator, Secretary of State

His mind had received the discipline which is characteristic of those who have had the benefit of the old-fashioned classical curriculum, and who have profited by their opportunities. His spoken and written language, in his early manhood, even in his familiar conversation and in unstudied correspondence, was that of a scholar—not merely correct and devoid of the gaucherie of the half taught, but elegant and precise, clear and terse. His familiarity with the works of the ancient classical writers seems to have had an important influence upon his own literary style, which was not an imitation of that of any other, but is suggestive of having been formed on the best models. His acquaintance with those works enabled him on occasion to enrich his own thoughts and words with apposite references to them, and with apt quotations. He had, too, acquired a taste for the best literature of all times, which he never ceased to gratify by reading omnivorously, avoiding only that which was trashy and sensational. Above all the college had imparted to him that thirst for knowledge, embracing all branches, all principles, all details, which is the trait of the true scholar.

His instructors discerned more in him than was revealed to his fellow students. The family fortunes were low, and his father was unable to help him to the further education which he desired—a preparation for the bar. He was obliged to postpone the gratification of that wish and resort to teaching for a time, in order to earn his living and provide means for future study.

—Edward Stanwood

Appleton's Encyclopedia

Read by Edward Bok, 1863-1930
Editor, Ladies Home Journal
1921 Pulitzer Prize Winner

When my school-days had ended, the question of self-education had become an absorbing thought. I had mastered a schoolboy's English, but six years of public-school education was hardly a basis on which to build the work of a lifetime. I saw each day in my duties as office boy some of the foremost men of the time. It was the period of William H. Vanderbilt's ascendancy in Western Union control; and the railroad millionaire and his companions were objects of great interest to me. I knew that some of the "great" men I saw had also been deprived of the advantage of collegiate training, and yet they had risen to the top. But how? I decided to read about these men and others, and find out. I could not, however, afford the separate biographies, so I went to the libraries to find a compendium that would authoritatively tell me of all successful men. I found it in *Appleton's Encyclopedia,* and determining to have only the best, I saved my luncheon money, walked instead of riding the five miles to my Brooklyn home, and after a period of saving, had my reward in the first purchase from my own earnings: a set of the Encyclopedia. I now read about all the successful men, and was encouraged to find that in many cases their beginnings had been as modest as my own, and their opportunities of education as limited.

HISTORY maketh a young man to be old without either wrinkles or gray hair, privileging him with the experience of age without either the infirmities or the inconveniences thereof.

—Thomas Fuller

Reading for Candidates
by Daniel Boorstin,
Former Librarian of Congress

Reading list for those who would be President:

Franklin of Philadelphia by Esmond Wright

Washington: *The Indispensible Man*
  by James Thomas Flexner

Thomas Jefferson and the New Nation
  by Merrill Peterson

The Age of Jackson by Arthur M. Schlesinger Jr.

Abraham Lincoln by Benjamin P. Thomas

The Age of Reform: From Bryan to F.D.R.
  by Richard Hofstadter

The Rise of Theodore Roosevelt by Edmund Morris

Woodrow Wilson: A Brief Biography by Arthur Link

American Diplomacy by George F. Kennan

American Caesar: Douglas MacArthur 1880-1964
  by William Manchester

In the Shadow of FDR: From Harry Truman to
  Ronald Reagan by William E. Leuchtenburg

FDR by Ted Morgan

Dictionary of American Biography

Read by Catherine Drinker Bowen,
Author, 1897-1973

In the writing of biography, it is expedient to approach one's subject from the periphery, from the outside in—to study first the times, then move to the localities and persons of the immediate story. With Oliver Wendell Holmes it was first of all necessary to know the great names, the movers and shakers at the White House, in Congress and the law courts; to be familiar with them as one is familiar with names in newspapers of today and with current controversial events. Now at the outset of work I roamed and read in blissful desultory fashion: old histories like Woodrow Wilson's and James Ford Rhodes's; McLaughlin's *Constitutional History,* Washburn's *Sketches of the Judicial History of Massachusetts,* Frankfurter on Holmes, Cardozo on *Law and Literature,* Moses Aronson on juridical evolutionism. I read biographies and letters of Theodore Roosevelt, Mark Hanna and the political bosses. Even the *Federalist* papers must be reread, though I could not hope to encompass them with any thoroughness. I bought books by the dozen and the score and kept them by, where I could make notes on margins and endboards; the twenty-six volumes of my *Dictionary of American Biography* bristled with paper markers. I read at mealtime and I read in bed—not as a scholar reads, in order to form new judgments on fresh-discovered material, but as a reporter might read, to learn the background of the scenes I must depict.

And the more I learned about Oliver Wendell Holmes, Jr., the more insupportable it became to think of him as dead, cold and motionless beneath that stone at Arlington. I found myself possessed by a witch's frenzy to ungrave this man, stand him upright, see him walk, jump, dance, tell jokes, make love, display his vanity or his courage as the case might be.

Guide to Christ

Author- Solomon Stoddard, 1643-1729
Read by David Brainerd, 1718-1747
American Missionary to the Indians

I could not bear that all I had done should stand for mere nothing; as I had been very conscientious in duty, had been very religious a great while, and had, as I thought, done much more than many others who had obtained mercy. I confessed indeed the vileness of my duties; but then what made them at that time seem vile, was my wandering thoughts in them, rather than because I was all over defiled like a devil, and the principle corrupt from whence they flowed, so that I could not possibly do any thing that was good. Hence I called what I did by the name of honest faithful endeavors; and could not bear it, that God had made no promises of salvation to them.

I could not find out what faith was; or what it was to believe and come to Christ. I read the calls of Christ to the weary and heavy laden; but could find no way in which he directed them to come. I thought I would gladly come, if I knew how; though the path of duty were never so difficult. I read Stoddard's *Guide to Christ,* (which I trust was, in the hand of God, the happy means of my conversion,) and my heart rose against the author; for though he told me my very heart...and seemed to be very beneficial to me in his directions; yet he seemed to me to fail: he did not tell me anything I could do that would bring me to Christ, but left me as it were with a great gulph between me and Christ, without any direction how to get through. For I was not yet effectually and experimentally taught, that there could be no way prescribed, whereby a natural man could, of his own strength, obtain that which is supernatural, and which the highest angel cannot give.

Expeditio Cyri

Author-Xenophon, 434-355 B.C.
Read by Louis Brandeis, 1856-1941
Supreme Court Justice for 23 Years

His formal education began at Miss Wood's school in Louisville when he was seven, and he kept Goodrich's *First School Reader* as a memento of that year. He went on to the German and English Academy, where the principal wrote on his almost perfect report card, "Louis deserves special commendation for conduct and industry." The course of study he described in his letter was undertaken during his first year in the Louisville Male High School. During the following year, he studied belles lettres, Latin, Greek, pure mathematics, chemistry and technology, French and German. Among the schoolbooks he preserved were Xenophon's *Expeditio Cyri* in Latin and *Herodotos* by Heinrich Stein (the latter in Greek with German footnotes). One year later, when he was sixteen, the University of the Public Schools in Louisville awarded him a gold medal "for pre-eminence in all his studies." The gold medal winner each year was expected to make a speech at graduation, but Louis, "overcome with terror at the thought of making a speech," was spared that ordeal by the discovery on graduation morning that he had laryngitis.

Brandeis remained at the Annen-Realschule for three terms and justified his unorthodox admission by becoming an outstanding student. He took courses in French, Latin, German, literature, mineralogy, geography, physics, chemistry, and mathematics, and did so well that in March 1875, the faculty awarded him a prize "for diligence and good conduct." He was permitted to pick his prize and chose A. W. Becker's *Charackterbilder aus der Kunstgeschicte,* a book about Greek art.

—Philippa Strum

Works of Anthony Trollope, 1815-1882

Read by Robert Brookings, 1850-1932
Merchant, Philanthropist, Founder of the
Brookings Institution of Washington D. C.

His judgment remained steady and sane. The panic of 1929 brought no panic to him. He had been through panics before and had survived the hard times which followed them. He even welcomed "the slackening of the pace of the get-rich-quick" for the opportunity it gave to take an inventory. He himself sought the solution of the problem of the depression in no restoration of old alignments. He was at eighty still a pioneer.

He was a model of consideration, exacting only in his demands on his wife to be the medium of contact with the printed word. She read to him for hours, almost for days at a time, reading sometimes almost until she dropped. He had always been so indefatigable himself that it did not seem to occur to him that she might be fatigued. Without his eyes, he was like a caged eagle and he clamored for the clear reaches of the upper air. He liked Trollope and she read him the complete works, seventeen volumes of them. He found his relaxation in odd places. "I am very tired," he said on one occasion. "I wish you would read me the Constitution of the United States." His taste for trading was still keen and he pleaded for the stock reports twice daily.

He spent the greater part of a winter under the skillful care of the great Wilmer in Baltimore, who operated on his eyes again and again, first for glaucoma and then for cataract. As the clouds lifted, he learned to read again, first the largest letters, then gradually, the rest. Wilmer marvelled at the determination of the octogenarian, fitting himself again to play a part in the world.

—Hermann Hagedorn

The Life of Abraham Lincoln
Read by William Jennings Bryan, 1860-1925
U. S. Congressman, Author, Orator

...have been reading *The Life Of Abe Lincoln.* It is quite interesting. He was ambitious and is the most humble statesman we have ever had. He had an eloquence which seemed born of inspiration. He spoke the truth and with it won the hearts of his hearers. As a lawyer he was a perfect model. He only wished justice for his clients and always got it. He was scrupulously honest, once walking three miles to return six and a half cents he had taken by mistake. He is a good character for study.

Lincoln's profound insight as shown in his *Ten Guidelines:*

You cannot bring about prosperity by discouraging thrift.

You cannot help small men by tearing down big men.

You cannot strengthen the weak by weakening the strong.

You cannot lift the wage earner by pulling down the wage payer.

You cannot help the poor man by destroying the rich.

You cannot keep out of trouble by spending more than your income.

You cannot further brotherhood of men by inciting class hatred.

You cannot establish security on borrowed money.

You cannot build character and courage by taking away man's initiative and independence.

You cannot help men permanently by doing for them what they could and should do for themselves.

The Effects of Cross- and Self-Fertilization in the Vegetable Kingdom

Author- Charles Darwin, 1809-1882
Read by Luther Burbank, 1849-1926
Horticulturist, known as "The Plant Wizard"

Burbank had seemed a nurseryman with a good future in the business, but he never stopped thinking of his future in terms of plant experimentation and the imaginative plant breeding for which he became known and which finally put his name into Webster's as a verb.

Some of his hybridizing experiments had backed up his feeling that by putting Charles Darwin's theories to practical use, he could make nature and her variations in plants work for him. When *The Effects of Cross- and Self-Fertilization in the Vegetable Kingdom* appeared during his early nurseryman's days in California, he quickly got a copy. One sentence in the book especially seized him. It read:

"As plants are adapted by such diversified and effective means for cross-fertilization, it might have been inferred from this fact alone that they derived some great advantage from the process; and it is the object of the present work to show the nature and importance of the benefits to be derived."

Burbank's reasoning from this pregnant passage was: Why not get nature to use her cross-fertilizing magic for the joy and comfort of man? Though he had already interested himself by helping nature along with a little cross-fertilizing, he was quoted later as saying that this sentence of Darwin's was "my starting point." Darwin, as he saw it, had drawn the plans, and now it was up to someone else to put them to work. Burbank elected himself that someone.

—Ken and Pat Kraft

Miracle at Philadelphia

Author- Catherine Drinker Bowen, 1897-1973
Read by Warren Burger, 1907-
Supreme Court Chief Justice

Reading *Miracle at Philadelphia* again, I find it as rewarding and as enthralling as I did 20 years ago. Anyone who wants to understand our system—its virtues and its flaws—will find more here than in any single work I know.

Why does this book resonate as it has through the years? Catherine Bowen spent long periods of time reading widely about the events that took place in Philadelphia during that hot summer of 1787. Then she put her fine mind to work, thinking long and hard about how 55 individuals—with widely differing opinions about how (and whether) a nation with a strong central government should be formed—could achieve this miracle. She created a narrative intelligible to the general reader and as exciting as a detective story. Later, in a book called *Biography: The Craft and the Calling,* Mrs. Bowen explained what she had tried to do: "What I wished was not to have readers exclaim, 'How grand a scene and how significant!'—but as the hot summer advanced, to ask anxiously, 'Are they going to sign this Constitution, will it go through? Or are these 55 delegates simply talking themselves into an impasse?'"

And so it is that *Miracle at Philadelphia* is perennially new. Mrs. Bowen brings to us the texture, the intrigues and the voices of the time—the scholarship of Madison, the organizational genius of Hamilton, the quiet, cohesive leadership of Washington. She makes us feel a part of that summer in Philadelphia. She shows us how the delegates dressed, where they stayed in the city, how they spent their off hours. Soon we come to know these people almost as we know our own contemporaries.

Iliad

Author- Homer, 800 B.C.
Read by Elihu Burritt, 1810-1879
Blacksmith, Reformer,
Lecturer on International Peace

He studied Homer's *Iliad,* of which he knew nothing, and with only a dictionary to help him.

"The proudest moment of my life," he once wrote, "was when I had first gained the full meaning of the first fifteen lines of that noble work. I took a short triumphal walk, in favor of that exploit."

He was an ardent reader of books from childhood up, and he was enabled to gratify this taste by means of a very small village library, which contained several books of history, of which he was naturally fond. This boy, however, was a shy, devoted student, brave to maintain what he thought right, but so bashful that he was known to hide in the cellar when his parents were going to have company.

When he was about half through his apprenticeship he suddenly took it into his head to learn Latin, and began at once through the assistance of the same elder brother. In the evenings of one winter he read the *Aeneid* of Virgil; and, after going on for a while with Cicero and a few other Latin authors, he began Greek. During the winter months he was obliged to spend every hour of daylight at the forge, and even in the summer his leisure minutes were few and far between. But he carried his Greek grammar in his hat, and often found a chance, while he was waiting for a large piece of iron to get hot, to open his book with his black fingers, and go through a pronoun, an adjective, or part of a verb, without being noticed by his fellow-apprentices.

—James Parsons

Books: A Father's Best Friend

William Byrd II, 1674-1744
Colonial Official, Founder of Richmond

Byrd's ambition blazed more for his children than himself, or rather for himself through his children. He had a somewhat sketchy education, as can be noted from the consistent misspelling and eccentric grammar of his letters. When had he had time for learning? Nevertheless he valued it and sought it. He often wrote to John Clinton of London, ordering books: "Either Mr. Boyle's or any other English author [on stones and minerals], and Salmon's 'Polygraphicae.'" He also ordered many books on theology—he was deeply religious—and, as a change of pace, he desired Clinton to send him *The Turkish Spy*. One order for books alone came to almost a thousand dollars by today's standards.

He recognized his own lack of education, regretted it, and sought to remedy it. Furthermore, he was absolutely determined that his children should have the best education in the world. This certainly was not to be had in Virginia, where there were no schools and children were gathered in some plantation house or other and taught by the local clergyman. That was not good enough for William Byrd's children. In 1681, when his little son, William, was seven years old, he was put aboard a ship with a cargo of tobacco and skins consigned to Perry and Lane. William was consigned to "Father Horsmanden." The tobacco and furs would pay for the finest education England could give. This was a genuine sacrifice on Byrd's part, for he saw the son, on whom all his hopes and love centered, only twice more in his life.

Will was already far better educated than his father ever would be. Thus Byrd had a father's rarest satisfaction, that of seeing his son turning into exactly the sort of man he hoped the boy would become.

—Alden Hatch

History of America

Author- William Robertson, 1721-1793
Read by John C. Calhoun, 1782-1850
Senator, Secretary of State, Vice President

The year 1795 marked a turning point in the life of young John Calhoun. It was the year, too, when he knew personal loss, the desolation that comes when those closest are torn away. It was the year when he studied his first books, learning then what a great and undreamed-of world lay inside them. So far, he had had only a few months of schooling. When he was seven or eight, he had trudged several miles a day through the almost unsettled frontier country to a log-cabin school at Brewers.

John had no time to be lonely. For there were books in the Waddel home, and in books the boy could find escape from more sad reality. He took to the library. Almost forgetting to eat or sleep, he consumed Rollin's *Ancient History,* Robertson's *America,* and *Charles the Fifth,* the large edition of Cook's *Voyages,* Brown's *Essays,* and a volume and a half of John Locke on the *Human Understanding.*

The choice of books was limited, theology, of course, predominating; but without hesitation John had unearthed the works of history and philosophy. His luck was good: Parton has called *Charles the Fifth* the best book ever written for a boy. John gained a knowledge of the past from the histories and travel books; and of the world of abstractions from the *Essays of Locke,* which laid solid foundations for all his subsequent thought.

He was not dissatisfied with his lonely, hard working life. A contemporary account tells of a farmer who rode by the Calhoun lands, and there saw John, hard at work in a field, whistling cheerfully, with a book 'tied to the plow.'

—Margaret Coit

History of the Roman Republic

Author- Adam Ferguson, 1723-1816
Read by Thomas Carlyle, 1795-1881
Scottish Essayist, Historian,
Lord Rector of Edinburgh University

I believe you will find one important thing not much noted, that there was a very great deal of deep religion in both Greece and Rome. This is pointed out by the wiser kind of historians, and particularly by Ferguson, who is very well worth reading on Roman History. He points out the profoundly religious nature of the Roman people, notwithstanding their ruggedly positive, defiant and fierce ways. They believed that Jupiter Optimus Maximus was lord of the universe, and that he had appointed the Romans to become the chief of nations, provided they followed his commands—to brave all danger, all difficulty, and stand up with an invincible front, and be ready to do and die; and also to have the same sacred regard to truth of promise, to thorough veracity, thorough integrity, and all the virtues that accompany that noblest quality of man, valour—to which later the Romans gave the name of 'virtue' proper (virtus, manhood), as the crown and summary of all that is ennobling for a man. In the literary ages of Rome this religious feeling had very much decayed away; but it still retained its place among the lower classes of the Roman people. I believe you will find in all histories of nations, that this has been at the origin and foundation of them all; and that no nation which did not contemplate this wonderful universe with awe-stricken and reverential belief that there was a great unknown, omnipotent, and all-wise and all-just Being, superintending all men in it, and all interest in it—no nation ever came to very much, nor did any man either, who forgot that. If a man did forget that, he forgot the most important part of his mission in this world.

History of the United States

Author-George Bancroft, 1800-1891
Read by Andrew Carnegie, 1835-1918
Industrialist and Philanthropist

Colonel James Anderson—I bless his name as I write—announced that he would open his library of four hundred volumes to boys, so that any young man could take out, each Saturday afternoon, a book which could be exchanged for another on the succeeding Saturday. My friend, Mr. Thomas N. Miller, reminded me recently that Colonel Anderson's books were first opened to "working boys," and the question arose whether messenger boys, clerks, and others, who did not work with their hands, were entitled to books. My first communication to the press was a note, written to the *Pittsburgh Dispatch*, urging that we should not be excluded; that although we did not now work with our hands, some of us had done so, and that we were really working boys. Dear Colonel Anderson promptly enlarged the classification. So my first appearance as a public writer was a success.

My dear friend, Tom Miller, one of the inner circle, lived near Colonel Anderson and introduced me to him, and in this way the windows were opened in the walls of my dungeon through which the light of knowledge streamed in. Every day's toil and even the long hours of night service were lightened by the book which I carried about with me and read in the intervals that could be snatched from duty. And the future was made bright by the thought that when Saturday came a new volume could be obtained. In this way I became familiar with Macauley's essays and his history, and with *Bancroft's History of the United States*, which I studied with more care than any other book I had then read. Lamb's essays were my special delight, but I had at this time no knowledge of the great master of all, Shakespeare, beyond the selected pieces in the school books.

The Making of a Pioneer
Kit Carson, 1809-1868
Trapper, Frontiersman, Soldier

The family's first son was born before the wilderness had been pushed back, and was named Moses. He learned to handle firearms before he was taught to read, and no sooner could he walk than he was placed on the unsaddled back of a horse. Younger brothers were given the same treatment, and as there were no schools in the district, the children were taught their letters and numbers by their mother, a woman who believed passionately in another American Dream, that every child deserves the best education his parents can give him.

Kit, who acquired his nickname in infancy, enjoyed many of civilization's benefits in his first years. The family drank water from a well that Carson, Senior, had dug, and several hearths kept the clapboard house warm. Mrs. Carson baked her own bread, of course, but made it from finely ground wheat flour purchased from peddlers. She was determined to give him an even better education than had been afforded his brothers, and although some of his biographers claim he was illiterate—she may have taught him the alphabet when he was only three or four. The child was precocious, and by the time he was five supposedly could read verses from the King James Bible.

In one significant respect, Kit Carson departed from the pattern of America's folk-supermen. He enjoyed reading, and as a mature man owned a library of between one hundred and two hundred books. He wrote with clarity, if not precision, but disliked writing; he felt more comfortable with a rifle in his hand than with a quill pen. It was not accidental that he reached the rank of a brigadier general of volunteers in the Union Army during the Civil War. He certainly was no scholar, but had acquired a sufficient education to feel at home with stars on the shoulder-boards of his uniform.

—Noel Gerson

The Making of a Pioneer

Gulliver's Travels

Author- Jonathan Swift, 1667-1745
Read by Daniel Boone, 1734-1820
Explorer

Daniel Boone, who liked to read when he had the chance, testified later that his party "had with us for our pleasure" a book. It was *Gulliver's Travels.* They were whiling away a long evening in camp with Swift's account of Glumdelick and its inhabitants, the Lulbegruds, when Indians approached. When the hunters had driven them off, Neeley remarked whimsically that they had disposed of the Lulbegruds. Amused by this unexpectedly literary aspect of wilderness warfare, they gave the creek near camp a name from Swift. It is still called Lulbegrud Creek.

—John Bakeless

Lives of Illustrious Men

Author- Plutarch, 46-120 A.D.
Read by Samuel Morse, 1791-1872
Inventor of the Electromagnetic Telegraph

Samuel was a good student. When he finished the lessons assigned to him, he hunted for books to read that were not part of his regular courses. One of his favorites was Plutarch's *Lives of Illustrious Men.* When Samuel read about the accomplishments of great men, he wanted to grow up to be like them.

Samuel was only thirteen when he wrote an excellent paper on the "Life of Demosthenes" which he sent to his father. At fourteen, he was thoroughly qualified to enter college and was accepted by Yale.

—Wilma Hayes

Let Us Now Praise Famous Men

Author- James Agee, 1909-1955
Read by Jimmy Carter, 1924-
39th President of the United States

Julia Coleman made sure he listened to classical music. "She would make me do it," he said. "And she'd make sure that I learned the famous paintings, and the author, and the artists, and she gave me lists of books to read."

When he was about twelve, she called him in and introduced him to Tolstoy's *War and Peace.* Even though it did not turn out to be about cowboys, which was Carter's first impression, it did prove to be one of his favorite books. As a classic account of Napoleon's epic and ultimately unsuccessful struggle against Russia, *War and Peace* instilled into Carter a bent toward what in America in the 1970s would be regarded as an appeal through populism.

Arthur Schlesinger, Jr., has suggested that Carter is theologically fuzzy in admiring both Tolstoy and Reinhold Niebuhr. But E. Brooks Holifield, professor of American religious history at Emory University, disagrees. "Carter was not taken with Tolstoy's pacifism or his religious ethics," Holifield wrote in the *New Republic.* "He was impressed, rather, with Tolstoy's insistence in *War and Peace* that the course of history is determined not by powerful, competent and ruthless leaders (not even by generals) but by the inclinations, passions, will power, courage, prejudices and inarticulate aspirations of the masses. Niebuhr would not have been uncomfortable with that notion."

In going up and down the land Carter has been careful not to sever his roots. He says his favorite book is James Agee's *Let Us Now Praise Famous Men,* a report on sharecropper life.

—David Kucharsky

Conflict and Crisis

Author- Robert Donovan, 1912-
Read by Rosalynn Carter
Wife of U. S. President Jimmy Carter

"If you can't stand the heat, get out of the kitchen," Jimmy would say on such occasions. Earlier in the administration, he had told me one day when I was complaining about all of the controversial problems we had to face, "If you think we have problems, I'm going to send you something when I get back to my office and you'll see we have a gravy train!" He sent me Robert Donovan's book about Harry Truman, *Conflict and Crisis,* and he was right. Truman's problems seemed insurmountable in the last days of the war and the time immediately following. He said that all the time he was in the White House, he looked forward to one week without a crisis—and it never came. To paraphrase Harry Truman: "The heat comes with the kitchen." It always has; it always will. And I enjoy the battle and the confrontations, but I also like to win.

Excerpt from Conflict and Crisis...

"Vigorous, hardworking, simple, he had grown up close to the soil of the Midwest and understood the struggles of the people on the farms and in the small towns—a larger segment of America then than now."

"He also became an insatiable reader, delving into a remarkable miscellany from Plutarch and the Bible to military lore and American history. He had absorbed a good deal of knowledge about the presidency. On the whole, though, Truman was more steeped in history than subtle about it. He had a great repertoire of tales about battles and generals, kings and presidents, and admired strong men of action. His store of historical anecdotes made him an engaging conversationalist. In his particular way, Truman was an educated man."

Little Men and Little Women

Author- Louisa May Alcott, 1832-1888
Read by George Washington Carver, 1860-1943;
Agricultural Scientist; Black Educator;
Fellow, Royal Society of Arts

From the time he was virtually a baby in the woods he wanted to know the name of every stone, insect, flower he saw. He had a book given him by Aunt Sue—Webster's old *Blue-Backed Speller*—that had a picture of a man climbing a high cliff on the top of which stood a temple of learning. Few people thereabouts could even write, but George had studied the Speller until he knew every word. However, it did not reveal the names of the birds, so he made up names to suit himself. Having once tasted of the fruit of knowledge and caught a glimpse of the mysteries hidden in words, he could not rest content.

He had not made knowledge a part of himself until he had done something with it; abstractions had to be made concrete. When stray copies of *Little Women and Little Men* found their way out to those parts, he said, "I can do that. I can write a book." And straightway he wrote a long, long story after what he considered was the general manner of Miss Alcott.

George looked with longing at the doors of the schoolhouse closed to him and announced grandly that someday he was going to have a school of his own where boys would learn to do cooking and housework the same as girls.

He liked to quote Tennyson's lines:

> Hold you here, root and all, in my hand,
> Little flower—but if I could understand
> What you are, root and all, and all in all,
> I should know what God and man is.

The Ethics of Freedom

Author- Jacques Ellul
Read by J. Richard Chase
President of Wheaton College

Freedom is the heart cry of mankind. I constantly cry out for freedom: Freedom from routine, a life that seems to be one long meeting, the judgment of others, the pressure and even desire to conform to the tacky web of our culture, the tendency to float downstream, the need for applause, the haunting sins and errors of the past.

"If the Son sets you free, you will be free indeed" (John 8:36). Upon this foundation, Ellul's book has been a rich source of stimulation and help to me.

Ellul writes, "God is the liberator and on this ground man is authorized to hope and to live out hope. Because he has experienced the act of liberation this man knows that hope is not vain. Only the free man can hope, since the breaking of his bondage guarantees all the rest. While man is still a slave, there is no real hope for him."

Yet, in another sense, freedom is demanding. I find both insight and challenge in Ellul's blunt statement, "There is no worse present than freedom." His expansion of this concept is sobering:

"Freedom is the most crushing burden that one can lay on man. In his vanity and boasting man pretends that he wants to be free. He also has a visceral fear of confinement, conditioning, and servitude. What he calls his love of freedom, however, is really his rejection of imprisonment. It is a revolt against slavery, which he cannot tolerate. Once a little freedom is offered him, however, he starts back at the sight of the void which he must now fill, the meaning he must now provide, and the responsibility he must now carry. He prefers the happy state of belonging to a group. He wants a mediocre happiness which brings no risks."

Iliad and Odyssey

Author—Homer, 850-800 B.C.
Read by Rufus Choate, 1799-1859
U.S. Senator & Congressman

Let me remind you that Scott is not the only writer of romance who has made his fiction the vehicle of authentic and useful information concerning the past, and thus earned the praise of a great historian. Let me remind you of another instance, the most splendid in literature. The *Iliad* and *Odyssey* of Homer,—what are they but great Waverly Novels! And yet what were our knowledge of the first 400 years of Grecian history without them! Herodotus, the father of history, devotes about twenty-five duodecimo lines to the subject of the Trojan Wanderer; and without meaning any disrespect to so revered a name—so truly valuable a writer—I must say that this part of his narrative is just about as interesting and instructive as an account in a Castine newspaper, that in a late, dark night a schooner from Eastport got upon Mt. Desert Rock, partly bilged, but that no lives were lost, and there was no insurance. Unroll now, by the side of this, the magnificent cartoons on which Homer has painted the heroic age of the bright clime of Battle and of Song! Abstracting your attention for a moment from the beauty and grandeur and consummate art of these compositions—just study them for the information they embody. We all know that critics have deduced the rules of epic poetry from these inspired models; and Horace tells us that they are better teachers of morality than the Stoic doctors—Chrysippus and Crates.

History is not history unless it is the truth.
—Abraham Lincoln

Mark Twain and Family

By Clara Clemens

Now and again Father entertained us at dinner—when no guests were present—by relating the contents of books he was reading, such as *Gulliver's Travels, The Arabian Nights,* or sea stories. More than once I wondered how Father could think, talk, and eat all at once in so vehement a manner. This capacity, added to his restless pacing the floor between courses at table, gave the meal a lively character. He never took any lunch, because he did not wish to break into his work or his billiards in the middle of the day, but sometimes he sat with us during part of this meal. Frequently he brought the old German nonsense rhymes called *Struwelpeter* to the lunch table and read them aloud with great emphasis. Even now, I can recollect how he laughed each time when he came to the lines—

"Am Brunnen Stand ein grosser Hund
Trank Wasser dort mit seinen Mund."

At one time he was inclined to read Browning aloud at the table, but Mother objected, declaring she would not be able to understand a single word amid the clatter of knives and forks and the exclamations of joy over griddlecakes or ginger-bread continually sounding in the air.

Among our favorite books were *At the Back of the North Wind, The Days of Bruce, The Children of the New Forest, Robinson Crusoe,* and *The Prince and the Pauper.* Like most small children, we clamored for stories descriptive of unusual people or events, and of such books we could never get enough. That a little boy should be able to take a ride in the beautiful hair of the North Wind and float up among the stars seemed too good to be true, even within the magic covers of a book, as we never could get quite enough of this lovely story, Father had to invent some more.

Byron and Moore

Read by Grover Cleveland, 1837-1908
22nd President of the United States

At Clinton in the winter of 1850-51, Grover attended the town academy at the foot of College Hill—called the Clinton Liberal Institute—where he studied doggedly but without brilliancy. "He was then, as I remember," his sister Margaret writes, "a lad of rather unusual good sense, who did not yield to impulses— he considered well, and was resourceful—but as a student Grover did not shine. The wonderful powers of application and concentration which afterwards distinguished his mental efforts were not conspicuous in his boyhood."

The school was small, with but two teachers. In a class of three Grover struggled through four books of the *Aeneid,* using a battered copy of his father's, without notes, and envying his richer classmates their new editions, with large print and explanatory glosses to help them over the difficult passages.

Cleveland, a tall, slender, sandy-haired youth of sixteen, had felt keenly the death of his father, of whose fine qualities he talked much; that he was thoughtful, reserved, disinclined to make friends, and a hard student; and that he was already planning to follow law as a profession. All this is doubtless true. Miss Crosby further says that he showed a keen appetite for history, which probably means that he read the old-fashioned texts, Rollin's *Ancient History* and Goodrich's *American History,* used in the school curriculum; and that he had a liking for Byron and Tom Moore. Beyond question Cleveland at this age was fond of poetry. William and he took turns in reading aloud several evenings a week to the blind pupils, and he recited verse with unusual spirit.

—Allan Nevins

Compendium of Knowledge

Read by Samuel Colt, 1814-1862
Inventor of the Revolver, 1836

He was disciplined for disturbing the Sabbath by firing a horse pistol, possibly the one he had rebuilt. The legacy of the sour religious zealots who had founded New England was still strong. Blue laws forbade running on the Sabbath or even walking in the garden—or anywhere else, for that matter, except "reverently to and from church." The disciples of the Christ who had preached universal love forbade kissing of husband and wife on the Sabbath—even prescribed that "no mother shall kiss her child upon the Sabbath-day."

Little wonder that Sam's shattering of the Sabbath quiet with a large-caliber pistol offended Connecticut's sensibilities and provoked punishment. Though Sam was a miserable student of the classical curriculum, he discovered in the farmer's library the encyclopedic *Compendium of Knowledge* and was entranced. Reading that volume, which supposedly summarized all of man's knowledge, inflamed his mind with imaginative applications of science to solving man's practical problems.

Sometime during 1828 or 1829, when Sam was about fourteen, he enrolled at Amherst Academy, a new school but already famed for its faculty. The high-powered teachers apparently did not impress Sam, however, for he was often disciplined.

Sam got into serious trouble, again over firearms. School regulations prohibited discharging firearms "either in shooting at game or at mark, or for amusement in any manner." Sam was caught firing his trusty horse pistol and fled to Ware rather than sit through a session with the formidable Reverend Royal Ashburn, president of the school's board.

—Bern Keating

The Making of a Naval Hero

Admiral George Dewey, 1837-1917
Spanish-American War Hero

Excerpt of letter from Admiral Dewey

Gentlemen, let us study Ticonderoga, Crown Point and Bennington; let us study the lives and teachings of the accomplished patriots, Washington, Hamilton, the Adamses, Jay, Jefferson and Madison on the one side, and those rough and ready sons of freedom, Ethan Allen and General Stark and Seth Warner on the other. Let us learn and teach the principles upon which our government has grown to its great and beneficent proportions; let us enforce the lesson that American liberty is the preservation of American opportunity for every man to rise above the condition in which he was born, and to receive the full fruit in honors from his fellow citizens and in protection from his country of the results which have come to him by his talents, his industry, his wisdom, his prudence, his thrift and his good citizenship.

John Paul Jones, 1747-1792
Revolutionary War Naval Hero

John was fond of good literature. He read the books that pleased the average gentleman of his era—Shakespeare and Ossian, Addison's *Cato,* Thomson's *Seasons* and Young's *Night Thoughts.* He loved sentimental writings, and wrote sentimental verses himself. But one trait of this romantic era he did not share—an appreciation of natural scenery. During his career he visited some of the most beautiful parts of the world, yet not once in his voluminous correspondence does he indicate any appreciation of them.

—Samuel Eliot Morison

Natural History

Author- Pliny, 23-79 A.D.
Read by Christopher Columbus, 1451-1506
Discoverer of America

Ferdinand's assertion that his father studied at the University of Pavia is disproved not only by the well-preserved matriculation records of that ancient foundation, but by the internal evidence of Christopher's Latin, which shows that it was learned after Spanish had become the language of his thought. The absence of Italian in the preserved writings of Columbus, excepting for a stray word of phrase, is a great talking point of the *Colon Espanol* sect. The earliest bit of writing that can possibly be his, a postil or marginal note dated 1481 on one of his books, is in bad Spanish; and when he annotated an Italian translation of Pliny's *Natural History* in later life, all but one of his postils are Spanish translations of the Italian text; that one is in very bad Italian. None of the authors to whom he alludes wrote in Italian; the beauty of the *Divine Comedy*, with Ulysses' last voyage and the play of light on the ocean, apparently was unknown to Columbus.

Columbus certainly visited Galway in Ireland, a natural port of call on Iceland voyages, for on the margin of his copy of Aeneas Sylvius's *Historia Rerum* he wrote, "Men of Cathay which is toward the Orient have come hither. We have seen many remarkable things, especially in Galway of Ireland, a man and a woman of extraordinary appearance in two boats adrift"—flat-faced Finns or Lapps, probably. "The author says that the northern ocean is neither frozen nor unnavigable."

—Samuel Eliot Morison

Russell Conwell & Books

Clergyman, Author—"Acres of Diamonds" and President of Temple University; 1843-1925

Every *real* book we *really* read gives us greater faith in the *goodness* and the *nobility* of life. As Lowell says, "Adds another block to the climbing spire of a great sould." The other sort which "swarm from the cozy marshes of immoral brains," the sort also who "rack their brains for lucre," do the devil's work for him, and are as baneful as the company of fools and vulgarians. Show an observant man your bookshelves, and he'll tell you what you are. The man who does not *love* some great book is not worth the time we spend in his company; we are fortunate if we are not in some way contaminated by him. If we knew the road they have traveled, we should likely find that those of modern times who have merited the crown of kings and queens for their stronger *moral* state and their *truer thoughtful* state have had most to do with some literature of knowledge and power; that they especially oftenest consulted the books of the greatest and wisest in their difficulties, and had been spurred on by their messages to the thoughts and the deeds which made them worthy.

It is fortunate that to-day the greatest of books are the common property of the printers of the world, for they are on this account the cheapest, and many of them can be had for the price of a poor man's dinner. It needs many a page to record even the names of the men and women who have become *somebody* and have done *something* just reading some one worthy book which had fallen into their hands. Many believe that Franklin is the greatest American that has yet appeared, and he has said that "Cotton Mather's *essays to do good* gave me a turn of thinking which, perhaps, had an influence on some of the principal future events of my life."

Essays

Author- Thomas Macaulay, 1800-1859
Read by Calvin Coolidge, 1872-1933
13th President of the United States

Office hours were from eight to about six o'clock, during which I spent my time in reading Kent's *Commentaries* and in helping prepare writs, deeds, wills, and other documents. My evenings I gave to some of the masters of English composition. I read the speeches of Lord Erskine, of Webster, and Choate. The essays of Macaulay interested me much, and the writings of Carlyle and John Fiske I found very stimulating. Some of the orations of Cicero I translated, being especially attached to the defense of his friend the poet Archias, because in it he dwelt on the value and consolation of good literature. I read much in Milton and Shakespeare and found delight in the shorter poems of Kipling, Field and Riley.

The books in the office soon appeared too ponderous for my study, so I brought a supply of students' text books and law cases on the principal subjects necessary for my preparation for the bar. These enabled me to gain a more rapid acquaintance with the main legal principles, because I did not have to read through so much unimportant detail as was contained in the usual treatise prepared for a lawyer's library, which was usually a collection of all the authorities, while what I wanted was the main element of the law.

Thoughts from Macaulay:

"Few of the many wise apothegms which have been uttered from the time of the seven sages of Greece to that of Poor Richard, have prevented a single foolish action."

"A great writer is the friend and benefactor of his readers."

Sebastopol

Author- Leo Tolstoy, 1828-1910
Read by Stephen Crane, 1871-1900
War Correspondent; Author,
"The Red Badge of Courage"

Stephen was remembered by his classmates as a friendly boy, although moody and rebellious (as his sister Agnes had been); he was liked by all except those teachers whose classes he cut in preference for the baseball diamond.

An indifferent schoolboy in such studies as mathematics and science, he was far in advance of his colleagues in history and literature (thanks to Agnes' tutoring him as a youngster). By calling Tennyson's poetry "swill" he got into a fist fight which cost him part of a tooth sometime that spring. He endured the ordeal of memorizing and reciting "The Charge of the Light Brigade," an agony he recast in his English years into "Making an Orator," a Whilomville story. Abram Lincoln Travis, his fellow student at Claverack, where Travis later taught after graduating from Syracuse University in 1894, remembers him as a voracious reader of all 19th Century English writers and of the classics of Greece and Rome. Plutarch's *Lives* was his constant companion, and he could quote from Tennyson's "In Memoriam" and Bryant's "Thanatopsis" and was familiar with the English and American poets. And of course he knew the Bible well. That his readings all his life were miscellaneous and desultory is evidenced by the "List of Books/Brede Place."

He declared that Count Tolstoy was the world's foremost writer. He had read Tolstoy's *Sebastopol*, but he was bored by Henry James' *Reverberator* (1888), a study of journalism. Years later he became Henry James' close friend.

—R. W. Stallman

Darius Green
and His Flying Machine

Author- John Trowbridge, 1827-1916
Read by Glenn Curtiss, 1878-1930
Inventor; Early Aviator; Industrialist

Of the two children, the boy was his grandmother's favorite, and he in turn held for her a deep and abiding affection. Her influence on his upbringing was more profound than Lua's; indeed, there seems never to have been a really close tie between Glenn and his mother. As might be expected, Ruth Curtiss indoctrinated her grandson in the moral precepts of Methodism, and yet she was much more to him than a spiritual superintendent. She it was who allowed him to erect a homemade incubator in an upstairs room and have baby chicks overrunning the house. Before he was of school age, Grandmother Curtiss often read to him, and one literary curiosity which he never tired of hearing was *Darius Green and His Flying Machine.* This humorous poem, lampooning man's efforts to fly, was having a vogue at the time, in booklet form with comic illustrations. Ruth Curtiss told her wide-eyed grandson that she had personally known its author, John T. Trowbridge, when she was a girl in Ontario County. The verses narrated how a gangling farmer lad decided that if birds could fly, so could he; how he built a device of "wings strapped to his arms, and a tail." When he tested it from the hayloft window of his father's barn, he hit the ground hard, and concluded:

"Wal, I like flyin' well enough,"
He said: "but the' ain't sich a thunderin' sight
O' fun in't when ye come to light."

Glenn and his grandmother regarded the misadventures of Darius Green as hilarious. In time to come, J. T. Trowbridge would make a trip into Boston to see Glenn fly.
—C. R. Roseberry

Our Penal Machinery and Its Victims

Author- John Altgeld, 1847-1902
Read by Clarence Darrow, 1857-1938
Defense Attorney, Orator

His brain began to clear from the miasma of adolescence; he found himself leaving home on Monday morning with a package of books under his arm, the novels of Balzac, the poetry of Pushkin or Baudelaire, the political satire of Voltaire, the *Odyssey* of Homer or the *Republic* of Plato. He spent his late afternoons and evenings reading with the eager gusto of the awakening mind that is beginning to question, search, evaluate.

His nature drew him back to the books. A banker of Ashtabula introduced him to Henry George's *Progress and Poverty*, which excited both his imagination and his critical faculties, starting him on the jagged, boundless road toward economic justice. A police judge by the name of Richards gave him a copy of *Our Penal Machinery and Its Victims*, by John P. Altgeld, which turned his mind to thinking about crime and prisons. His intellectual vigor renewed, he again began reading in history and political economy and the verses of the *Rubaiyat* and hungered for someone with whom to discuss them. He consumed the works of Walt Whitman, who was anathema in Ashtabula, as were the European novelists with whom he felt a kinship of spirit: Flaubert, Turgenev, Zola. He wanted to discuss free trade and free thought, states' rights and single tax, socialism, paganism; he wanted to hear theories built up or torn apart by educated and trained minds. He wanted to meet people who knew the outside world, who could lead him to new books and philosophies, who argued from the premises of logic rather than prejudice.

He was slowly, awkwardly, painfully, coming of age.

—Irving Stone

Wonders of the World

Read by Charles Darwin, 1809-1882
Naturalist, Author, "The Origin of Species"

Looking back as well as I can at my character during my school life, the only qualities which at this period promised well for the future, were, that I had strong and diversified tastes, much zeal for whatever interested me, and a keen pleasure in understanding any complex subject or thing. I was taught Euclid by a private tutor, and I distinctly remember the intense satisfaction which the clear geometrical proofs gave me. I remember, with equal distinctness, the delight which my uncle (the father of Francis Galton) gave me by explaining the principle of the vernier of a barometer. With respect to diversified tastes, independently of science, I was fond of reading various books, and I used to sit for hours reading the historical plays of Shakespeare, generally in an old window in the thick walls of the school. I read also other poetry, such as Thomson's 'Seasons,' and the recently published poems of Byron and Scott. I mention this because later in life I wholly lost, to my great regret, all pleasure from poetry of any kind, including Shakespeare. In connection with pleasure from poetry, I may add that in 1822 a vivid delight in scenery was first awakened in my mind, during a riding tour on the borders of Wales, and this has lasted longer than any other aesthetic pleasure.

Early in my school days a boy had a copy of the *Wonders of the World,* which I often read, and disputed with other boys about the veracity of some of the statements; and I believe that this book first gave me a wish to travel in remote countries, which was ultimately fulfilled by the voyage of the Beagle.

Thoughts on Personal Religion

Author- Edward Goulburn, 1818-1897
Read by Jefferson Davis, 1808-1889
President of the Confederacy

December 7, 1865 [from prison]

My Beloved Wife,

I am deeply impressed by the kindness of the Bishop, and that of the priests who have so nobly shown their readiness to do their Master's work in relieving the afflicted and protecting the fatherless. They have sent thus the sweetest solace to one in the condition of Him who went down from Jerusalem to Jericho. I feel with you, that God has been very good to us.

I have been reading *Thoughts on Personal Religion,* by Dr. Goulburn. His instructions as to prayer have impressed me particularly. When we shall pass into the future state of pure intelligence, so as to judge not external signs but by the inner motives, how different men will appear to each other from the estimates of their carnal soul!

Though my prison life does not give me the quiet of solitude, its isolation as to intercourse affords abundant opportunity for turning the thoughts inward; and if my self-love, not to say sense of justice, would have resisted the reckless abuse of my enemies, I am humbled by your unmerited praise. It teaches me what I ought to be.

December 8th. Another day has succeeded the night. The sun has risen bright, and the cold bracing air invites animal life to activity. To me there is the same monotonous round of prisoner's life in military confinement. I am, however, thankful for the power to bear, and trustful that the power will be given to me to bear in patience.

Ever affectionately, your Husband Jeffn. Davis

Iliad

Author- Homer, 850 B.C.
Read by Varina Davis, 1826-1906
Wife of Confederate President Jefferson Davis

October 23, 1865

My Beloved Dear Husband,

I have appealed again and again to go to you, but never an answer. President Johnson stated to one of a committee who called upon him that my applications were not in a proper spirit. Perhaps he may change his mind. I do not know. If so, how gladly will I come to you.

What do you think I have been reading? A literal translation of Homer's *Iliad*. It has new beauty to me divested of Pope's swelling rhyming translation. I really have forgotten myself to a pitch of high enthusiasm over it a great many times. My heart actually beats when I come to such battles as the one in which "Jove withdrew Hector from the weapons." And when Achilles slept and the ghost of Patroclus came to him like to himself and then "Art forgetful of me, Achilles?" "Thou didst not neglect me when alive."—But all these things you know and you love to think of them.

Your letters are the sweetest books to me. I live upon one until another comes, and then I am not so ungrateful as to throw the old one by. Would to God you could write daily. Can you not describe your room? Are the sentinels with you at night? Why is your sleep broken? Tell me even what is in your room—what clothes have you. Do tell me every little thing. How infinite are the questions I might ask— how deep and tender is the love with which every thing of yours is surrounded. When I read of the heroic and good, you are my exemplar better than man can depict. Seven times tried in the fiery furnace—brighter than refined gold.

Your devoted Wife, Varina

My Father and I

By Cecil B. DeMille, 1881-1959
Academy Award-winning Film Director,
"The Ten Commandments"

I remember Father best there at Pompton, for I was then 11 years old. I remember best the evenings, I think, when he read to us a chapter from the Old Testament, a chapter from the New, and often a chapter from American or English or European history or from Thackeray or Victor Hugo or some other classic. He liked to have his head rubbed while he read, and Bill and I used to take advantage of that to prolong the evening's reading. Father had a beautifully modulated voice and a fine sense of dramatic values in what he read. He made everything real.

He once said, "The dramatist is a camera, and his photography of life must be true if he would reach men's hearts." His reading of the Bible and the classics of literature reached a boy's heart; and he was unconsciously prophetic when, back in 1889, he spoke of his work in terms of photography and a camera. I have had a good deal to do with photography and cameras since then. *The King of Kings* and *The Ten Commandments* were born in those evenings at Pompton, when father sat under the big lamp and read and a small boy sat near his chair and listened.

For father it was a time of contentment. The time of struggle was over. He was on the crest of life. My mind keeps going back to that Christmas, 1892, our first at Pamlico. Millie Dowling had given father a complete set of the works of Ruskin. Father wrote in his diary about this: "not since Kingsley have I met an author who has so taken hold of me. Strange to say, he comes just at the time I need him. God is over all." It was a very happy Christmas. It was father's last Christmas on earth.

Waverly Novels

Author—Sir Walter Scott, 1771-1832
Read by Chauncey M. Depew, 1834-1928
U.S. Senator

Every community has a public-spirited citizen who unselfishly devotes himself or herself to the public good. That citizen of Peekskill in those early days was Doctor James Brewer. He had accumulated a modest competence sufficient for his simple needs as a bachelor. He was either the promoter or among the leaders of all the movements for betterment of the town. He established a circulating library upon most liberal terms, and it became an educational institution of benefits. The books were admirably selected, and the doctor's advice to readers was always available. His taste ran to the English classics, and he had all the standard authors in poetry, history, fiction, and essay.

No pleasure derived in reading in after-years gave me such delight as the *Waverly Novels.* I think I read through that library and some of it several times over.

The excitement as the novels of Dickens and Thackeray began to appear equalled almost the enthusiasm of a political campaign. Each one of those authors had ardent admirers and partisans. The characters of Dickens became household companions. Every one was looking for the counterpart of Micawber or Sam Weller, Pecksniff or David Copperfield, and had little trouble in finding them either in the family circle or among the neighbors.

Even if the time for action has gone by, the time for extracting a lesson from history is ever at hand for those who are wise.

—Demosthenes

The Adventures of Tom Sawyer

Author- Mark Twain, 1835-1910
Read by Walt Disney, 1901-1966,
Cartoonist, Film Producer

As he lay in his bed at night, he could hear the steam engines hooting across the prairie, and by day he could hike to the railroad tracks and watch the huge locomotives go roaring past, pulling the brightly colored passenger cars on the route to Kansas City. The engineers, leaning from their cabs, never failed to return his wave. And when a freight train passed, he drew waves not only from the engineer, but from the brakeman on the caboose, and from the hobos, catching a free ride in the boxcars. Walt liked the freight trains best.

Since there were no grammar schools close enough to the Disney home, Walt was spared the discipline of school life until he was seven. His mother, a former schoolteacher, provided him with the necessary elementary training, teaching him his numbers, and his colors, as well as how to read and write. She was a loving tutor, whom Walter adored.

Once he had been taught how to read, Walter read everything he could find. And there was plenty to find. His father had been educated through high school—not too usual for a young man in Mr. Disney's day—and enjoyed a lively interest in politics. So Walt read Elias Disney's political newspapers, and also borrowed books from his friend, Doc Sherwood. The boy's greatest reading pleasure came when he discovered Mark Twain. Hannibal—where Samuel Clemens had spent his boyhood, and which served as a setting for so many of his books—was only sixty miles away. And since the passing of a half century had not greatly changed the life of a Missouri boy, Walt found many echoes of his own youthful pleasures in the adventures of Tom Sawyer and Huck Finn.

—Bob Thomas

History of the Modern World

Author- Paul Johnson, 1928-
Read by Pete Domenici
U. S. Senator, New Mexico

One of the most recent books I've read and enjoyed is *History of the Modern World* by Paul Johnson:

"John Conrad (himself an Easterner) had been the only major writer to reflect this pessimism, working it into a whole series of striking novels: *Nostromo* (1904), *The Secret Agent* (1907), *Under Western Eyes* (1911), *Victory* (1915). These despairing political sermons, in the guise of fiction, preached the message Thomas Mann was to deliver to central Europe in 1924 with *The Magic Mountain*. For Conrad the war merely confirmed the irremediable nature of man's predicament. From the perspective of sixty years later it must be said that Conrad is the only substantial writer of the time whose vision remains clear and true in every particular. He dismissed Marxism as malevolent nonsense, certain to generate monstrous tyranny; Freud's ideas were nothing more than 'a kind of magic show'. The war had demonstrated human frailty but otherwise would resolve nothing, generate nothing. Giant plans of reform, panaceas, all 'solutions', were illusory. Writing to Bertrand Russell on October 23, 1922 (Russell was currently offering 'solutions' to *The Problem of China,* his latest book), Conrad insisted: 'I have never been able to find in any man's book or any man's talk anything convincing enough to stand up for a moment against my deep-seated sense of fatality governing this man-inhabited world...The only remedy for Chinamen and for the rest of us is the change of hearts. But looking at the history of the last 2,000 years there is not much reason to expect that thing, even if man has taken to flying...Man doesn't fly like an eagle, he flies like a beetle.'"

McGuffy's Eclectic Reader

Author- William McGuffey, 1800-1873
Read by Maj. Gen. "Wild Bill" Donovan,
1883-1959, World War II Intelligence Officer

What made the Donovans' upbringing unusual was Timothy Donovan's attention to moral theology, "the science of the laws which regulate duty." Through this preoccupation and through the other aspects of Timothy Donovan's regimen, WJD's concern with God, country, honor, and duty was unusually marked, even for that virtuous era.

Timothy Donovan introduced his children to the Gaelic Revival, and he taught them the decisive value of books—"great men are men who read"—in a man's career. Throughout his life, wherever he was, whatever he was doing, WJD always read two or three books a week, often a book a day, almost all of them about military, historical, or political affairs, many of them old volumes, and some of them in Latin or French—WJD learned to read and speak Latin and French well.

Also for the mind was that amazing book in American temporal history, *McGuffey's Eclectic Reader,* which not only assisted the improvement of the mind but also provided an introduction to what one social historian of the times would call "integrity, honesty, industry, temperance, true patriotism, courage, politeness, and all other moral and intellectual virtues." For WJD, to whom patriotism became a guiding light, *McGuffey's* became a life force, helping shape his actions as the volumes did for four generations of Americans of all classes. For the object of *McGuffey's,* as a preface stated, was not only to "present the best specimens of style in the English language" and "to impart valuable information" but also to "exert a decided and healthful moral influence."

—Anthony Brown

Columbian Orator

Read by Frederick Douglass, 1817-1895
Black Anti-slavery lecturer, newspaper editor

Everything contributed to his enlightenment and prepared him for that freedom for which he thirsted. His occasional contact with free colored people, his visit to the wharves where he could watch the vessels going and coming, and his chance acquaintance with white boys on the street, all became a part of his education and were made to serve his plans. He got hold of a blue-back speller and carried it with him all the time. He would ask his little white friends in the street how to spell certain words and the meaning of them. In this way he soon learned to read. The first and most important book owned by him was called the *Columbian Orator.* He bought it with money secretly earned by blacking boots on the street. It contained selected passages from such great orators as Lord Chatham, William Pitt Fox, and Sheridan. These speeches were steeped in the sentiments of liberty, and were full of references to the "rights of man." They gave to young Douglass a larger idea of liberty than was included in his mere dream of freedom for himself, and in addition they increased his vocabulary of words and phrases. The reading of this book unfitted him longer for restraint. He became all ears and all eyes. Everything he saw and read suggested to him a larger world lying just beyond his reach. The meaning of the term "Abolition" came to him by a chance look at a Baltimore newspaper.

—Booker T. Washington

NAPOLEON to his troops in Egypt: "From the height of these pyramids forty centuries look down on us."

—Unknown

Ethics Demonstrated
in Geometrical Order

Author- Baruch Spinoza, 1632-1677
Read by Will Durant, 1885-1981
Educator; Author, "The Story of Civilization"

I was beginning to adjust myself to a life of vain hypocrisy when I encountered Baruch Spinoza. I had been made librarian, and was allowed to wander freely among those precious shelves. There I came upon White's translation of Spinoza's *Ethics Demonstrated in Geometrical Order* (1674). I took the book to my room and studied every word of it. No other book (barring the Bible) ever impressed me so lastingly. Not only by its metaphysics, but even more so by its logical order, its stoic conclusions, and its obvious goodwill to all men. Probably Spinoza's character affected me as much as his philosophy, and I found them more concordant than in most thinkers.

Finally, in January, 1910, I announced my second defection to Father Mooney. He bore with me with saintly patience; and as if to ease the transition for me and my parents he asked me to resume my former duties as a lay teacher in college. I gladly agreed, for I loved Seton Hall, and dreaded a return to disappointed family and a gossipy parrish, or a mad leap from rural isolation to the physical and mental chaos of New York.

Some of my ardor went into reading. In the seminary I had had little time for literature; now, eager to play a part in the literary world, I frequented the bookstores and public library of Newark, and carried away armfuls of Ibsen, Hauptmann, Shaw, Wells, Arnold Bennett, Flaubert, Maupassant, Anatole France, Whitman, Jack London, Upton Sinclair...I joined other swelling spirits in forming a Social Science Club, at whose meeting one or another of us read a prepared paper as the cue for a general discussion.

Victor Hugo, 1802-1885

Read by Thomas Alva Edison, 1847-1931
Inventor; Engineer;
First Inductee into the Inventor's Hall of Fame

With his mother he found study easy and pleasant. The quality of the education she gave him may be judged from the fact that before he was twelve years old he had studied the usual rudiments and had read with his mother's help, Gibbon's *Decline and Fall of the Roman Empire*, Hume's *History of England*, Sear's *History of the World*, Burton's *Anatomy of Melancholy*, and the *Dictionary of Sciences*.

They even tried to struggle through Newton's *Principia*, but the mathematics were too much for both teacher and student. To this day Edison has little personal use for arithmetic beyond that which is called "mental." He said to a friend, "I can always hire some mathematicians, but they can't hire me."

His father always encouraged his literary tastes, and paid him a small sum for each book which he mastered. Although there is no fiction in the list, Edison has all his life enjoyed it, particularly the works of such writers as Victor Hugo. Indeed, later on, when he became a telegraph operator, he was nicknamed by his associates "Victor Hugo Edison"—possibly because of his great admiration for that writer.

When he was about eleven years old he became greatly interested in chemistry. He got a copy of Parker's *School Philosophy*, an elementary book on physics, and tried almost every experiment in it.

—William Meadowcroft

HISTORY is the biography of great men.

—Thomas Carlyle

Critique of Pure Reason

Author- Immanuel Kant, 1724-1804
Read by Albert Einstein, 1879-1955
Physicist, 1921 Nobel Prize winner;
Originator of the theory of relativity

"He showed a particular inclination toward physics and took pleasure in conversing on physical phenomena. I gave him therefore as reading matter Bernstein's *Popular Books on Physical Science* and *Buchner's Force and Matter,* two works that were then quite popular in Germany. The boy was profoundly impressed by them. Bernstein's work especially, which describes physical phenomena lucidly and engagingly, had a great influence on Albert, and enhanced considerably his interest in physical science."

He began to show keenness for mathematics, and Talmey gave him a copy of Spieker's *Lehrbuch der ebenen Geometrie,* a popular textbook. Thereafter, whenever the young medical student arrived for the midday meal on Thursdays, he would be shown the problems solved by Einstein during the previous week.

"After a short time, a few months, he had worked through the whole book of Spieker. He thereupon devoted himself to higher mathematics, studying all by himself Lubsen's excellent works on the subject. These, too, I had recommended to him if memory serves me right. Soon the flight of his mathematical genius was so high that I could no longer follow. Thereafter philosophy was often a subject of our conversations. I recommended to him the reading of Kant. At that time he was still a child. Only thirteen years old, yet Kant's works, incomprehensible to ordinary mortals, seemed to be clear to him. Kant became Albert's favorite philosopher after he had read through his *Critique of Pure Reason* and the works of other philosophers."

On War

Author- Karl von Clausewitz, 1780-1831
Read by Dwight D. Eisenhower, 1890-1969
34th President of the United States

The commander of our brigade was a practical officer, down to earth, equally at home in the company of the most important people in the region and with any of the men in any regiment. One change in my attitude he accomplished quickly—with profound and endless results. In asking me a casual question, General Conner discovered that I had little or no interest left in military history.

We talked for a time and he went through the library and picked out two or three historical novels. "You might be interested in these." he said quietly. I remember that one of them was *The Long Roll* by Mary Johnston, and another *The Exploits of Brigadier Gerard* in the Napoleonic Wars. A third was *The Crisis* by the American Winston Churchill. They were stirring stories and I liked them.

After I read the first of these books, General Conner questioned me closely about the decisions made—why they were made and under what conditions. "What do you think would have been the outcome if this decision had been just the opposite?" "What were the alternatives?" And so I read Grant's and Sheridan's memoirs, and John Codman Ropes on the Civil War. I read Clausewitz's *On War* three times and a volume that was the Comte de Paris' Army of the Potomac narrative, but only certain chapters that bore upon campaigns we were discussing. He had me read Fremantle's account of the Battle of Gettysburg, as well as that of Haskell.

I can never adequately express my gratitude to this one gentleman, for it took years before I fully realized the value of what he had led me through. In a lifetime of association with great and good men, he is the one more or less invisible figure to whom I owe an incalculable debt.

The Dictionary

Read by Millard Fillmore, 1800-1874
13th President of the United States

During the months of attending the mill machines, he became painfully aware of his ignorance. In previous years he had taken all the schooling the surrounding country could offer, but this had given him only a slight exposure to the three "R's." He could read, to be sure, but almost nothing except the Bible and a few spelling and reading books were available. Years later he described the Family Library as "a Bible, a hymn book, and an almanac." His enlightenment began at seventeen when neighbors organized a circulating library and he bought a share in it. Voraciously he attacked the books. No method plotted the course of his reading; it was aimless, but extensive. Immediately one lesson emerged. He recognized the woeful limitations of his vocabulary. He purchased a dictionary, and, determined to learn the meaning of every unknown word, he set up his own school on a desk in the shop. In a spare moment as he passed between the wooden mill-machines, he looked up a word, and fixed its meaning in his memory while changing rolls.   —Robert J. Rayback

Thoughts on The Dictionary:

"A word or a form of speech is not good because it is in the dictionary; it is in the dictionary because it was good before it was put there."—Francesco Maria Zanotti

"Dictionaries are like watches; the worst is better than none, and the best cannot be expected to go quite true ."   —Samuel Johnson

"The responsibility of a dictionary is to record the language, not set its style."   —Philip Gove

Life of Washington

Author- Parson Weems, 1759-1825
Read by Sydney Fisher, 1856-1927
Historian; Author, "The Evolution
of the Constitution"

Fisher, for whom the exposure of historical myths was a specialty, regarded Weems as "a writer of the highest order of popularity." He had a fabulous influence, and "in that sense" he was "the ablest historian we have produced." Weems, he wrote, "will live forever. He captured the American people. He was the first to catch their ear. He said exactly what they wanted to hear. He has been read a hundred times more than all the other historians and biographers of the revolution put together." One may well differ with Fisher's final assessment.

The Life and Memorable Actions of Washington, published in 1800, was written for the edification of the young, but absorbed the youthful of all ages. Weems had a superlative talent for storytelling. He made the most obdurate indifference quicken into interest. The peerless character who materialized by Weems' deft use of words was already the national idol. All the shining attributes with which he endowed his subject were the commonplace attributes, honored by everyone and capable of universal emulation. There but for the grace of a devil's luck any could go, for hard work, perseverance, and temperate living were the opportunities of all men. Weems was one of the earliest exemplars of a sturdy American literary genre, the biography of success. And the cult of success, even though hardened into a sentimental axiom by unimaginative dullards, is deep in the American grain. He was the pioneer Horatio Alger of American literary culture, the author of the most popular biography of American letters.

—Bert James Lowenberg

Little Journeys

Author-Elbert Hubbard 1856 - 1915
Publisher-The Roycrofters
Read by Henry Ford 1863 - 1947

Elbert Hubbard's writings in *The Philistine* and in the *Little Journeys*, and his famous experiment in book making at East Aurora, made him one of the interesting American characters of his time. He had a rare faculty of expression and he used it to serve the cause of common sense in this country.

Elbert Hubbard demonstrated the power of an idea when conceived by an independent mind and supported by intelligent industry. His Shop became a place of pilgrimage to men and women who were interested in the hadicrafts and who dreamed of a greater idealization of common life. Whether Mr. Hubbard made a permanent contribution toward that end, the event will declare, but certainly he served to keep the thought alive in his time.

I visited him at East Aurora and was a reader of the *Little Journeys* from the first. There has been so much interest in the personality and work of Elbert Hubbard that this volume descriptive of the man by one who worked with him will be eagerly sought by readers. A biography of Elbert Hubbard should find a permanent place in our libraries.

"Get your happiness out of your work or you will never know what happiness is."

—Elbert Hubbard

The Making of a Composer

Stephen Foster, 1826-1864
Song Writer; Member, American Hall of Fame

Morrison Foster tells of his brother's personality.

"He was very simple in his tastes, and no matter how well his income justified it, he shrank from everything like display. The simplest forms of food satisfied him. Indeed, he never appeared to care for what was set before him on the table. If it appeased hunger it was all he cared for. His companions were seldom ever musicians. Outside of his own studies and performances he seemed to prefer to get away from music and musical topics. But he was very fond of the society of cultured people and men of genius in walks entirely different from his own."

There are numerous references to Stephen's love for reading in reminiscences of his family and friends, and it may be that we have direct evidence of the kind of literature he read. On the inside back cover of his manuscript book, turned upside down, Stephen wrote a list of books and authors, with amounts written after each name. Two possibilities are suggested by this list. One, that it comprised books he had purchased, with an estimate of what they had cost, and the other that before he went to New York in 1860 he planned to sell his collection of books, and was figuring what they should bring.

Here is the list, and the reader may judge Stephen's taste for himself:

Bleak House..........$ .60		Webster........ .35
(Illegible) 1.50		Maryott........ .40
Harp [er's?]............ 1.00		(Illegible).... .30
Webster................. 2.00		Hutten...........60
Scott...................... .50		Meadow...... .25
Cowper .... .25		$8.50

—John Howard

An Essay on Projects

Author- Daniel DeFoe, 1660-1731
Read by Benjamin Franklin, 1706-1790
Statesman, Publisher, Inventor

From a child I was fond of reading, and all the little money that came into my hands was ever laid out in books. Pleased with the *Pilgrim's Progress*, my first collection was of John Bunyan's works in separate little volumes. I afterward sold them to enable me to buy R. Burton's *Historical Collections*; they were small chapmen's books, and cheap, forty or fifty in all. My father's little library consisted chiefly of books in polemic divinity, most of which I read, and have since often regretted that, at the time when I had such a thirst for knowledge, more proper books had not fallen in my way, since it was now resolved I should not be a clergyman. Plutarch's Lives was there, in which I read abundantly, and I still think that time spent to great advantage. There was also a book of DeFoe's, called *An Essay on Projects*, and another of Dr. Mather's, called *Essays to do Good*, which perhaps gave me a turn of thinking that had an influence on some of the principal future events of my life.

This bookish inclination at length determined my father to make me a printer, though he had already one son (James) of that profession. In 1717, my brother James returned from England with a press and letters to set up his business in Boston. In a little time I made great proficiency in the business, and became of a useful hand to my brother. I now had access to better books. An acquaintance with the apprentices of booksellers enabled my sometimes to borrow a small one, which I was careful to return soon and clean. Often I sat up in my room reading the greatest part of the night, when the book was borrowed in the evening and to be returned early in the morning, lest it should be missed or wanted.

Caesar, Virgil, Horace, Homer

Read by John C. Fremont, 1813-1890
Western Explorer; Civil War
General; California Governor

In the year 1827, a very respectable lawyer came to my school with a youth, John Fremont, apparently about sixteen, or perhaps not so much (14), of middle size, graceful in manners, rather slender, but well formed, and upon the whole what I should call handsome; of a keen, piercing eye, and a noble forehead, seemingly the very seat of genius. The gentleman stated that he found him given to study, that he had been about three weeks learning the Latin rudiments, and had resolved to place him under my care for the purpose of learning Greek, Latin, and Mathematics, sufficient to enter Charleston College. I very gladly received him, for I immediately perceived he was no common youth, as intelligence beamed in his dark eye, and shone brightly on his countenance, indicating great ability, and an assurance of his future progress. I at once put him in the highest class, and although at first inferior, his prodigious memory and enthusiastic application soon enabled him to surpass the best. In the space of one year he had with the class, and at odd hours he had with myself, read four books of Caesar, Cornelius Nepos, Sallust, six books of Virgil, nearly all Horace, and two books of Livy; and in Greek, all Graeca Minora, about the half of the first volume of Graeca Majorca, and four books of Homer's Iliad. And whatever he read, he retained. I was myself utterly astonished, and at the same time delighted with his progress. He was designed for the church, but when I contemplated his bold, fearless disposition, his powerful inventive genius, his admiration of warlike exploits, and his love of heroic and adventurous deeds, I did not think it likely he would be a minister of the Gospel. He was always the very pattern of virtue and modesty.

—Dr. John Roberton

Abraham Lincoln

Read by J. Paul Getty, 1892-1976
American Oil Executive

I repeat the words of Abraham Lincoln:

"You cannot bring about prosperity by discouraging thrift. You cannot help the wage-earner by pulling down the wage-payer. You cannot further the Brotherhood of Man by encouraging class hatred. You cannot help the poor by destroying the rich. You cannot keep out of trouble by spending more than you earn. You cannot build character and courage by taking away a man's initiative. You cannot help men permanently by doing for them what they could and should do for themselves."

It is intriguing to speculate what socialist politicians will do if they have their way and nationalize all business. The capitalist goose that lays the golden tax-eggs will be transmuted into a money-losing socialist crow. Who will provide the funds for the salaries—and the secretaries, chauffeured cars, globe-hopping junkets and other perquisites—of senators, congressmen, Members of Parliament and the bureaucratic hordes? The prospect is one that might be profitably pondered by professional business-baiters and by all who reject Abraham Lincoln's dicta: "You cannot help the wage-earner by pulling down the wage-payer. You cannot help the poor by destroying the rich."

This is as Abraham Lincoln saw it. This is as I see it. This is as I hope a very great number of people will come to see it again. If they do, our society's chances of surviving and seeing a peaceful, prosperous future will be vastly increased.

But it is up to each and every one of you to make the decisions and take the actions. Whatever you may decide, whatever you may do, I wish you—and yours—luck, health and happiness.

Bulwer's Novels

Author- Edward Bulwer-Lytton, 1803-1873
Read by Ulysses S. Grant, 1822-1885
18th President of the United States

Since he did not leave West Point, he had to find his own private escape within the school. In his *Memoirs* he wrote, "I did not take hold of my studies with avidity, in fact I rarely ever read over a lesson the second time during my entire cadetship. I could not sit in my room doing nothing. There is a fine library connected with the Academy from which cadets can get books to read in their quarters. I devoted more time to these than to books relating to the course of studies. Much of the time, I am sorry to say, was devoted to novels, but not those of a trashy sort." Here with his characteristic balance of boldness and conventionality, Grant credited himself with intellectual initiative and then, as quickly, apologized for it. Those books mattered to him; he felt it important to record his debt to them. They were good books, and reading them was fun. Grant read "all of Bulwer's then published" (which means nine historical novels), James Fenimore Cooper, Washington Irving, the naval adventure stories of Frederick Marryat, and the lively anecdotal novels of Charles Lever, the Irishman. Either the library's collection of Lever disappointed Grant, or (like the Duke of Wellington) he enjoyed the Lever so much that he wanted his own copies of the novels. In the spring of his last year at the academy Grant twice urged Lever's American publisher to fill his order for *Charles O'Malley* and *Harry Lorrequer*.

It is difficult to know how important this world of imaginative literature remained for Grant. In later life, he disliked discussing literary matters, perhaps because of his lack of formal training or possibly because he liked the books themselves better than the talk about them.

—William McFeely

Laws From Heaven
for Life on Earth

Author- William Arnot
Read by James Gray, 1851-1935
President, Moody Bible Institute

My conversion came while reading a book, *Laws From Heaven for Life on Earth*, by Rev. William Arnot of Edinburgh, Scotland. It was a series of brief homilies upon the Book of Proverbs addressed to young men. I did not care for my Bible, but this book had a strong attraction for me.

On a memorable night in the quiet of my own room, after an exciting evening among worldly people, my eye fell on this sentence: "Every soul not already won to Christ is already lost."

It was an arrow of conviction to my soul. Quicker than I can express it, an overwhelming sense of my lost and hopeless condition fell upon me. I knew that I was not won to Jesus, and yet I knew that I ought to be. There was nothing in my life, professedly Christian and outwardly clean as it was, to indicate that I belonged to Him, or that He possessed or controlled me. Hell seemed open to receive me, and my soul was hanging over the abyss....

The prayer of the publican came to me: "God, be merciful to me a sinner!" I am not ashamed to say that in agony I uttered it with my face on the floor.

And God heard it. He always hears that prayer. He put the everlasting arm under me that night.

I cannot but believe that had I died during that period, moral youth that I was and church member besides, I should have died in my sins.

The highways of history are strewn with the wreckage of the nations that forgot God.

—Unknown

The Columbian Orator

**Read by Horace Greeley, 1811-1872
Founder & Editor, New York Tribune;
Democratic Presidential candidate**

Horace learned to read before he had learned to talk; that is, before he could pronounce the longer words. No one regularly taught him. When he was little more than two years old, he began to pore over the Bible, opened for his entertainment on the floor, and examine with curiosity the newspaper given him to play with. He cannot remember a time when he could not read, nor can any one give an account of the process by which he learned, except that he asked questions incessantly, first about the pictures in the newspaper, then about the capital letters, then about the smaller ones, and finally about the words and sentences. Allowing that nature gives to every child a certain amount of mental force to be used in acquiring the art of reading, Horace had an overplus of that force, which he employed in learning to read with his book in positions which increased the difficulty of the feat.

He was the possessor of three books, the *Columbian Orator*, Morse's *Geography*, and a spelling book. From the *Columbian Orator*, he learned many pieces by heart, and among others, that very celebrated oration which probably the majority of the inhabitants of this nation have at some period of their lives been able to repeat, beginning, "You'd scarce expect one of my age, to speak in public on the stage." One of his schoolfellows has a vivid remembrance of Horace's reciting this piece before the whole school in Londonderry, before he was old enough to utter the words plainly.

He had read the Bible through from Genesis to Revelations; had read the Pilgrim's Progress with intense interest, and dipped into every other book he could lay his hands on.

—James Parton

Essay on Human Understanding

Author- John Locke, 1632-1704
Read by Nathanael Greene, 1742-1786
Continental Army General
in the American Revolution

He was probably seventeen or eighteen when he met two men who first inspired and then guided him in his quest for higher learning.

Nathanael met William Giles in East Greenwich when the latter was a student at Yale. Giles found an eager listener for all he had to tell of the marvelous realm of higher education. Inspired by Giles, Nathanael thereafter was seldom seen without a book. Whenever possible, he made his way to the library.

Probably it was not long after he met Giles that Nathanael had the good fortune to come to know the Reverend Mr. Stiles, one day to become president of Yale, but at this time minister of The Second Congregational Church at Newport. According to tradition, Nathanael entered a bookstore at Newport and awkwardly made known his desire to buy a book on a certain subject. The bookseller questioned him as to title and author and the Reverend, who chanced to be in the store, overheard the dialogue. Observing the youth's perplexity, Stiles opened the conversation which presently led into a general discussion of books and authors. It was apparently through Stiles that Nathanael came to read Locke's *Essay on Human Understanding*, a book of unbounded influence on eighteenth-century thousands. Nathanael, whose Quaker upbringing afforded him a genuine taste for philosophical literature, found the deepest satisfaction in Locke.

—Theodore Thayer

Writers of the Enlightenment

Read by Albert Guerard, 1880-1959
Professor of Literature, Stanford University;
Author, "The Napoleonic Legend"

I recognize the kinship between my own thought and that of Locke, Montesquieu, Voltaire, Hume, Gibbon, just as close friends of mine feel themselves in deep harmony with Luther, Calvin, St. Augustine, and St. Paul. The quest of awareness which I am urging is ancient: it is the "Know thyself" of Greek philosophy. But in history, it has a definite name, the Enlightenment.

The Enlightenment was not ruled by crude formal logic. Not only did it inherit the "reasonableness" of the seventeenth century, but its acknowledged master, the guide of Montesquieu, Voltaire, d'Alembert, was Bacon and not Descartes. These men believed, not in abstract constructions, but in critical thought, serious inquiry, experimental science. This, incidentally, disposes of the accusation that they were frivolous. They smiled the delightful smile so well caught by La Tour, but they were also hard workers. Bayle's *Historical Dictionary*, Montesquieu's *Spirit of Laws*, Voltaire's *Century of Louis XIV* and *Essay on Manners*, Diderot's mighty *Encyclopaedia*, Buffon's monumental *Natural History*, Gibbon's *Decline and Fall*, are massive achievements, hard to match in any period. This very list disposes of a third charge that the Philosophes lacked historical sense. They did not worship the past, like some Romanticists, for its picturesque or sentimental appeal. They refused to accept without examination "the wisdom of prejudice." But it was their enemy Rousseau who grandly asserted: "First of all, let us brush aside all the facts!" The Philosophes studied the past earnestly, diligently. Montesquieu and Voltaire were the founders of modern history, emerging at last from the welter of chronicles, breaking the inflexible framework of dogma.

The Rise and Fall of the Third Reich

Author- William Shirer, 1904-
Read by John Gunther, 1901-1970
Foreign reporter; Author, "Inside Europe"

This is one of the most spectacular stories ever told. Mr. Shirer gives us a readable, percipient and closely documented history of the Third Reich, that is, of Adolf Hitler, who was both a criminal lunatic and a man of genius—one of the most appalling, atrocious varieties of madmen ever to deface the earth.

Hitler died in 1945, which means that hundreds of thousands of young people have no direct memory of his odious life and works. Even their elders, who should know better, are sometimes accustomed these days to shrug the Fuhrer off or even to give excuses for his murderous behavior. All such should read Mr. Shirer's Chapter 27, which sketches some elements of the new Hitler "order." It is the most appalling record of pure evil I have ever read.

Mr. Shirer tells the Hitler story from its beginnings; everything is here, in the most copious and telliing detail, from the early days in Vienna to the Beer Hall *Putsch* in Munich and, some years later, in 1933, the seizure of power from the senile Hindenburg. From this time on war was foredestined; and everybody should have known it, although some fatuous British, French and American diplomats and men of affairs were taken in. The cynicism with which Hitler manipulated opinion are not neglected in Mr. Shirer's pages.

Mr. Shirer's book is a study in frightfulness, yes—but it is something more than that as well. Its story has nobility, even grandeur, in that it proves (in the instance of Nazi Germany at least) that the guilty meet ignominious punishment for the most part and that, on balance, good triumphs over evil in the end.

The Wealth of Nations

Author- Adam Smith, 1723-1790
Read by Arthur Hadley, 1856-1930
Economist; Author,
"Standards of Political Morality"

It was reserved for Adam Smith to develop a philosophy of business which was in the highest and best sense of the word a moral philosophy. There have been a good many needless inquiries as to the reasons which make The *Wealth of Nations* superior in merit and influence to the many other acute economic writings in the latter part of the last century. The answer to these inquiries is a simple one. It was because Smith presented clearly to the reader the essentially moral character of business under modern conditions. His predecessors had generally thought of trade as a bargain, as a contest between buyer and seller, where the more skillful and more unscrupulous party gained the advantage over the other. Smith showed how under free competition the self-interest of the several parties, intelligently pursued, conduced to the highest advantage of the community. That Smith saw this truth, was his fundamental merit. That he was the first to see it in anything like its full scope, that he had the power to verify it, the candor to recognize its limits, the vigorous English in which to communicate his ideas to others, are facts which give The *Wealth of Nations* the place it deservedly holds in science and in literature. Not in economic science only, but in the whole field of morals have we learned from Adam Smith to expect a harmony of interests between the enlightened self-interest of the individual and the public needs of the community. The fact that the completeness of this harmony has been exaggerated by subsequent writers does not detract from the merit of its discoverer, but rather is a testimony to his power.

Edward Everett Hale & Books
1822-1909, Minister, Author,
"The Man Without a Country"

In the *New England Boyhood,* I have described our amusements. Meanwhile at home we were reading everything. Before I was eleven I had read Mungo Park and Claperton, Franklin's *Voyages* and *Parry's,* which were going on at that time. I had attacked Shakespeare and found it dull. I had been made to read more or less of Hume, which I found equally dull. But I had under my lee always a well-selected library. In our own private room, the attic of the house, we had *The Boy's Own Book,* one volume of *Don Quixote, The Treasury of Knowledge,* the sequel to *Harry and Lucy, Grimm's Fairy Tales,* and immense files of bound newspapers to which we occasionally went back.

It was a great grief to me when my older brother, at the age of thirteen, got hold of the Waverly Novels. For he was apt then to retire to one of the lower rooms to read his *Guy Mannering* or his *Ivanhoe,* and I was left alone.

My father had a collection of voyages and travels, which included a translation of Krusenstern's account of his voyage in the Pacific. This included a vocabulary of the language of the Marquesan Islands.

When Mr. Herman Melville subsequently published his book called *Typee,* we were quite at home in Marquesan Islands. I am afraid we were Imperialists before our time. It was a great grief to us to read that when Porter took possession of the islands in 1814 the United States did not choose to keep them. But all this is saying too much of boyish enterprises.

Caesar, Cicero and the Aeneid

Read by John Hancock, 1737-1793
President of the Continental Congress;
1st signer of the Declaration of Independence

In the good weather when there was early light the school day began at seven, so Johnny was up early and trudging off down the hill. The school itself was an old wooden structure crammed onto a small lot just behind King's Chapel, the Anglican church. It was two stories high, about forty feet wide where it faced the street, and twenty-five feet deep. The shingled gambrel-style roof had an incongruous-looking belfry perched atop. As Johnny walked up the steps the bell was pealing and would continue to ring until all the students were seated and the master appeared.

At his bench, hunched over his Greek and Latin texts, including *Aesop's Fables*, Eutropius' *Roman History*, and Ward's *Lily's Grammar*, Hancock began his career at Latin. By no means was he Lovell's best student, but, then, he was not the worst, either. But if he could be bad, he could also be good and share in the rewards, the highest of which was being allowed to work in Master Lovell's garden.

By his fifth year he was ready to begin "making Latin," so he was moved from his bench to a table, where he could begin to write. He translated from Caesar's *Commentaries*, Cicero's *Orations*, and the *Aeneid*. In his last year at the school the capstone was added—Xenophon and Homer.

The narrow curriculum provided for no frills. The purpose of the Latin Grammar School was to prepare a student in the tradition of the liberal arts so that he could follow the same path at college. Classical languages were the foundation, but with his mastery of the ancients he also acquired knowledge of history, philosophy, and theology.

—William J. Fowler, Jr.

War and Peace

Author- Leo Tolstoy, 1828-1910
Read by Oscar Handlin, 1915-
Historian; Pulitzer Prize for "The Uprooted"

In addition to its quality as an absorbing narrative, this book illuminates the complexity of the forces that shape history and their relation to human character. It also contains pertinent observations on the fallacies that entrap historians who fail to take account of those forces.

Thoughts from Tolstoy:

"In historical events great men—so called—are but the labels that serve to give a name to an event, and like labels, they have the least possible connection with the event itself. Every action of theirs, that seems to them an act of their own free will, is in an historical sense not free at all, but in bondage to the whole course of previous history, and predestined from all eternity."

"The strongest of all warriors are these two—Time and Patience."

"For us, with the rule of right and wrong given us by Christ, there is nothing for which we have no standard. And there is no greatness where there is not simplicity, goodness, and truth."

"Pure and complete sorrow is as impossible as pure and complete joy."

Sister Carrie

**Author- Theodore Dreiser, 1871-1945
Read by Moss Hart, 1904-1961
Librettist, Playwright; 1936 Pulitzer Prize
for "You Can't Take It With You"**

I can no longer remember which boy it was that summer evening who broke the silence with a question; "What's in those books you're always reading?" he asked idly. "Stories," I answered. "What kind?" asked somebody else without much interest.

Listening to a tale being told in the dark is one of the most ancient of man's entertainments, but I was offering them as well, without being aware of doing it, a new and exciting experience. The books they themselves read were the *Rover Boys* or *Tom Swift* or *G.A. Henty*. I had read them too, but at thirteen I had long since left them behind. Since I was much alone I had become an omnivorous reader and I had gone through the books-for-boys-series in one vast gulp. In those days there was no intermediate reading material between children's and grownups' books, or I could find none, and since there was no one to say me nay, I had gone right from *Tom Swift and His Flying Machine* to Theodore Dreiser and *Sister Carrie*. Dreiser had hit my young mind and senses with the impact of a thunderbolt, and they listened to me tell the story with some of the wonder that I had had in reading it.

It was, in part, the excitement of discovery—the discovery that there could be another kind of story that gave them a deeper kind of pleasure than the *Rover Boys*—blunderingly, I was giving them a glimpse of the riches contained outside the world of *Tom Swift*. Not one of them left the stoop until I had finished, and I went upstairs that wonderful evening not only a member of the tribe but a figure in my own right among them.

The Story of Civilization— Caesar and Christ

Author- Will Durant, 1885-1981
Read by Orrin Hatch
U. S. Senator, Utah

Over the years I have taken great pleasure in perusing each volume, as it was published, of *The Story of Civilization* by Will Durant. This continuing study has given me a long range perspective which has always been of significant value to me but which has been of particular use during my career in the Senate. New ideas, held up to the light of history, can be more readily understood and evaluated; their real meaning in the context of time becomes more clearly apparent. Each of these volumes is precious to me, but perhaps *Caesar and Christ* is my favorite. I commend them to you:

"The mind must be a citadel free from bodily desires, passions, anger, or hate. It must be so absorbed in its work as hardly to notice the adversities of fortune or the barbs of enmity. 'Every man is worth just so much as the things about which he busies himself.' He reluctantly concedes that there are bad men in this world. The way to deal with them is to remember that they, too, are men, the helpless victims of their own faults by the determinism of circumstance. 'If any man has done thee wrong, the harm is his own; it is thy duty to forgive him.' If the existence of evil men saddens you, think of the many fine persons you have met, and the many virtues that are mingled in imperfect characters. Good or bad, all men are brothers, kinsmen in one God; even the ugliest barbarian is a citizen of the fatherland to which we all belong. Does this seem an impracticable philosophy? On the contrary, nothing is so invincible as a good disposition, if it be sincere. A really good man is immune to misfortune, for whatever evil befalls him leaves him still his own soul."

The Discovers

Author- Daniel Boorstin, 1914-
Read by Mark Hatfield,
U. S. Senator, Oregon

Among the books which has most influenced my life is Daniel Boorstin's *The Discoverers* :

"Origen (185?-254) wrote in Alexandria some two centuries before Augustine, 'among all his predecessors and...among posterity as well who was the expectation of the nations.' Jesus Christ had taken mankind off the 'wheel.' The 'finality of Jesus,' elaborated by Augustine into a theory of history, would govern Christian thought in Europe for the next thousand years.

"While Christianity would be justified in history, its truths could not grow but were simply fulfilled. To the Jewish view of the past the Christians added their own sacred texts. The New Testament, they said, fulfilled the prophecies of the Old. Both Scriptures together were the one God's revelations not merely for a chosen people but for all mankind. While the Gospels were good news for everyone, they were not history in the Greek sense of inquiry, but were verifications of faith. The Christian test was a willingness to believe in the one Jesus Christ and His Message of salvation. What was demanded was not criticism but credulity. The Church Fathers observed that in the realm of thought only heresy had a history.

"When the literate leaders of Christianity made their record, they were not interested in inquiry. They had no need to seek answers, they had only to document them. During the Christian centuries in Europe these best minds in the Church developed their own techniques for using the past.

—Daniel Boorstin

Pilgrim's Progress

Author- John Bunyan, 1628-1688
Read by Nathaniel Hawthorne, 1804-1864
Author, "The House of the Seven Gables"

For the most part, Hawthorne's life in Maine was undisturbed by the irksome question of education. During the winter of 1818-1819, however, he was forced to go to school at nearby Stroudwater, under the direction of the Reverend Caleb Bradley, a Harvard graduate. Restless and unhappy, he waited until Uncle Robert had returned to Salem, then threatened to leave the school on his own. His mother and his more amenable Uncle Richard allowed the boy to come home.

Hawthorne nonetheless read a good deal during this period and was to form some opinions about his own education. He could recall reading, on rainy days in Maine, "in Shakespeare and 'The Pilgrim's Progress', and any poetry or light books within my reach." Interestingly, in view of his later development as a writer of allegories, his two favorite books of these earlier years were Spenser's *Faerie Queene* and Bunyan's *Pilgrim's Progress*, which he read and reread (and frequently alluded to) throughout his life. He could recall his pleasure as a small boy, standing on tiptoe to pull down books from his Grandfather Manning's shelf, shutting himself off in the pages of some barely comprehensible work, but understanding it more through sensibility than intellect. Only a solitary child, "left much to such wild modes of culture as he chooses for himself while yet ignorant what culture means," Hawthorne maintained, could develop the special intimacy with an author that he thought was worth having.

—James R. Mellow

The Analogy of Religion

Author- Joseph Butler, 1692-1752
Read by Patrick Henry, 1736-1799
Revolutionary War Statesman

While still a boy in his teens, and put prematurely to uncongenial attempts at shopkeeping and farmkeeping, he at any rate made the great discovery that in books and in the gathering of knowledge from books could be found solace and entertainment; in short, he then acquired a taste for reading. No one pretends that Patrick Henry ever became a bookish person.

He was particularly fascinated by Livy, which he read in the English translation; and then it was, as he himself related it to Judge Hugh Nelson, that he made the rule to read Livy through "once at least in every year during the early part of his life." He read also, it is apparent, the history of England and of the English colonies in America, and especially of his own colony; for the latter finding, no doubt, in Beverley and in the grave and noble pages of Stith, much material for those incisive opinions which he so early formed as to the rights of the colonies, and as to the barriers to be thrown up against the encroaching authority of the mother country.

There is much contemporaneous evidence to show that Patrick Henry was a deeply religious person. It certainly speaks well for his intellectual fibre, as well as for his spiritual tendencies, that his favorite book, during the larger part of his life, was Butler's *Analogy*, which was first published in the very year in which he was born. It is possible that even during these years of his early manhood he had begun his enduring intimacy with that robust book. Moreover, we can hardly err in saying that he had then also become a steady reader of the English Bible, the diction of which is stamped upon his style as unmistakably as it is upon that of the elder Pitt.

—Moses Tyler

The Greatest Thing
in the World

Author- Henry Drummond, 1851-1897
Read by Major Gen. Patrick Hessian
Chief of Army Chaplains

Henry Drummond's great little book had a profound influence on me:

"Everyone has asked himself the great question of antiquity as of the modern world: What is the 'summum bonum'—the supreme good? You have life before you. Only once can you live it. What is the noblest object of desire, the supreme gift to covet?

"We have been accustomed to be told that the greatest thing in the religious world is faith. That great word has been the keynote for centuries of the popular religion; and we have easily learned to look upon it as the greatest thing in the world. Well, we are wrong. If we have been told that, we may miss the mark. In the 13th chapter of I Corinthians, Paul takes us to Christianity at its source; and there we see, 'The greatest of these is love.'

"In these few words we have what one might call the spectrum of love, and analysis of love. Will you observe what its elements are? Will you notice that they have common names; that they are virtues which we hear about every day; that they are things which can be practiced by every man in every place in life; and how, by a multitude of small things and ordinary virtues the supreme thing, the 'summum bonum,' is made up?

"The spectrum of love has nine ingredients: patience, kindness, generosity, humility, courtesy, unselfishness, good temper, guilelessness, and sincerity. These make up the supreme gift, the stature of the perfect man."

The Adventures of Tom Sawyer

Author- Mark Twain, 1835-1910
Read by Eric Hodgins, 1899-1971
Vice-President, Time, Inc.

An incredible thing happened. I came across a copy of *The Adventures of Tom Sawyer* by Mark Twain, a name unknown to me. (He was still alive, with his white mane, white evening clothes, and a fully recognized genius. Perhaps it was just as well I did not know this: it might have made me suspicious of him.) He burst into my mind like a rocket. Here was a man who used words with grace and power, whose characters were real, and who could tell a rattling yarn.

But wonderful as these things were, there was a more wonderful thing still. Tom had been unfairly treated by Aunt Polly, he thought. Put to bed, he brooded and brooded on his sorrows. They were insurmountable, so "He turned his face to the wall and died." Here was an adult, a writer, who actually knew what it was like to be a boy. I had turned my face to the wall and died a thousand times in my eight years, and here was someone who understood and wrote about it. The effect was overwhelming.

I sought out all the Mark Twain I could find. *Tom Sawyer, Detective* didn't quite measure up, but then there was *Huckleberry Finn* and, above all, *Life on the Mississippi*. I think I must have spent a year reading and rereading those books. Why had my parents not put me wise? I didn't know, and still don't. In fact I can remember only one literary experience with my parents. By the light of a green-shaded lamp my father read aloud to my mother and me Dickens' *Our Mutual Friend*. It took a long time, and it passed largely over my head, but the words were pleasant to hear in my father's grave voice.

A School Teacher Makes a President

By Herbert Hoover, 1874-1964
31st President of the United States

At fifteen years of age, I left school to practice the profession office boy in a business firm in Salem, Oregon. One day there came into the office a Miss Gray. She was a tall lady in her thirties, with agreeable manners, kindly eyes and a most engaging smile. I was alone in the reception office. She announced that she was a schoolteacher and asked me about my schooling.

She asked if I was interested in reading books. She must have thought some wider scope in book reading was desirable from my replies to her questions as to what I had read.

Miss Gray asked me if I would go with her to the small lending library in town. At the library she said she wished to borrow a copy of Ivanhoe, and she gave it to me saying I would find it interesting. I read the book at the office between chores, and in the evenings. It opened a new world filled with alarms and excursions of battles, the pomp of tournaments, the tragedy of Rebecca's unrequited love, the heroism of the Black Knight and Locksley, and the destiny of Ivanhoe. Suddenly I began to see books as living things as was ready for more of them.

A few days later Miss Gray dropped in again and suggested David Copperfield, I can still remember the harshness of Murdstone, the unceasing optimism of Micawber and the wickedness of Uriah Heep. I have met them alive many times in afteryears.

And so, through books, my horizons widened, sometimes with Miss Gray's help, sometimes on my own initiative. I devoured samples of Thackeray and Irving, biographies of Washington, Lincoln and Grant.

Miss Gray's influence widened when I began the practice of my profession as an engineer, and it extended over the eighteen years which followed. In that work I had long days of travel, and many hours of waiting for things to happen on ships, railways and canalboats all over the world—from the United States to China, to Burma, to Mexico, to Australia, to Africa, to Canada and Russia. On one journey, thanks to Miss Gray's inoculation, I armed myself with paperbound volumes of Defoe, Zola, Balzac; on another, with such less exciting books as those of Herbert Spencer, James Mill and Walter Bagehot. Another time I took along Carlyle's *French Revolution,* Gibbon's *The History of the Decline and Fall of the Roman Empire,* and some more popular histories of Greece and Egypt. I also read books on Mohammed, Buddha and Confucius, as well as more American history.

With the coming of World War I and with official duties devouring my time and energy thereafter for many years, my book reading slackened. Nonetheless, Miss Gray's influence penetrated even as far as the White House. When I arrived at that residence in 1929, I found it was mostly bare of books except for the published papers of former presidents—incomplete at that. One day I mentioned this famine of representative American literature in the White House to John Howell, an old friend and a leading bookseller. Under his leadership and with the co-operation of the American Booksellers Association, some five hundred books were selected. Most of these I had read long ago, but they were much enjoyed by the many other inhabitants of the White House.

To me they were always a reminder of Miss Gray, and of the words of John Milton: "A good book is the precious lifeblood of a master spirit, embalmed and treasured up on purpose to a life beyond life."

Uncle Tom's Cabin

Author- Harriet Beecher Stowe, 1811-1896
Read by Oliver Wendell Holmes,
1841-1935
United States Supreme Court Justice

It was becoming impossible for Boston to maintain the middle course. Property versus freedom: both were sacred. A hard choice for New England to make. Dr. Holmes brought a book home from the Athenaeum: *Uncle Tom's Cabin*. Wendell was old enough, his father thought, to read something besides Fenimore Cooper. *The Pathfinder, The Deerslayer, The Prairie, The Last of the Mohicans, The Ways of the Hour*—week by week these titles appeared on the doctor's library card.

The Holmes children read *Uncle Tom's Cabin*, wept over little Eva, thrilled when Eliza crossed the ice. But to Dr. Holmes as to his children, these things were far off, would never touch their lives. The doctor's friend Ticknor, the publisher, remarked of Mrs. Stowe's book that it deepened the horror of slavery, but did not change a single vote. It occurred to few that war was coming. Howe had a letter from Theodore Parker, written from Italy. "What a pity," wrote Parker, "that the map of our magnificent country should be destined to be so soon torn in two on account of the negro, that poorest of human creatures, satisfied, even in slavery, with sugar cane and a banjo."

—Catherine Drinker Bowen

When I want to understand what is happening today or try to decide what will happen tomorrow I look back. A page of history is worth a volume of logic.

—Justice Holmes

Cause and Cure of Infidelity

Author- Rev. David Nelson, 1793-1844
Read by General Sam Houston, 1793-1863
President of Republic of Texas, Military Hero

In May, Houston was transferred to the U.S. First Infantry garrisoned at New Orleans.

He spent most of the winter recuperating in a French-built barracks by the river, reading the books that he had brought with him: the Bible his mother had given him, *Shakespeare,* Akenside's *Poems, Robinson Crusoe, Pilgrim's Progress,* and *The Vicar of Wakefield.*

Houston was familiar with Roman history. His much-thumbed copy of Caesar's *Commentaries,* supposed to have been carried in his saddlebags, has become a museum item. His favorite Roman character was Caius Marius (c. 155 B.C.-86 B.C.), a general, who had also been in exile. Among his other virtues as general and statesman, Marius displayed patience and the ability to recover after setbacks. Following his exile, he organized a well-disciplined army out of unpromising material and a demoralized soldiery and inflicted two decisive defeats on invaders. Houston especially admired Marius' ability to make a comeback. In 1831, on a brief excursion from Arkansas to Tennessee during his own forest exile, Houston had his portrait painted as Marius.

A stern realist in military matters, diplomacy, and statesmanship, Houston was suspicious about authoritarian doctrine that could not be subjected to rational analysis. Rev. Samson directed Houston's attention to Nelson's *Cause and Cure of Infidelity,* which the Senator bought and later gave to many persons who expressed skepticism of Christianity. Just as he had preached temperance when he was a hard drinker, he spread the Christian doctrine to unbelievers before he accepted it for himself.

—M. K. Wisehart

Shakespeare and Byron

Read by Julia Ward Howe, 1819-1910
Woman Suffrage Leader; Composer of
"The Battle Hymn of the Republic"

As it happened, Julia's enforced isolation had the effect of making her withdraw into herself. She turned to books instead of people and allowed "fiery feverish dreams" to fill her mind. "In the large rooms of my father's house I walked up and down perpetually alone, dreaming of the extraordinary things I should see and do. I now began to read Shakespeare and Byron and to try my hand at poems and plays." Such daydreams appealed to her far more than her schoolwork. At the age of eleven, she handed in a collection of poems to her teacher instead of the prose composition that had been assigned, and was rebuked for being overambitious. She persisted nonetheless, and by the age of fourteen she had succeeded in having several poems published in the New York *American.*

Her greatest pleasure, since she was discouraged from leaving the house except for an occasional drive with her sisters, was to go into Sam's new library and lose herself in one of the hundreds of volumes of German, French and Italian literature that filled the shelves. Joseph Cogswell had already introduced her to the works of various German authors and she had read some Byron, but it was in her brother's library that she found Victor Hugo, Balzac, George Sand and other European writers of the day. Sam encouraged her to read anything she wished, and Julia later remembered that the "sense of intellectual freedom" this reading gave her was "half delightful, half alarming."

—Deborah Pickman Clifford

Abridgement of the Law

Author- Matthew Bacon
Read by Andrew Jackson, 1767-1845
7th President of the United States

Andrew Jackson stated with pride that the stout mare carried "half a dozen books" over the windy summits of the Blue Ridge. Of these Matthew Bacon's *Abridgement of the Law* was the sheet anchor of the journeyman solicitor. Or so it seemed to Waightstill Avery who found himself opposed to young Mr. Jackson in a suit before the Superior Court at Jonesborough, where Jackson and McNairy had decided to tarry, finding it impossible to get through to Nashville in time to open court before the autumn session. Waightstill Avery, of Morganton, was a personage in North Carolina, a wise and scholarly old lawyer mellowed by the experiences of life. He liked Jackson and had gone out of his way to be helpful to him, but this did not deter him, in an address to the court, from twitting his adversary upon the liberal doses of Bacon that spiced his arguments.

Andrew squirmed in his seat, and, when Colonel Avery concluded, he blurted out, probably forgetting to suppress his Irish accent:

"I may not know as much law as there is in Bacon but I know enough not to take illegal fees!"

Silence in the log court-room. Colonel Avery arose to ask if Mr. Jackson meant to imply that he had taken illegal fees.

"I do, sir," replied Andrew Jackson.

"It's false as hell!" shouted Waightstill Avery.

Mr. Jackson was writing rapidly on a fly-leaf of his Bacon. He tore out the page and bowing—"Your obedient servant, sir"—presented it to Colonel Avery.

—Marquis James

The Swamp Fox

Read by Thomas "Stonewall" Jackson, 1824-1863
General, Confederate States of America

Young Tom's natural curiosity expanded as he broadened his knowledge, and by 1840 his inquiries extended beyond the classroom. Religious matters caught his interest and soon the earnest young man became a familiar figure in church. A daughter of one of the local Methodist ministers wrote that on several Sundays "Thomas Jackson, a shy, unobtrusive boy, sat with unabated interest in a long sermon, having walked three miles in order to attend." Tom's concern with spiritual affairs extended beyond formal church-going. Christianity he must study carefully so that he could share fully in its joys and duties. He began to read the Bible and soon became something of a Biblical scholar.

Religion opened a whole new world for young Jackson, and although careful never to force his views on anyone, he gladly would read the Scriptures or discuss theological matters if asked. In return for Tom's Scriptural instruction and the loan of his Bible, Joe Lightburn, one of Tom's best friends gave his highly prized copy of Parson Weem's *Life of Francis Marion*. The two boys must have been vastly influenced by the Bible and by The Swamp Fox. Both rose to be generals on opposite sides during the Civil War; Lightburn became a Baptist minister after the war, and Jackson thought about going into the ministry before the war. He talked of the ministry, and it appears that his deficiency in education and a fear of public speaking were all that kept him from this calling. There is little doubt that Tom's interest in religion began much earlier in life than is generally supposed.

—Frank Vandiver

Ordeal by Fire

Author- Fletcher Pratt, 1897-1956
Read by John Jakes
Author, "North & South"

In 1952, a year after I made my first writing sale—a science fiction story—I was reading widely in several fields of interest, one of them history. I chanced across a remarkable work retitled *A Short History of the Civil War* for its paperback edition. The author, Fletcher Pratt, originally published the book in the 1930's as *Ordeal by Fire.*

Pratt's book awakened my interest in the Civil War. But it did something even more important. With its fire-engine and its vivid, sometimes breathless prose, it showed me for the first time the real stuff of history: the sounds and colors; the quirky personalities behind the legendary names; the high drama—even melodrama.

Fletcher Pratt wrote all sorts of material during his career, from fantasy to excellent works on the naval history of the Civil War. For me, though, none ever matched *Ordeal by Fire.* I went on to admire other historians, the great Bruce Catton chief among them, but it was Pratt's book that set me firmly on my present path by showing me the excitement, and the challenge, of bringing the past to life through use of the particular detail instead of the gray generality.

It has been more than a decade since I re-read the book; long out of print, it is available only in a few libraries. Even its title has been replaced by another *Ordeal* by one of our finest academic historians, Dr. James McPherson of Princeton. I would not want to vouch for all of Pratt's facts and conclusions. Yet if you can find the book, I would recommend it for its matchless presentation of its unspoken premise: there is no greater drama than history, properly told.

Plutarch's Lives

Author- Plutarch, A.D. 46-120
Read by John Jay, 1745-1829
American Statesman,
President of Continental Congress

The instruction of the first year at King's College was devoted exclusively to Latin and Greek, but the curriculum for the second included rhetoric and "Repetitions to learn the Art of speaking." His indistinct articulation embarrassed him. His pronunciation of the letter *l* subjected him to the youthful, though cruel, ridicule of his fellow students. Added to this was a habit of reading too rapidly. John determined to correct both. He bought a copy of John Holmes's *Art of Rhetoric made easy...for the practice of the Studious Youth of Great Britain and Ireland,* and shut himself up daily in his room. There, before a mirror, practicing a full stop after each word, he overcame his faults and laid the foundation for that "quiet, limpid style" for which he was afterward noted. The same assiduous method he employed to improve his English compositions. During his preparation for an English essay he placed paper and pencil by his bedside that he might record ideas and phrases that came to him during the night. At the same time he began the reading of his twenty-one volumes of Cicero. He read deeply in Rowning's *Compendius System of Natural Philosophy* and John Clarke's translation of Suetonius. With a more utilitarian view he turned to Atkinson's *Epitome of the Art of Navigation* and William Hume's *Surveying Improved.* On November 25, 1762, he noted on a flyleaf of one of his books a momentous date in the history of the institution that has become the world's largest university, for "on this day happened the first examination of the students that ever was in King's College."

About this time his father presented him with a volume of *The Humorist: Being Essays on Several Subjects,* perhaps hoping that it might supply an element that he observed was not conspicuous in his son. It supplied little humor but did sharpen John's power of sarcasm, which he controlled with difficulty. During his college career he enjoyed the friendship of the pious and learned Dr. Johnson. Among the students of King's College McPherson's *Ossian* enjoyed a vogue; in one of his books John had copied Ossian's "Address to the Sun," a bombastic bit of rhetoric. Dr. Johnson observed with distress the absence of any mention of God in the address: that fault he sought to remedy by adding to Ossian's Address a passage which began: "But it is only this decaying Body that can fade and dye, my soul shall continue to live and flourish in immortal youth; it shall dwell with the great Father of the Universe and enjoy unfading bliss," and ended "Amen." This the students dutifully added to Ossian and the incipient spirit of paganism was repulsed. In his third year John read through the tragedies of Seneca, the *Ethics* of Aristotle and the works of Livy and Isocrates, as well as Locke's *Essay on Human Understanding.* More important in its permanent influence on Jay was Plutarch's *Lives,* which shaped the thoughts of many youths in Europe and America in the eighteenth century, inculcating an intense admiration of Plutarch's idealized picture of the stoical virtues of republican antiquity.

—Frank Monaghan

PRESIDENTS OF THE UNITED STATES

The Life of Washington
Author- Jared Sparks, 1789-1866
Read by James Buchanan, 1791-1868
15th President of the United States

In 1853 when Marshall College merged with Franklin College, Buchanan accepted the presidency of the Board of Trustees of the new institution and spent considerable time helping to select a suitable location in Lancaster for the campus. His renewed associations with academic people led him to expand his library and to do more reading. He at last had time to look at the five volume *Life of Washington* by Jared Sparks, and to study Madison's newly published notes on the Constitutional Convention and Elliott's *Debates* on its ratification. He dipped into the works of Byron and read a good many of Sir Walter Scott's novels and the writings of Charles Dickens. —Philip Klein

English History, Shakespeare and the Bible
Read by Zachary Taylor, 1784-1850
12th President of the United States

Zachary was an educated man, no matter what his enemies said. For this there is the evidence of no less a figure than Jefferson Davis, a most cultivated person, who had been raised in the best drawing room tradition. Zachary Taylor was one of the most deeply read and profoundly learned men in military history that he had ever known. He encouraged his own children to study French and to read English history, Shakespeare and the Bible. He sent his children to the best private schools he could afford. One must say that Zachary had a profound appreciation of formal education, although his own had been sketchy, and he was by all standards a self-educated man. —Edwin Hoyt

The American Speaker

Read by Andrew Johnson, 1808-1875
17th President of the United States

A certain charm attaches to Andy's efforts at an early age to satisfy his itch for learning. There were no free schools in Raleigh and money for tuition was out of the question for "Aunt Polly," hard put to support Andy and his brother by taking in washing and weaving clothes on her loom. So Andy found his own school—in the shop of master-tailor James J. Selby. It was the custom of the journeymen tailors, while they sat cross-legged about the shop doing their cutting and sewing, to hire a man to read to them from newspapers, magazines, novels, poems, plays and the debates of Congress. For hours on end the reading went on, and for hours on end, once young Andy had discovered this unorthodox institution of learning, he could be found among the tailors, dark-eyed and eager, listening and learning.

One of the paid readers took note of the boy's interest and gave him the volume he was using. From this book; with the aid of a primer and an alphabet provided by one of the tailors, Andy taught himself to read. The book was an 1810 edition of The American Speaker which, despite its title, was a collection of orations by famous Members of Parliament.

—Milton Lomask

What are all histories but God manifesting Himself, that He hath shaken and tumbled down, and trampled upon everything that He hath not planted.

—Oliver Cromwell

Advice to Law Students

By Thomas Jefferson, 1743-1826
3rd President of the United States
Author of the Declaration of Independence

from his correspondence:

The enclosed letter to C. Lewis near Charlottesville will show you what I have supposed could be best done for you there. It is a general practice to study the law in the office of some lawyer. This indeed gives to the student the advantage of his instruction. But I have ever seen that the services expected in return have been more than the instructions have been worth. All that is necessary for a student is access to a library, and directions in what order the books are to be read. This I will take the liberty of suggesting to you, observing previously that as other branches of science, and especially history, are necessary to form a lawyer, these must be carried on together. I will arrange the books to read into three columns, and propose that you should read those in the first column till 12 o'clock every day; those in the 2d from 12 to 2; those in the 3d after candlelight; leaving all the afternoon for exercise and recreation, which are as necessary as reading: I will rather say more necessary, because health is worth more than learning.

1st—Coke on Littleton. Coke's 2d. 3d. & 4th. institutes. Coke's reports. Vaughn's reports. Salkeld's. Ld. Raymond's. Strange's. Burrow's. Kaim's Principles of equity. Vernon's reports. Peere Williams. Precedents in Chancery. Tracy Atheyns. Verey. Hawkin's Pleas on the crown. Blackstone. Virginia laws.

2d—Dalrymple's feudal system. Hale's history of the Com. law. Gilbert on Devises. Uses. Tenures. Rents. Distresses. Ejectments. Executions. Evidence. Sayer's law of costs. Lambard's circonantia. Bacon, voce Pleas & Pleadings. Cunningham's law of bills. Molley de jure maritimo. Locke on government. Montesquieu's Spirit of law. Smith's wealth of nations. Beccaria. Kaim's moral essays. Vattel's law of nations.

3d—Mallet's North antiquit'. History of England in 3 vols. folio compiled by Kennet. Ludlow's memoirs. Burnet's history. Ld. Orrery's history. Burke's George III. Robertson's hist. of Scotl'd. Robertson's hist. of America. Other American histories. Voltaire's historical works.

Should there by any little intervals in the day not otherwise occupied fill them up by reading Lowthe's grammar, Blair's lectures on rhetoric, Mason on poetic & prosaic numbers, Bolingbroke's works for the sake of the stile, which is declamatory & elegant, the English poets for the sake of style also.

As Mr. Peter Carr in Goochland is engaged in a course of law reading, and has my books for that purpose, it will be necessary for you to go to Mrs. Carr's, and to receive such as he shall be then done with, and settle with him a plan of receiving from him regularly the before mentioned books as fast as he shall get through them. The losses I have sustained by lending my books will be my apology to you for asking your particular attention to the replacing them in the presses as fast as you finish them, and not to lend them to anybody else, nor suffer anybody to have a book out of the Study under cover of your name. You will find, when you get there, that I have had reason to ask this exactness.

Booker T. Washington

Read by Dr. Laurence C. Jones
Principal, Piney Woods Country Life School

During my sophomore year I heard our President, Dr. George E. MacLean, use the phrase, "Nobless Oblige," and one day in the botany class Professor Thomas H. Macbride explained to me its meaning. More than ever I realized that because of the superior advantages for schooling that had been mine, I was morally obligated to pass the opportunity on to those less fortunate than myself. I believe I had always had a subconscious desire to be a school teacher, but I had also cherished a desire to engage in the poultry business. One of my fondest dreams was to realize money enough from this business some day to cross the ocean and see the countries of the Old World. "Nobless Oblige," however, taught me that my duty was down in the black belt among the less fortunate of my people.

This conviction came to me strongly in my junior year through the "Industrial Art" class work of Professor Clark Fisher Ansley. It was seminar work, and during the latter half of the year I was assigned the task of developing a theme on the work of Dr. Booker T. Washington. I proceeded to read and re-read this leader's books and to look up every magazine article listed in the various indexes. The result was that I got together an interesting amount of material and for the first time realized the meaning of the poet's phrase, "Our echoes roll from soul to soul," when I learned that Mark Hopkins taught General S.C. Armstrong, and that General Armstrong taught and inspired Booker T. Washington. Most of the class members had been given an hour each to the topics assigned, but I was so full of my subject that I was given six hours. A member of the class who was on the staff of the city papers gave a review of each lecture to the various papers. I called the attention of the class to the fact that the Negro race had many other great men, distinguished in various lines, who simply happened not to be so well known as Dr. Washington. One of the highest expressions of Negro life and achievement, I said, was to be found in the life, personality and writings of Dr. W.E.B. DuBois. From industrial training to the scholarship of Dr. DuBois seemed a long step, but it showed the possibilities of the Negro. I further said that Dr. DuBois was not opposing industrial education but that his great contention was that there was not so much a "Negro Problem" as a "Human Problem," as Frederick Douglass once said, and that industrial education was no more a means for the complete development of the Negro than any other kind of education. I also read some passages from the beautiful and fascinating "Souls of Black Folk," which book so impressed me that I decided to purchase a copy and present it to my English teacher, Miss Mary G. Chawner, in appreciation of the interest and help she had given me in my courses.

During my last two summers in Iowa City I realized my Pilgrim Hotel ambition by becoming a night clerk at one of the local hotels. Several of the guests registered their prejudice by going to the landlord, but he told them that he was running the hotel, and I went on with my work. One evening at the close of my senior year— commencement week, 1907—while I was waiting at table, a gold watch was presented to me by the members of the Delta tau Delta Fraternity; and next to the ovation given me in Marshalltown this was the greatest surprise of my life. Then came commencement day and with it the Secretary of War, William Howard Taft, who delivered the graduation address. Once more I had completed a prescribed course of study. Once more I looked out upon the world and realized how little I really knew.

—Laurence Jones

Serious Call to a
Devout and Holy Life

Author- William Law, 1686-1761
Read by Samuel Johnson, 1709-1784
Author, "Dictionary of the English Language"

Despite his determination to vex the tutors in his own college, Johnson did not altogether neglect his studies. In his room at the top of the staircase above the main gateway, he had over a hundred volumes from his father's stock, mostly Greek and Roman classics, volumes of poetry, and religious books; and these he studied with as much diligence as he could muster, reading Homer and Euripides "solidly." He also picked up William Law's *Serious Call to a Devout and Holy Life,* "expecting to find it a dull book (as such books generally are) and perhaps to laugh at it." But he was profoundly impressed by it; it made him think about religion "in earnest," and from this time forward religion was "the predominant object of his thoughts; though with the just sentiments of a conscientious Christian, he lamented that his practice of its duties fell far short of what it ought to be."

He was profoundly affected by what he read. He was so shocked by Cordelia's death in *King Lear* that he could scarcely bear to look at the closing scenes of the play again until he was obliged to do so as its editor. The first time he read the ghost scene in *Hamlet* he was so frightened he ran out of the basement kitchen and up the stairs to the street to have people of flesh and blood about him. Yet he rarely finished a book. His eye skimmed over the lines, the pages were turned with astonishing speed, his capacious memory retained the substance of what he had read. But before the end was reached he would put the book aside and pick up another, or go out to walk in the fields or compose something of his own.

—Christopher Hibbert

Literature is My Utopia

By Helen Keller, 1880-1968
Blind Author, Lecturer

"Literature is my Utopia. Here I am not disfranchised. No barrier of the senses shuts me out from the sweet, gracious discourse of my friends. They talk to me without embarrassment or awkwardness."

Helen Keller is totally blind; yet she has read far more books than most people who can see. She has probably read a hundred times as many books as the average person and she has written seven books herself. She made a motion picture of her own life and acted in it. She is totally deaf, yet she enjoys music far more than many people who can hear.

Mark Twain once said: "The two most interesting characters of the nineteenth century are Napoleon and Helen Keller." When Mark Twain said that, Helen Keller was only fifteen years old. Today she still remains one of the most interesting characters of the twentieth century.

Helen Keller was born perfectly normal. For the first year and a half of her life, she could see and hear like other children and had even begun to talk. Then suddenly she was overwhelmed by catastrophe. She was struck down by an illness which left her deaf, dumb and blind at the age of nineteen months and blighted her whole existence.

—Dale Carnegie

Reading is the loom on which one's inner garments are woven. Shoddy reading clothes both mind and heart in shoddy garments.

—A.P. Gouthey

Lord Byron, 1788-1824

Read by John F. Kennedy, 1917-1963
35th President of the United States

Because he was so frequently bedridden, Jack was the only Kennedy who became a reader, consuming parables like *Pilgrim's Progress* and romances like *King Arthur and His Knights*. (Family friend Kay Halle recalled that the first time she saw him, thirteen-year-old Jack was in the hospital working his way through Winston Churchill's *The World Crisis*.)

Jack became a close friend of a tall intellectual from Yale named Chuck Spalding, who saw a side of Jack the others didn't—a literary and thoughtful side. Both of them were Anglophiles, which Spalding recognized as having Oedipal overtones for Jack given the Ambassador's attitudes. They both read books like Cecil's *Life of Melbourne* and *Pilgrim's Way* by John Buchan. Spalding became a sort of Jack Kennedy specialist, fascinated with him because he was so different from the other Kennedys.

Chuck Spalding felt it was instructive that Jack was fascinated by Byron: "He'd read everything about him and read most of the poetry too. There were a lot of similarities. Byron too had that conflict between irony and romanticism; he too wanted the world to be better than it was; he also had the disability—the club foot—and the conviction of an early death."

—Peter Collier and David Horowitz

"When power leads man toward arrogance, poetry reminds him of his limitations. When power narrows the areas of man's concern, poetry reminds him of the richness and diversity of his existence. When power corrupts, poetry cleanses, for art establishes the basic human truths which must serve as the touchstone of our judgment."

—JFK, address at Amherst College, 1963

My Father

By Rose Fitzgerald Kennedy, 1890-
Mother of President John F. Kennedy

So often, it seems, people get their college degrees and then are content to let mental facilities atrophy from disuse. My father, on the contrary, and perhaps because of being denied the credentials of an education, retained his appetite for knowledge and became an avid reader. He had wonderful azure blue eyes and boundless curiosity, so he read everything within reach: books, magazines, and, of course, many newspapers. Everything in print seemed to be grist for him—and when he found something that struck him as interesting, important, or in some way useful, he would cut the item out of the magazine or paper with a small penknife he carried. Then, to be sure he wouldn't lose it, quite often he would pin it (with a straight pin; he carried a supply) on his lapel or, when that area was filled, almost anywhere else on the front of his jacket. One of my earliest vivid recollections is of his sitting in a chair surrounded by newspapers, penknife in hand and neatly (always neatly, like a surgeon) excising something pertinent.

He kept on doing this all his life. Eunice says that one of her own enduring images of him—one of those impressions that somehow are selected and stored in the mind from among the many—was when he was well along in years, probably in his seventies. He was visiting us at Hyannis Port and was sitting in his favorite perch there, a chair at the far end of our big, bright, comfortable living room, with a sea view and the sunlight streaming in behind him. "There were masses of newspapers all over the floor around him, and he was clipping. He wouldn't get through a page or two without pulling out something. And he'd say, 'Now look at this! Look what the women are doing'—anyway, always he'd be finding something interesting."

Commentaries on
the Laws of England

Author- William Blackstone, 1723-1780
Read by James Kent, 1763-1847
Chief Justice of the New York Supreme Court

"When the college was broken up in 1779 by the British, I retired to a village, and, finding Blackstone's *Commentaries*, I read the four volumes. Parts of the work struck my taste, and inspired me, at the age of fifteen, with awe, and I fondly determined to be a lawyer."

After his graduation, his father found a place for him in the law offices of Attorney-General Egbert Benson, where he remained until admitted to the New York Supreme Court Bar in 1785. He has told with much detail what was the method of his study and what books he read. Among these were Grotius' *Puffendorf,* Smollett's *History of England,* Rapin's *English History,* Hale's *History of the Common Law* and Blackstone again.

Writing in 1782, he said: "Law, I must frankly confess, is a field which is uninteresting and boundless. Notwithstanding, it leads forward to the first stations in the State. The study is so encumbered with voluminous rubbish and the baggage of folios that it requires uncommon assiduity and patience to manage so unwieldy a work. Yet this adage often serves to steel my courage and smooth the rugged moments of despair: 'The harder the conflict the more glorious the triumph.'

"At the June circuit, 1786, I saw Edward Livingston, and he had a pocket Horace and read some passages to me, assuming that I well understood Horace. I said nothing, but was stung with shame and mortification. I purchased immediately Horace and Virgil, a dictionary and a grammar, and a Greek lexicon and grammar, and the Testament, and formed my resolution, promptly and decidedly, to recover the lost languages."

—Malcolm MacLean & Elizabeth Holmes

Christianity and the Social Crisis

Author- Walter Rauschenbusch, 1861-1918
Read by Martin Luther King, 1929-1968
Minister, Civil Rights Leader
1964 Nobel Peace Prize Winner

For Martin, what mattered most was the exploration that Crozer Theological Seminary encouraged. The first year emphasized Biblical criticism, and coming as he did from a literalistic background, Martin found Professor Enslin's liberal interpretation of the New Testament fascinating. In Enslin's teaching, the Apostle Paul emerged as a profound ethical thinker, Jesus came to life as a new kind of prophet, the life of the early Christians was delineated in the context of their times and the world around them. It began to make a different and more relevant kind of sense than it had before. Martin also found a theological basis for the perspective on society which had been evolving from his own experiences, and one which accorded well with Enslin's Biblical views. Walter Rauschenbusch's *Christianity and the Social Crisis* provided the key. First published in 1907, at the height of the trust-busting Progressive era of Theodore Roosevelt, it communicated an excessive optimism about bringing the Kingdom of God on earth in the near future—a failure that Martin King was quick to note. But what left "an indelible imprint," as King later wrote, was Rauschenbusch's insistence "that the gospel deals with the whole man, not only his soul but his body; not only his spiritual well-being but his material well-being. It has been my conviction ever since reading Rauchenbusch that any religion which professes to be concerned about the souls of men and is not concerned about the social and economic conditions that scar the soul, is a spiritually moribund religion only waiting for the day to be buried."

—William R. Miller

Louis L'Amour & Books

Awarded the Congressional Gold Medal for his contribution to Western Literature

Books surge and spill and twine through almost every room of his house. They march along one entire wall of the large living room and collect in piles on every flat surface. They stand guard in the home gymnasium where he tries to work out daily, and gather in stacks atop the glass table in his sun-washed family room. They parade in shelves along the hallways and take over completely in his cavernous bedroom. And he knows where everything is.

"These are all on archaeology," he says, indicating several shelves in the living room. "Here's one on the fall of the Byzantine Empire and—I love these volumes—*Leland's Itinerary* in England and Wales." But there's not much fiction: "I only read fiction on planes," he explains. Two long shelves hold the myriad works of Louis L'Amour. "It makes me feel good to see them, but I'm more conscious of what I haven't done."

When Boorstin, the author of a recent book on exploration, visited L'Amour, he was delighted to discover the "best collection of Marco Polo books I ever saw in private hands." Beyond are his trophies— awards, keys to a score of cities, framed hononary degrees—"That's a thrill for a guy who didn't get out of the tenth grade."

Later, he leads the way into his workroom—"A writer's dream room," he calls it—where a capacious desk sits between a fireplace and a window beyond which Sunset Boulevard traffic roars. "It doesn't bother me, it's like the sound of the sea." The floor-to-ceiling shelves contain about 8,000 books. "I'm in my own world here, I can transport myself to another time and place and put myself there."

—Donald Dale Jackson

NOBODY ever outgrows Scripture; the book widens and deepens with our years.

—Spurgeon

THE BOOK

THE Scriptures teach us the best way of living, the noblest way of suffering, and the most comfortable way of dying.

—Flavel

Patriots & the Book

The word of God tends to make largeminded, noble-hearted men.

—Henry Ward Beecher

No nation is better than its sacred book. In that book are expressed its highest ideals of life, and no nation rises above those ideals. No nation has a sacred book to be compared with ours. This American nation from its first settlement at Jamestown to the present hour is based upon and permeated by the principles of the Bible. The more this Bible enters into our national life the grander and purer and better will that life become.

—David Josiah Brewer

This great book...is the best gift God has given to man...But for it we could not know right from wrong.

—Abraham Lincoln

The whole hope of human progress is suspended on the ever-growing influence of the Bible.

—William H. Seward

I believe that the Bible is to be understood and received in the plain and obvious meaning of its passages; since I cannot persuade myself that a book intended for the instruction and conversion of the whole world, should cover its true meaning in such mystery and doubt, that none but critics and philosophers can discover it.

—Daniel Webster

I have always said, I always say, that the studious perusal of the sacred volume will make better citizens, better fathers, and better husbands.

—Thomas Jefferson

Patriots & the Book

So great is my veneration for the Bible that the earlier my children begin to read it, the more confident will be my hope that they will prove useful citizens to their country, and respectable members of society.

—John Quincy Adams

The Bible holds up before us ideals that are within sight of the weakest and the lowliest, and yet so high that the best and the noblest are kept with their faces turned ever upward. It carries the call of the Saviour to the remotest corners of the earth; on its pages are written the assurances of the present and our hopes for the future.

—Williams Jennings Bryan

Hold fast to the Bible as the sheet-anchor of your liberties; write its precepts in your hearts, and practice them in your lives. To the influence of this book we are indebted for all the progress made in true civilization, and to this we must look as our guide in the future. "Righteousness exalteth a nation; but sin is a reproach to any people."

—Ulysses S. Grant

It is impossible to mentally or socially enslave a Bible-reading people.

—Horace Greeley

There is a Book worth all other books which were ever printed.

—Patrick Henry

What you bring away from the Bible depends to some extent on what you carry to it.

—Oliver Wendell Holmes, Sr.

Refuge in the Bible

Clara Barton, 1821-1912
Founder of the Red Cross

Clara was eighteen when she stood before her first class, the New Testament in her hand open at the Sermon on the Mount. "All who could read, read a verse each, I reading with them in turn," she later recalled. Instinctively she had found a sure beginning, although fear and uncertainty had troubled her as she stepped lightly "over the dewy, grass road" to District School Number Nine on a scented May morning in 1839.

The little schoolhouse was along the road from Sally's home. A clergyman, a lawyer, and a justice of the peace had just signed her first teaching certificate. Her family had helped her "to look larger and older" by getting her a tightly fitted green dress with velvet facings, longer and more adult in cut than the "two little old waifish dresses" she owned at that time.

Clara's luxuriant brown hair, her one vanity, was parted in the middle and squared back from her wide forehead. Thick clusters of ringlets hung bunched over her ears. Her high-planed cheekbones and wide mouth, curving up at the corners, gave maturity to her face. Her dark brown eyes were wise and merry. Her waist was slim, her hands noticeably small. If not a beauty, Clara looked healthy and animated, bright and sympathetic, on her first day as a teacher. Actually, in spite of the family tradition in teaching, she had no idea how to handle her pupils and was too tongue-tied to address them directly. Thus she sought refuge in the Bible.

—Ishbel Ross

For All People

Sarah Grimke, 1792-1873
Anti-Slavery and Woman's Rights Advocate

Every Sunday afternoon the Grimke girls taught Bible classes in the colored school. It seemed obvious to her that the slave children hungered for the gospel message. Why could she not teach them to read the Bible? Why give them the word of the Saviour secondhand?

It was explained to her that slaves had no use for reading; it would make them restless and rebellious. Their minds were not fitted for such pursuits; it would strain them and make them unfit for the labor they must do. Besides, it was against the law.

How could that be? Sarah refused to believe it. One can well imagine that Judge Grimke, ever approving of an inquiring mind, took that opportunity to instruct his daughter by presenting her with the irrefutable evidence of the printed word.

"AN ACT FOR THE BETTER ORDERING AND GOVERNING OF NEGROES AND SLAVES...any person who shall teach any slave to write or to employ any slave as a scribe in writing, shall forfeit 100 pounds."

Printed law or entrenched social custom, Sarah found it impossible to accept either. "My great desire in the matter would not be totally suppressed, and I took an almost malicious satisfaction in teaching my little waiting-maid at night, when she was supposed to be occupied in combing and brushing my long locks. The light was put out, the keyhole screened, and flat on our stomachs, before the fire, with the spelling-book under our eyes, we defied the laws of South Carolina."

It was the one act of open defiance she recorded in all the years of childhood and it ended in discovery. The slave girl barely escaped a whipping and Sarah was summoned before her father, who lectured her sternly on the enormity of her transgression.

—Gerda Lerner

P.T. Barnum & the Bible

During the Rev. Mr. Lowe's ministrations at Bethel, he formed a Bible class, of which I was a member. Once, I remember, I drew the text, Luke x.42: "But one thing is needful; and Mary hath chosen that good part which shall not be taken away from her." *Question,* "What is the one thing needful?" My answer was nearly as follows:

"This question 'what is the one thing needful?' is capable of receiving various answers, depending much upon the persons to whom it is addressed. The merchant might answer that 'the one thing needful' is 'plenty of customers, who buy liberally, without beating down and pay cash for all their purchases.' The farmer might reply, that 'the one thing needful is large harvests and high prices.' The lawyer might be of opinion that 'it is an unruly community, always engaged in bickerings and litigations.' The clergyman might reply, 'It is a fat salary with multitudes of sinners seeking salvation and paying large pew rents.' The bachelor might exclaim, 'It is a pretty wife who loves her husband, and who knows how to sew on buttons.' The maiden might answer, 'It is a good husband, who will love, cherish and protect me while life shall last.' But the most proper answer, and doubtless that which applied to the case of Mary, would be, 'The one thing needful is to believe on the Lord Jesus Christ, follow in his footsteps, love God and obey His commandments, love our fellow-man, and embrace every opportunity of administering to his necessities.' In short, 'the one thing needful' is to live a life that we can always look back upon with satisfaction, and be enabled ever to contemplate its termination with trust in Him who has so kindly vouchsafed it to us, surrounding us with innumerable blessings, if we have but the heart and wisdom to receive them in a proper manner."

Sergeant York and the Bible

1887-1964
U.S. Army Sergeant, World War I hero

The Major then went on and said that the United States of America was an earthly government and its servants must fight for it whenever its liberties was threatened, and he reminded me that Christ said we must render unto Caesar the things that are Caesar's. And the Major 'lowed that Christ meant by this to emphasize the duties of Christians to their government. Major Buxton ended by quoting from Ezekiel:

"He heard the sound of the trumpet, and he took not warning, his blood shall be upon him. But he that taketh warning shall deliver his soul.

"But if the watchman see the sword come and blow not the trumpet, and the people be not warned, if the sword come and take any person from among them, he is taken away in his iniquity; but his blood will I require at the watchman's hands."

The Major made a great impression on me that night. He had kinder opened my eyes to things which were in the Bible, which I knowed were there, but which I hadn't thought of as he had thought of them.

I spent considerable time turning the Major's arguments over in my mind that night and I worried and prayed 'most all through the night until reveille. The next morning I wrote in my little diary:

"Camp Gordon, Georgia. Ho, these were trying hours for a boy like me, trying to live for God and do His blessed will, but yet I could look up and say:

Oh Master, let me walk with Thee
In lonely paths of service free,
Tell me Thy secret, help me to bear,
The strain of toil, the fret of care."

And then the Lord would bless me and help me to bear my hard toiles.

Excerpts from John Brown's Last Letter to his Family

American Abolitionist, 1800-1859

Charlestown, Prison, Jefferson Co.,Va.
November 30, 1859

My Dearly Beloved Wife, Sons, Daughters, & Everyone:.

As I now begin what is probably the last letter I shall ever write to any of you; I conclude to write you all at the same time...I am waiting the hour of my public murder with great composure of mind, & cheerfulness: feeling the strongest assurance that in no other possible way could I be used to so much advance the cause of God; & of humanity: & that nothing that either I or all my family have sacrificed or suffered: will be lost.

I beseech you every one to make the Bible your dayly and nightly study; with a childlike honest, candid, teachable spirit: out of love and respect for your husband; and father: and I beseech the God of my Fathers; to open all your eyes to a discovery of the truth. You cannot imagine how much you may soon need the consolations of the Christian religion.

Circumstances like my own; for more than a month past; convince me beyond all doubt: of our great need: of something more to rest our hopes on; than merely our own vague theories framed up, while our prejudices are excited; or our vanity worked up to its highest pitch.

Oh do not trust your eternal all upon the boisterous Ocean, without even a Helm; or Compass to aid you in steering. I do not ask any of you; to throw away your reason: I only ask you, to make a candid & sober use of your reason: My dear younger children will you listen to the last poor admonition of one who can only love you? Oh be determined at once to give your whole hearts to God; & let nothing shake; or alter; that resolution. You need have no fear of regreting it.

Do not be vain; and thoughtless: but sober minded. And let me entreat you all to love the whole remnant of our once great family: "with a pure heart fervently." Try to build again: your broken walls: & to make the utmost of every stone that is left. Nothing can so tend to make life a blessing as the consciousness that you love: & are beloved: & "love ye the stranger" still. It is ground of the utmost comfort to my mind: to know that so many of you as have had the opportunity; have given full proof of your fidelity to the great family of man.

Be faithful until death. From the exercise of habitual love to man: it cannot be very hard: to learn to love his maker. I must yet insert a reason for my firm belief in the Divine inspiration of the Bible: notwithstanding I am (perhaps naturally) skeptical: (certainly not, credulous.) I wish you all to consider it most thoroughly; when you read the blessed book; & see whether you can not discover such evidence yourselves. It is the purity of heart, feeling or motive: as well as word, and action which is everywhere insisted on; that distinguish it from all other teachings; that commends it to my conscience; whether my heart be "willing & obedient" or not. The inducements that it holds out; are another reason of my conviction of its truth: & genuineness: that I cannot here omit; in this my last argument for the Bible.

Eternal life; is that my soul is "panting after" this moment. I mention this; as reason for endeavouring to leave a valuable copy of the Bible to be carefully preserved in remembrance of me: to so many of my posterity; instead of some other things of equal cost.

The Bible & Modern Infideltiy

By Erastus Otis Haven, 1820-1881
President, University of Michigan

The most substantial of all existences is soul. The first thing known to exist to every one is I, myself, I. From that proposition as a centre all else is perceived. Manipulation cannot create. Organization of matter cannot educe emotion and thought, unless emotion and thought previously exist in the matter. They are perceived to be distinct by the same power that perceives them to exist. A piece of gold cannot be hammered so thin as to begin to shout or cry out in agony. Thread cannot be spun so fine as to think. There is no thought in the electric flash, no emotion in mere motion. A lower substance cannot be manipulated into a higher substance.

The Bible recognizes soul as an entity. It assumes this as it assumes also the existence of God. It does not attempt to prove either, both are assumed. They are, indeed, the invisible, ever-present framework on which the whole structure is built. Some have maintained that the Old Testament does not teach immortality! Poor, feeble-minded, and blind literalists! Would they have had the inspired writers of the Old Testament imitate children who, when drawing pictures on their slates, write under them. "This is a house," "This is a horse?" Must God be under the necessity of saying again and again, "This being is immortal?"

Alfred Russel Wallace, the modern co-discoverer and able defender of Darwin's dogma of natural selection—the process by which, in nature's multitudes of kinds of living creatures struggling for existence the strong and the fit conquer and destroy the weak and the unsuitable—a theory the beauty and truth of which careful observation will not allow us to deny, but at the same time which does not profess to reveal the origin of forces or existences, and least of all, to shut out Mind—the great organizer and executor of law—has at length, as the supreme result of his protracted investigations, arrived at the conclusion similar to that believed by the great Christian chemist, Faraday, that all force is will-born, and thus that the whole universe is not merely dependent on, but actually is, the will of higher intelligences or of one Supreme intelligence. It has often been said that the true poet is a seer, and in the noble verse of an American poetess we find expressed what may prove to be the highest fact of science, the noblest truth of philosophy:

> God of the Granite and the Rose!
> Soul of the Sparrow and the Bee!
> The mighty tide of Being flows
> Through countless channels, Lord, from thee.
> It leaps to life in grass and flowers,
> Through every grade of being runs.
> While from Creation's radiant towers
> Its glory flames in Stars and Suns.
>
> How unwise not to claim fellowship
> with the Great Spirit that builds and
> upholds the universe.
>
> The soul of man is larger than the sky,
> Deeper than ocean or the abysmal dark
> Of the unfathomed centre. Like that ark
> Which in its sacred hold uplifted high,
> O'er the drowned hills, the human family
> And stock reserved of every living kind;
> So in the compass of the single mind
> The seeds and pregnant forms in essence lie
> That make all worlds.
>
> —H. Coleridge

The Book

Read by Joseph Thompson, 1819-1879
American Congregational Clergyman;
Founder of "The New Englander"

The Bible holds a position independent among the books of the world. It cannot be classed with scientific works; it cannot be classed with historical works, though containing both science and history. It does not properly belong to the department of mental philosophy; not is it a treatise upon either ethics or morality. Upon all these department it trenches, and yet it does not belong to any of them. It stands independent. Poetical in language, grand and sublime, yet the Bible is not a poem; legislative and philosophical, it is neither a book of government nor of logic. It is a book for all times and for the whole world. It stands alone as "the Book."

Bound in one cover, or divided into the Old and New Testaments, it in reality comprises 66 productions, the work of some forty different authors. But these authors did not write in concert, in the design of making one thought, upon independent topics, and yet there is such a harmony among them that it points directly to some one general superintendence. Again, they wrote in different countries. Hence, though the writers were of one race, it is difficult to conceive of any circumstances that could have been more diverse than those in which they wrote. Amid the widest contrasts for sixteen centuries, these writers prepared the books which compose our Bible.

In estimating these books in respect to their unity, we must take into account the difference of social position and intellectual culture among their authors. What are the probabilities that these men, differing in their position and culture in addition to all the other circumstances I have enumerated, would have written at all in harmony? What is the probability they would at all agree?

But they agree throughout in their representation of the character of God. Everywhere in the Bible God appears as a spirit, and everywhere His attributes are represented as infinite. The oneness of God is taught, or rather is assumed equally by all the writers of the Bible. Whether it be the Father, Son, or Spirit, the oneness of God is always asserted. The holiness of God is everywhere presented as the sum of all His attributes, His crowning excellence. Now, this view of the character of God, uniform in the Bible, is also peculiar to the Bible. Some of the ancient philosophers approached to the idea of one only God, but the Bible alone presents a God—a spirit of infinite attributes, of infinite holiness—one God. Nowhere does mythology approach to the idea of a God of holiness. This is purely Biblical teaching. Now, how came it to pass that these men, writing at such divers times, in such divers circumstances, and divers manners, represented God the same? It must have been because God inspired them.

It has an unity of purpose, and a sublimity and purity of conception, unrivaled among the books of the world.

Christ did not come to establish a new system of truth, but to complete an old system. His disciples recognized his connection with the Old Scriptures. He fulfilled all these Scriptures; they were all verified in Him. In the height of the kingdom of Israel David sang in his prophetic Psalms of a coming One before whom he was to bow as his Lord. All the prophecies point to Christ, and all of them were fulfilled in Him. Here is a unity of plan in the redemption of mankind to which I call your attention. All the emblems and type met in Christ, when the Lamb slain from the foundation of the world was offered once for all for sin.

There is unity in the Biblical history in regard to the establishment of the kingdom of Christ. From the very first it was foretold, and Christ himself proclaimed it.

Theodore Roosevelt on the Bible

From a discourse delivered in the Presbyterian Church, Oyster Bay, N.Y., June 11, 1901:

There are certain truths which are so very true that we call them truisms; and yet I think we often half forget them in practice. Every thinking man when he thinks, realizes what a very large number of people tend to forget, that the teachings of the Bible are so interwoven and entwined with our whole civic and social life that it would be literally—I do not mean figuratively, I mean literally—impossible for us to figure to ourselves what that life would be if these teachings were removed. We would lose almost all the standards by which we now judge both public and private morals. All the standards toward which we, with more or less resolution, strive to raise ourselves. Almost every man who has by his life-work added to the sum of human achievement of which the race is proud, almost every such man, has based his life-work largely upon the teachings of the Bible. Sometimes it has been done unconsciously, more often consciously, and among the very greatest men a disproportionately large number have been diligent and close students of the Bible at first hand.

Lincoln—sad, patient, kindly Lincoln, who, after bearing upon his weary shoulders for four years a greater burden than that borne by any other man of the nineteenth century, laid down his life for the people whom, living, he had served so well—built up his entire reading upon his early study of the Bible. He had mastered it absolutely; mastered it as later he mastered only one or two other books, so that he became almost "a man of one book," who knew that book, and who instructively put into practice what he had been taught therein.

Mere Honesty Not Enough

A man must be honest in the first place; but that by itself is not enough. No matter how good a man is, if he is timid he cannot accomplish much in the world.

So, besides being honest, a man has got to have courage, too. And these two together are not enough. No matter how brave and honest he is, if he is a natural born fool, you can do little with him. Remember the order in which I name them. Honesty first; then courage; then brains. And all are indispensable; we have no room in a healthy community for either the knave, the fool, the weakling, or the coward.

You may look through the Bible from cover to cover, and nowhere will you find a line that can be construed into an apology for the man of brains who sins against the light. On the contrary, in the Bible, taking that as a guide, you will find that because much has been given to you much will be expected from you; and a heavier condemnation is to be visited upon the able man who goes wrong than upon his weaker brother, who cannot do the harm that the other does, because it is not in him to do it.

Home and Church Training

So I plead, not merely for training of the mind, but for the moral and spiritual training of the home and the church; the moral and spiritual training that have always been found in this book, which in almost every civilized tongue can be described as "The Book," with the certainty of all understanding you when you so describe it.

The teaching of the Bible to children is, of course, a matter of especial interest to those of us who have families. Older folks often fail to realize how readily a child will grasp a little askew something that they do not take the trouble to explain. We cannot be too careful in seeing that the biblical learning is not merely an affair of rote, so that the child may understand what it is being taught. And, by the way, I earnestly hope that you will never make your children learn parts of the Bible as punishment. Do you not know families where this is done? For instance: "You have been a bad child—learn a chapter of Isaiah." And the child learns it is a disagreeable task, and in his mind that splendid and lofty poem and prophecy is forever afterward associated with an uncomfortable feeling of disgrace. I hope you will not make your children learn the Bible in that way, for you can devise no surer method of making a child revolt against all the wonderful beauty and truth of Holy Writ.

The immense moral influence of the Bible, though of course infinitely the most important, is not the only power it has for good. In addition there is the unceasing influence it exerts on the side of good taste, of good literature, of proper sense of proportion, of simple and straightforward writing and thinking.

The Bible does not teach us to shirk difficulties, but to overcome them. That is a lesson that each one of us who has children is bound in honor to teach these children, if he or she expects to see them become fitted to play the part of men and women in our world.

What the Bible Teaches

If we read the Bible aright, we read a book which teaches us to go forth and do the work of the Lord; to do the work of the Lord in the world as we find it; to try to make things better in this world, even if only a little better, because we have lived in it. That kind of work can be done only by the man who is neither a weakling nor a coward; by the man who in the fullest sense of the word is a true Christian, like Great Heart, Bunyan's hero. We plead for a closer and wider and deeper study of the Bible, so that our people may be in fact as well as in theory, "doers of the Word and not hearers only."

The Bible Means To Me

by William Randolph Hearst, 1863-1951
Newspaper Publisher

The Bible means to me the accumulation of the wisdom of the ages, and the inspiration which God has given to those most worthy to receive it, and which He gives to all His people who come to Him prayerfully for help and guidance.

It means also the expression and establishment of moral and religious standards which we may all strive to achieve, and are the better for the striving, even if we do not entirely attain them,

I believe for the Bible to have its full didactic effect upon the minds of men it should retain not only the enduring basis of its teachings but also the dignity and authority of its ancient phraseology.

When I turn to the Bible for comfort and encouragement, for courage and confidence, for renewed faith in the goodness and guidance of God, I want the familiar passages to speak to me in the same words that have given me help and inspiration before, in the words that I learned in my youth and that have been with me more or less definitely and distinctly through the years.

Those words have come to mean and to be the word of God.

When the wording has been changed, it does not seem to have the same effect and authority.

I think the Bible should be the Rock of Ages, indestructible and inimitable, both in its teaching and its wording.

In 1940, prior to our entry into the Second World War, he wrote:

"The trouble with most Christians is that they do not believe in Christianity."

The Bible at the Alamo

by Colonel Davey Crockett

The following extract from his posthumous work...

Feb. 24, 1836. Very early this morning the enemy commenced a new battery on the banks of the river, about three hundred and fifty yards from the fort, and by afternoon they amused themselves by firing at us from that quarter. (February)-25th. The firing commenced early this morning, but the Mexicans are poor engineers, for we haven't lost a single man, and our outworks have sustained no injury. Our sharpshooters have brought down a considerable number of stragglers at a long shot. The Bee-hunter keeps the whole garrison in good heart with his songs and his jests, and his daring and determined spirit. He is about the quickest on the trigger, and the best rifle shot we have in the fort. I have already seen him bring down eleven of the enemy, and at such a distance we all thought it would be waste of ammunition to attempt it. His gun is first-rate, quite equal to my Betsey, though she has not quite as many trinkets about her. This day a small party sallied out of the fort for wood and water, and had a slight skirmish with three times their number from the division under General Sesma. The Bee-hunter headed them, and beat the enemy off, after killing three. On opening his Bible at night, of which he always reads a portion before going to rest, he found a musket ball in the middle of it. 'See here, colonel,' said he, 'how they have treated the valued present of my dear little Kate of Nacogdoches.' 'It has saved your life,' said I. 'True,' replied he, more seriously than usual; 'and I am not the first sinner whose life has been saved by this book.' He prepared for bed, and before retiring he prayed, and returned thanks for his providential escape; and I heard the name of Catherine mingle in his prayer.

A taste for books, which is still the pleasure and glory of my life.

—Gibbon

THE BOOKS THAT SHAPED THE HISTORY MAKERS

I love to lose myself in other men's minds.
When I am not walking, I am reading;
I cannot sit and think. Books think for me.

—Lamb

Memoirs of the War in the Southern Department of the United States

Author- Henry Lee, 1756-1818
Read by Robert E. Lee, 1807-1870
Commander-in-Chief, Confederate Army

There was one historical work he probably could not resist. That was the new edition of his father's *Memoirs of the War in the Southern Department*. The work was in a single volume, and though poorly printed by Peter Force, it contained some useful notes and addenda. Robert doubtless had read the first edition in boyhood, but now he could bring to bear on the book something of the understanding of a soldier, and could appreciate more fully the military qualities of his father.

"Light-Horse Harry" Lee, it will be remembered, had written late in life that "mankind admired most the hero; of all, the most useless, except when the safety of a nation demands his saving arm." Yet it was plain to Robert that his father had loved military life and had possessed high ability in it. Washington had thought so. After the Paulus Hook affair he had praised Henry Lee for displaying "a remarkable degree of prudence, address, enterprise, and bravery." Greene often mentioned Lee in orders. "Everybody knows I have the highest opinion of you as an officer," he told Lee in the correspondence preceding Lee's resignation from the army in 1782.

What were the military qualities, then, that Robert Lee discovered in his father when he read the new edition of his Memoirs? The answer could not be without some effect on the education of the son as a soldier.

Perhaps the most notable quality of Henry Lee, the soldier, as revealed again in his book, was his ability in creating and maintaining an *espirit de corps*. His command, the biographer of Greene admitted, "was, perhaps, the finest. . . that made its appearance on the arena of the Revolutionary War." When his men behaved with bravery, "Light-Horse Harry" saw to it that they were rewarded.

He was careful not to expose them or himself needlessly, and was always so vigilant that after the episode at the tavern, he was never surprised. The animals of his command received almost as much attention at his hands as did the men. If his command deserved credit, he saw that they got it. "No officer," said Johnson, "was ever more devoted to the interests of his own corps or his own fame."

The effect upon Robert of the probable reading of this edition of his father's *Memoirs* does not show in any of his letters but it must have confirmed him in his determination to follow the career of a soldier. In ways that neither biographer nor psychologist may fathom, it is possible, also, that Robert's admiration for his father led him to magnify and to copy the military virtues of the sire. The morale of the Army of Northern Virginia may have been inspired in 1781, though it was not until 1862 that the army itself was created.

Encouraged by this showing and relieved after April, I of his mathematical teaching, Robert had more time for independent reading during the late winter and early spring of 1828 than in any other period of his cadetship. Between January 26 and May 24, he drew fifty-two books from the library. They covered a wide field—navigation, travel, strategy, biography, and history. His principal interest seems to have been in seamanship and in the works of Alexander Hamilton, for he borrowed Atkinson's *Navigation* seven times, and the second volume of Hamilton's *Works* no less than nine times during this period. This volume contains *The Federalist*, which Lee must have read very thoroughly. He indulged himself, moreover, in a reading of a French edition of Rousseau's *Confessions*.

—Douglas Southall Freeman

Life of Washington

Author- Parson Weems, 1759-1825
Read by Abraham Lincoln, 1809-1865
16th President of the United States

Lincoln himself is authority for the statement that certain of these books impressed him for life. He declared February 21, 1861, "May I be pardoned if I mention that away back in my childhood, the earliest days of my being able to read, I got hold of a small book, such as one as few of the younger members have ever seen— Weems' *Life of Washington*. I remember all the accounts there given of the battlefields and struggles for the liberties of the country, and none fixed themselves upon my imagination so deeply as the struggle here at Trenton, New Jersey. The crossing of the river, the contest with the Hessians, the great hardships endured at this time, all fixed themselves on my memory more than any single Revolutionary event; and you all know, for you have all been boys, how these early impressions last longer than any others. I recollect thinking then, boy even though I was, that there must have been something more than common that these men struggled for."

The temptation is strong to associate with the chiseled sentences of his First Inaugural Address, for example, the direct clear statement and the simple diction of DeFoe and of Bunyan. The fabled stories of Aesop suggest his own highly anecdotal manner, such as he used extensively in the forties. The rhythmical gait of the Gettysburg Address and of the Second Inaugural suggests of certain lilting verse of the Bible; his precise legal phraseology, such as he employed at Cooper Union, for example, hints of the language of the Constitution. It is reasonably certain that his early reading directed his attention to rules of syntax, to the value of and to the technique or organic composition.

—Earl Wellington Wiley

My Father and I

Anne Morrow Lindbergh, 1907-
Aviator; wife of Charles Lindbergh;
Author- "North to the Orient"

My father was a curious, hungry, and ceaseless learner, an inveterate reader of history, philosophy, economics (Herodotus, Plutarch's *Lives*, and Plato were ranged beside Froude, Bagehot, and Prescott).

With such a propensity for teaching, it is not strange that much stress was put on our education, both moral and intellectual. It started early in the home with nightly prayers and evening reading by our mother from the meritorious *Heidi, The Book of Saints and Friendly Beasts*, and *Little Women*, progressing to the Greek myths and the classics. On Sunday evenings there were Bible stories and sometimes sermons on the green sofa in her bedroom. (This hour was in addition to early morning prayers, kneeling down in a row by our parents' big bed, followed by regular church service.) Our father also occasionally read to us from *The Just So Stories* and *The Jungle Book*. But his teaching was not entirely recreation. Breakfasts were sometimes made horrendous by the public practice of our multiplication tables or questions of addition or subtraction that were shot at us from the head of the table. To this day if someone asks me suddenly: "How much is 7 times 8?" my mind blanks to the child's frozen landscape of panic. There were, of course, vacations, but along with physical recreation our minds were not allowed to idle. If summering in New England, we always had our reading lists and suitcases of books. The communal family reading took on a more relaxed tone in summer, appropriate to wicker armchairs and shady verandas. Trollope and Jane Austen, I remember, or even something as entertaining as Mark Twain or O. Henry.

Outline of History

Author- H. G. Wells, 1866-1946
Read by Charles Lindbergh, 1902-1974
Pioneer Aviator; 1st man to make a solo
non-stop flight across the Atlantic Ocean

From his wartime journals:

September 3, 1939

Spent the morning writing and making plans. We listened to the King's speech over the radio at 1:00. I read Fisher's *History of Europe* in between thinking about the European situation and what action I should take in this country. It is hard to concentrate on anything but the aspects of the war.

November 20

Day at Englewood—dictating, writing, and reading. Two trips to school for inspection of work and conferences with Connie Chilton. Have finished second reading of Fisher's third volume and am now rereading Whitehead's *Adventures of Ideas*.

January 21, 1940

I spent the rest of the afternoon reading Wells' *Outline of History.* I read it many years ago, and I think it gives one a general grasp of the sweep of human history better than any other book I know. Of course, Wells leaves much to be desired, but I admire his vision and his courage in these volumes, and I enjoy his opinions and eccentricities—they are both stimulating and provocative. What the volumes lack is much more than made up by what they contain.

Anne is reading *The Medieval Mind* by Taylor. I hope to start it soon.

May 16, 1941

Spent the morning writing and reading Ouspensky's *A New Model of the Universe.* Arrived at New York City one hour late. Drove directly to Lloyd Neck. Evening with Anne, discussing developments while away.

Atlas Shrugged

Author- Ayn Rand, 1908-1982
Read by Robert Livingston
U.S. Congressman, Louisiana

Ayn Rand's philosophy and spellbinding story of the independent man pitted against the institutions of bureaucracy was what inspired me to run, run, and rerun for the United States Congress once Congressman Herbert announced his retirement.

Through reading *Atlas Shrugged*, I learned that hard work and a positive attitude can move mountains and beat incredible odds. It certainly worked for me. And had I not read that book, I might never have known it:

"The man who refused to judge, who neither agrees nor disagrees, who declares that there are no absolutes and believes that he escapes responsibility, is the man responsible for all the blood that is now spilled in the world. Reality is an absolute, existence is an absolute, a speck of dust is an absolute and so is a human life.

"There are two sides to every issue: one side is right and the other is wrong, but the middle is always evil. The man who is wrong still retains some respect for truth, if only by accepting the responsibility of choice. But the man in the middle is the knave who blanks out the truth in order to pretend that no choice or values exist, who is willing to sit out the course of any battle, willing to cash in on the blood of the innocent or to crawl on his belly to the guilty, who dispenses justice by condemning both the robber and the robbed to jail, who solves conflicts by ordering the thinker and the fool to meet each other halfway. In any compromise between food and poison, it is only death that can win. In any compromise between good and evil, it is only evil than can profit. In that transfusion of blood which drains the good to feed the evil, the compromiser is the transmitting rubber tube."

The Count of Monte Cristo

Author- Alexandre Dumas, 1802-1870
Read by Huey Long, 1893-1935
U.S. Senator, Governor of Louisiana

The Longs were among the literary elite. According to the memories of surviving family members, they had access to the works of Shakespeare, Dickens, Poe, and other English and American classics, and to such periodicals as the *Saturday Evening Post*, the *Progressive Farmer*, and the *Youth's Companion*. The most often-read book was the Bible, if only because Mrs. Long insisted on reading aloud from it at evening gatherings. Second in popularity was a history of the world by Ridpath. A colorful although superficial work, it stressed the role of powerful leaders. It became one of the favorites of young Huey, who also manifested a consuming interest in a biography of Napoleon.

But by far his favorite work was *The Count of Monte Cristo*, whose hero meted out harsh revenge to all his enemies. Years later, when he was a United States senator he was walking down a street in New York City with a friend and spied the book in the window of a shop. He announced that he was going in to buy a copy and asked the friend if he wanted one. This man replied that he had read the book as a boy. "I read it then too," Huey said, "but I read it every year."

The boy Huey may have had only a dim perception that his destiny was to lead others, but deliberately or not he read works that would help equip him for this role. His literary fare, like that of the young Lincoln, may have been narrow, but it was the kind that somebody deliberately preparing to be a politician might well have chosen. For what he was going to be, Huey Long derived more value from his program of self-education than he did from the Winnfield educational system.

—T. Harry Williams

Four Things Men Live By

Read by Henry Luce, 1898-1967
Publisher; Editor; Founder of
"Time," "Life" and "Fortune" Magazines

Luce's need to combine idealism with pragmatism accompanied the birth pangs of *Sports Illustrated*.

"Sport has aspects of creativity. Man is an animal that works, plays and prays. As a boy, I remember reading a book titled *Four Things Men Live By*. These four things were Love, Work, Play and Prayer. No important aspect of life should be devalued. And if play does correspond to some important elements in spiritual man, then it is a bad thing for it to be devalued. And sport has been devalued. It does not get serious attention. The new magazine will be a re-evaluation of sport to put it in its proper place as one of the great modes of expression..."

As a summation of his thoughts about the relation of sport to the human spirit, Luce cited a passage from Faust in a context nobody but he would discover:

> Only he deserves his liberty and life
> Who must conquer them each day anew...
> Such is the turbulent scene I long to see,
> To stand on free soil among free people,
> Then to the fleeting moment I could say:
> Stay, you are so good.
> The traces of my earthly days
> Then could vanish into eternity.

"Is Sports the goal of life? Certainly not. There are deeper things to be pursued—Art, Religion, Good Morals, all the high 'ideals.' But if you ask most any American what he's going to do next weekend, what's he going to do next summer, what's he planning now for his pursuit of happiness—one sure part of the answer will be something to do with Sport."

—John Kobler

Essays

Author- Francis Bacon, 1561-1626
Read by Hamilton Wright Mabie, 1845-1916
Lawyer; Editor; Author,
"American Ideals, Character and Life"

No one comes in contact with Bacon without receiving a deep impression of his power, but it is safe to say that his readers do not love him. They are somewhat in awe of him. Montaigne has a rich background, but he keeps himself easily in the fore; he is the central figure and dominates the subject. Bacon, on the other hand, withdraws himself and puts us in direct contact with his themes and his thought. In Montaigne personality is the chief element of charm and interest; in Bacon the compelling power resides in a noble treatment of great matters. Bacon's personal contribution to his work is the quality of his mind, the affinities of his thought, revealed in his selection of themes, and the greatness of his manner. There is little egotism; there is rather the disposition to leave the stage clear for the actors. The bare list of Bacon's topics has an educational quality—"Of Death," "Of Great Place," "Of Empire," "Of Ambition," "Of Honour and Reputation," "Of the True Greatness of Kingdoms and Estates."

In his dealings with his readers Bacon never violates his trust. In no other kindred body of writing is there more weight of thought, more concentration of intellectual power, or loftier dignity of manner. In a certain noble eloquence the essays have never been surpassed; if they have not the long organ roll of Milton's and Hooker's prose, they have the same massive quality touched and vivified by imagination.

The Making of a General

Lt. Gen. Arthur MacArthur, 1845-1912
Civil War Congressional Medal of Honor winner, Father of Gen. Douglas MacArthur

Arthur is not creative, like Major General Lew Wallace in Santa Fe, who spends these years writing *The Fair God, Ben Hur,* and *The Prince of India,* but he is a great reader of other men's books, and sends for them by the trunkful. It is not light fare. An efficiency report filed in the Adjutant General's Office the year after the closing of the frontier will note that MacArthur had pursued "investigations in political economy," inquiries into "the colonial and revolutionary period of American history," a "comparison of the American and English constitutions," and an "extensive investigation into the civilization and institutions of China," together with studies of the works of Gibbon, Macaulay, Samuel Johnson, Thomas Malthus, David Ricardo, John Stuart Mill, Henry Carey, Walter Bagehot, Thomas Leslie, and William Jevons. That spring he will receive a Doctor of Laws degree from the National Law School in Washington, and the fact that Judge MacArthur held an influential position as regent of the school cannot obscure the son's extraordinary achievements in self-education despite the most discouraging handicaps.

Both the range of his knowledge and the isolation of his years on the frontier are important to an understanding of Arthur's immense influence on his children. Douglas eventually inherited over four thousand books from his father. From him and them he acquired a remarkable vocabulary; a mastery of Victorian prose, a love of neo-Augustan rhetoric, and a ready grasp of theory.

—William Manchester

Crime and Punishment

Author- Fyodor Dostoevski, 1821-1881
Read by Gen. Douglas MacArthur, 1880-1964
World War II Commander, U. S. Forces Far East

In the Phillipines:

Most evenings were spent at the movies, as before, or reading in the library. (Like MacArthur's mother, Jean was forever giving him biographies of Confederate generals; among them Douglas S. Freeman's four-volume life of Lee, G.F.R. Henderson's two volumes on Stonewall Jackson, and J. A. Wyeth's *Nathan Bedford Forrest*.) A speed reader, MacArthur could get through three books a day; sitting in his favorite rocking chair he would also pore over magazines and newspapers.

In New Guinea:

Unable to sleep, and missing his small family, MacArthur spent long evenings in the bungalow's library. An earlier tenant had been highly literate; the shelves were packed with books in several languages. Unless he was preoccupied with battle reports, the General would pace the room hour after hour, a volume open in his left hand, reading of Papuan aborigines, native lore, and anthropology, or, if he was in the mood for European literature, the works of Zola, Shaw, Ibsen, and others. Phrases from this cultural smorgasbord would find their way into the aureate communiques he dictated to Diller each morning. Durdin wrote, "He can quote Shakespeare, the Bible, Napoleon, Mark Twain, and Lincoln in expounding a single idea," and Johnson reported that he drew "for parallel and metaphor on ... a statement by Plato, or sometimes on a passage from Scripture." Curiously, neither correspondent mentioned the book the General enjoyed most: Dostoevski's *Crime and Punishment*.

—William Manchester

Memoirs of the Cardinal de Retz

Author- Jean Francois de Gondi, 1614-1679
Read by James Madison, 1751-1836
4th President of the United States

Thomas Martin lived at Montpelier for the next two years, teaching the younger children and guiding James's studies and reading. These ranged as widely as the books the rector brought with him.

Combined with *The Spectator,* Martin's library need have contained only three particular works to account for the full contents of Madison's "Commonplace Book," compiled at some period in his early youth. The notebook opens with short excerpts from the *Memoirs of the Cardinal de Retz,* who rose and fell in the France of Louis XIV. Retz had a gift for aphorisms, and Madison picked out many that carried a warning for public men:

"It is more unbecoming a Minister to speak foolishly than to act foolishly."

"Patience works greater effects than activity."

Extracts from the *Essays of Montaigne* demonstrate a growing ability to analyze and synthesize literary material. Bringing together from different parts of an essay the common thought of Socrates and Plato that men should treat slander with silence and overthrow it by their conduct, Madison injected the thought: "A reputation grounded on true virtue is like the sun that may be clouded, but not extinguished." Throughout his life he ignored slanders.

A keen interest in literature was displayed in excerpts from the Abbe Dubos's *Critical Reflections on Poetry and Painting.* In condensing both Montaigne and Dubos, he occasionally sharpened their utterances. A long and ponderous sentence by Dubos was cut to read, "the most delicious banquet without an appetite is insipid."

—Irvin Brant

Self-Help

**Author- Samuel Smiles, 1812-1904
Read by Orison Swett Marden, Author, 1850-1924**

"Smiles's *"Self-Help"* was a wonderful stimulus to me, and I believe it has proved the turning-point in the careers of tens of thousands of youths. Nothing else is more fascinating than the romance of achievement under difficulties. The youth full of hope, bubbling over with enthusiasm, reads the life-stories of men and women who have succeeded under difficulties, and he says to himself, "Why can't I do it?" To which something within him replies, "I can, and I will!"

Excerpt from *Self-Help*

"The chief use of biography consists in the noble models of character in which it abounds. Our great forefathers still live among us in the records of their lives, as well as in the acts they have done, which live also; still sit by us at the table, and hold us by the hand; furnishing examples for our benefit, which we may still study, admire and imitate. Indeed, whoever has left behind him the record of a noble life, has bequeathed to posterity an enduring source of good, for it serves as a model for others to form themselves by in all time to come; still breathing fresh life into men, helping them to reproduce his life anew, and to illustrate his character in other forms. Hence a book containing the life of a true man is full of precious seed. It is a still living voice: it is an intellect. To use Milton's words, "It is the precious life-blood of a master-spirit, embalmed and treasured up on purpose to a life beyond life." Such a book never ceases to exercise an elevating and ennobling influence."

—Samuel Smiles

Locke & Montaigne

Read by Francis Marion, 1732-1795
American General & Patriot

Job, who was only eighteen months older than Francis, and understood his brother, opened his mouth to defend the culprit, but lost his courage when his father glared at him.

"It has been a tradition in this family to read the works of John Calvin, the essays of Montaigne, the plays of Pierre Corneille. We nourish the spirit and the mind. But Francis must walk alone."

"Francis has always accepted his reading assignments in good faith, Papa," Job said in a low voice.

"He does not read them for pleasure. He prefers the philosophy of the Englishman, Locke."

The younger Gabriel was the only man present able to say what was in everyone's mind. "After all, Papa we are British subjects."

"Have you read Locke?" his father demanded. "I spent several months studying him this past winter. I wanted to see why Francis should be so fascinated by him." Gabriel looked disgusted. "The man preaches freedom. Personal liberty. The right to choose and plot one's own course as one wishes. No wonder Francis reads him. Those who reject discipline must find an excuse, and Francis has discovered a philosopher who can be idolized by the lazy."

The brothers exchanged glances, knowing that someone would have to intervene strongly before their father completely lost his temper and launched into an endless tirade. They silently elected Isaac, long the student of the family, whose chances of escaping parental wrath were relatively good.

He accepted the unpleasant assignment. "Francis isn't lazy, Papa. He just prefers to do things in his own way."

—Noel B. Gerson

Why I Know There Is A God

Author- Fulton Oursler, 1893-1952
Read by Catherine Marshall, 1914-
Wife and biographer of Peter Marshall,
Chaplain of U.S. Congress

If the girl who is not sure that she is a Christian will make a definite act of giving herself to God, even though she feels nothing at all, in God's eyes that is a real transaction—done, finished. As soon as she accepts the truth of this, God will handle her emotions. Eventually she will feel different. Eventually she will feel God's presence. The emotions trail behind the will. In the interval, she must not be led astray by ephemeral emotional responses to a date that turns out badly or ants that invade the picnic basket.

Does this sound too simple? Actually, I believe it to be the only principle that makes entering the Christian life possible. It is a theory that works in real life. I think of what happened in the case of the late Fulton Oursler— for years editor of *Liberty* magazine and senior editor of *Readers' Digest* at the time of his death.

At thirty, Mr. Oursler was a self-styled agnostic. As he described himself, he was "genially loyal to ethical standards when they did not interfere too much with what I wanted to do. But I sneered at God as an elaborate self-deception and did all that I could to tear down the faith of those close to me."

Then trouble surrounded Fulton Oursler in all phases of his life. *Liberty* went under, so he was out of a job. At the same time there were health and marriage difficulties. There came the day when he realized that he was absolutely helpless to do one thing for himself.

What happened then is vividly described by Oursler himself in a book he later wrote, *Why I Know There Is a God*. On a blustery day with dark clouds lowering, the distraught man wandered down Fifth Avenue in New

York City. He stopped in front of a church—self-conscious, filled with conflicting emotions, but knowing that unless he got help he had come to the end of the way. For the first time in years, he ventured inside a church. Let him tell the rest of it in his own words:

"In ten minutes or less I may change my mind," he prayed. "I may scoff at this—and love error again. Pay no attention to me then. For this little time I am in right mind and heart. This is my best. Take it and forget the rest; and if You are really there, help me."

What Mr. Oursler did in the quiet church was what Hannah Smith meant by setting the rudder of the will and disregarding everything else—conflicting thoughts, contrary feelings. And God must have accepted this as the real decision of the real man, exactly as Hannah insisted that He always does. Within two weeks Fulton Oursler's problems began to resolve.

"Only chance would explain it to the unbelieving, because nothing either I or anyone else did contrived the events. The complications dissolved...by what the rationalist would call a series of beautiful coincidences God literally took over my life, took it out of my hands."

The more impressive proof that God accepted Fulton Oursler's gift of his will that day in the church is the massive contribution to the religious life of the nation that Mr. Oursler made during the remainder of his life. A knowing, spirited faith replaced his former agnosticism. Lost in emptiness, he found direction. His enthusiasms, his intensity, his insatiable love of a good story that had once poured into murder mysteries, plays, and movie scripts he now dedicated to the building up of faith in others. Since that experience his work includes some eighteen books, and endless succession of articles, and his column "Modern Parables," syndicated in about a hundred newspapers. When he was stricken with a heart attack on May 23, 1952, his *The Greatest Story Every Known* was interrupted in mid-sentence.

Daddy Long Legs

Author- Jean Webster, 1876-1916
Read by Gen. George C. Marshall, 1880-1959
U.S. Army Chief of Staff; Secretary of State;
1953 Nobel Peace Prize Winner

His reading over the years was voluminous and wonderfully diffuse. Biography, personal accounts of military expeditions, and general works on American and European history fascinated him, and he sought relaxation in popular Westerns and occasional novels. Once he astounded his officer students at Fort Benning by revealing that he found his pointers on the writing of a good term paper in a current fiction favorite, *Daddy Long Legs*. Some of his associates deplored his lack of academic accomplishments, saying he had made no proper study of Clausewitz and had only textbook knowledge of other masters of the art of war. Like most officers of his generation, he had read little in political theory, international economics, or advanced science. In these matters he was not far behind most of his military and political contemporaries. In one particular, the duties of a soldier in a democracy, he was better informed than most. By inheritance, by training, and by prolonged work with civilians, he was aware of the strength and weakness of democratic government, and he was wholly prepared to fit his role to that system.

Marshall's education came primarily from constant study of his trade. He learned what made the Army work and then sought to improve the way in which it accomplished its purposes. Although a "student" by Army standards, he was not known as an original thinker. He was a pragmatic military scientist, tinkering with what he had until it worked better, rather than the intuitive genius who changes the nature of warfare.

—Forrest Pogue

History of the Peloponnesian War

Author- Thucydides, 471-400 B.C.
Read by Thomas Masson, 1866-1934
Editor, Saturday Evening Post

The lack of accurate knowledge of our own American history is certainly widespread and a matter for concern. When, in my own dense ignorance, I first began to look into American history, I found it necessary to go back to England, and from England to Rome. Rome got her culture from Greece. Cicero learned oratory in Athens. Among all the writers of Rome, the divine Virgil alone stands out as an original source.

In Greece, I found my historical starting point in Thucycides' *History of the Peloponnesian War*, the greatest history ever written and a model for all time. It is here we find the sources of democracy, of imperialism, of everything humanity displays, in the original package. No one can compare the funeral oration of Pericles with Lincoln's Gettysburg Address, without being startled by their similarity. I should place Thucydides' history (in Jowett's admirable translation) as first on my list; and next, Gibbon's *Decline and Fall of the Roman Empire*, a monumental work written in sonorous prose, more than 800,000 words in length, and which would take at least 60 or 70 days to read through, reading one hour a day. In the life of Olive Schreiner, author of *The Story of an African Farm* and one of the great women of our modern world, her husband said she kept this book at her bedside, and read it continuously. I know of no better background to the reading of American history than the companionship of these two books.

The Making of a Leader

Cotton Mather, 1662-1727
Influential Colonial Clergyman,
Author, "Wonders of the Invisible World"

Fortunate indeed was Cotton Mather that to him reading was the greatest of delights. In his father's book-lined study, he learned before he could read that love of books for which he was always noted. In 1676, two days after the great fire that destroyed his father's church and house, the family bent their energies to drying the books which, chief of their possessions, had been saved. Cotton Mather was the son and grandson of authors; books on his father's shelves bore the names of John Cotton, of Richard Mather, and of Increase Mather himself. Certainly the *Bay Psalm Book*, of which Richard Mather was part author, had its place there—that pious but halting verse version of the Psalms of which the authors said: "...we have respected rather a plain translation, then to smooth our verses with the sweetness of any paraphrase, and so have attended Conscience rather than Elegance, fidelity rather than poetry, in translation the Hebrew words into English language, and Davids poetry into English meter; that so we may sing in Sion the Lords songs of prayer according to his own will." John Cotton spoke particularly of its virtue in being closer to the original and free from "divers other defects (which we cover in silence)" of the version hitherto in use. But all the books in this library were not pious, though there were tracts, sermons, and church histories in abundance. There were also almanacks, medical books, secular histories, the *Body of Chemistry*, travel books, Herbert's poems, and more than a five-foot shelf of classics in Greek and Latin, including Aesop and Plautus, and even Ovid's *Art of Love*. Here was amusement enough for any studious boy.

History of the United States From the Compromise of 1850

Author- James Ford Rhodes, 1848-1927
Read by William McKinley, 1843-1901
25th President of the United States

Like most uneducated men, William McKinley, Sr., longed that his children rise above his own station through education. Though lacking diplomas and degrees, the elder McKinley was not ignorant. Both he and his wife tried hard to maintain adequate intellectual standards in the midst of the arduous duties of child-raising. Hume's *History of England*, Gibbon's *Decline and Fall*, and the early works of Dickens graced the scant library shelves alongside the Bible in their household. The better monthly magazines were read carefully by every member of the family old enough, and saved to be passed on to the less fortunate. Though the family lacked intellectual pretensions, they encouraged study.

His reading was scattered and eclectic, though he liked history, biography, and non-fiction in general. In the past he had digested great quantities of dusty tables and labyrinthine figures on the tariff, but that was no longer possible or necessary. He did manage occasionally to read some of the gift volumes sent to him, including James Ford Rhodes' *History*. "...It has been so engaging that I have gone well into the night in perusing it," he wrote the author.

In the back of his mind McKinley regretted his inability to read much, feeling perhaps that gathering information largely from men was really not as good or as rewarding as gathering it from books. "You make me envious," he told Theodore Roosevelt somewhat wistfully in 1901. "You've been able to get so much out of books..."

—H. Wayne Morgan

The Autobiography of Benjamin Franklin

Author- Benjamin Franklin, 1706-1790
Read by Thomas Mellon
Financier, Philanthropist

Thomas Mellon, the founder of one of America's greatest fortunes, was a 14-year-old living on a farm outside Pittsburgh when he stumbled upon a copy of the autobiography. "I had not before imagined any other course of life superior to farming," he said later, "but the reading of Franklin's life led me to question this view. For so poor and friendless a boy to be able to become a merchant or a professional man had before seemed an impossibility; but here was Franklin, poorer than myself, who by industry, thrift and frugality had become learned and wise, and elevated to wealth and fame. The maxims of 'Poor Richard' exactly suited my sentiments... I regard the reading of Franklin's *Autobiography* as the turning point of my life."

Not long after he discovered Franklin, Mellon set out from his home in Poverty Point, Pennsylvania for Pittsburgh, 21 miles away, with 99 cents in his pocket. Years later, the financier put a statue of Franklin in his bank, and later in life he printed 1,000 copies of the autobiography to give to the young people who flocked to him for assistance or advice.

—Peter Baida

Read much, but not many books
Reading makes a full man
Meditation a found man
Discourse a clear man

—Benjamin Franklin

Works of Epictetus, 90 A.D.

Read by James Monroe, 1758-1831
5th President of the United States

Jefferson exerted a decisive influence on Monroe's life. At the time, Monroe, who was floundering about and had no idea what to do with himself, badly needed advice and encouragement. The Governor advised his protege to prepare for a career in politics by studying law. Following Jefferson's advice, Monroe re-entered William and Mary early in 1780 and joined William Short and Mercer in reading law under Jefferson's direction. Jefferson disapproved of the current habit of utilizing apprentices to the law, but also read those books which illuminated the fundamental principles of the social order and gave meaning to the law. His pupils mastered the thorny but liberal Coke, followed by the more graceful but Tory-minded Blackstone. Jefferson further assigned the statutes of Virginia, of which he had one of the few complete collections. As an advocate of the case method in an age in which law cases were rarely reported, he made his own extensive compilation available to his students. As the crowning glory to the course of study he added what might be termed the "Great Books" as viewed by an American *philosopher*—a catalogue from which St. Thomas and Aristotle were excluded with the same impartial rigor with which they are now included. The list Jefferson prepared for Monroe was probably much like the one he sent to Fulwar Skipwith a decade earlier. It included Locke, Bolingbroke, Rousseau, Montesquieu, Algernon Sidney and Hume, among the moderns. To represent the ancients he recommended Plutarch, Tacitus, Cicero, and his own favorite Epictetus, who appealed equally to Monroe. As a man of sensibility as well as sense, Jefferson did not omit the most characteristic novelists of the age—Smollett, Richardson and Sterne.

—Harry Ammon

The Will of God and a Man's Lifework

Author- Henry Wright
Read by John R. Mott, 1865-1955
Chairman, International Missionary Council;
Y.M.C.A. Leader; Nobel Peace Prize winner

No church or men's society should count itself as having attained. "If a man's reach doth not exceed his grasp, what's a heaven for?"

Having prepared and agreed upon a program with which to challenge men, the leaders of the Church should seek to enlist each man in some one or more specific pieces of work. Each man among the latent forces of the Church is under obligation to engage in Christian service. With God's help it must be pressed upon him that he has a responsibility which is individual, untransferable, and urgent. This is a will of God for him. In this connection attention should be called to one of the most useful books ever written, *The Will of God and a Man's Lifework*, by Professor Henry Wright, of Yale. This book and the simple public talks and personal conversations of its author have to my knowledge led hundreds of men to become lay workers. Once let a man become convinced that God has a plan and a definite work for him, and that no other man can perform it, and you introduce into his life a motive and a motivating power which will enable him to transcend his handicaps and limitations and will carry him through all opposition. When we have committed definite responsibility to a man, we should trust him with it. We should not only be willing to take risks but should actually take them. Men respond to trust. They rise to great heights when faith is manifested in them. We should stand behind them and encourage them and in every way possible strengthen their hands. We should see that full credit and recognition are accorded to them.

Works of William Penn, 1644-1718

Read by Lucretia Mott, 1793-1888
Quaker Minister; Co-director of first
Woman's Rights Convention, 1848

At twenty-five having resigned her position as teacher, she began close study of the Bible and theological books. She had four children to care for, did all her sewing, even cutting and making her own dresses; but she learned what every one can learn—to economize time. Her house was kept scrupulously clean. She says: "I omitted much unnecessary stitching and ornamental work in the sewing for my family, so that I might have more time for the improvement of my mind. For novels and light reading I never had much taste; the ladies' department in the periodicals of the day had no attraction for me." She would lay a copy of William Penn's ponderous volumes open at the foot of her bed, and drawing her chair close to it, with her baby on her lap, would study the book diligently. A woman of less energy and less will-power than young Mrs. Mott would have given up all hope of being a scholar. She read the best books in philosophy and science. John Stuart Mill and Dean Stanley, though widely different, were among her favorite authors.

—Sarah Bolton

THOUGHTS OF WILLIAM PENN:
"Truth often suffers more by the heat of its defenders than from the arguments of its opposers."

"They that love beyond the world cannot be separated by it. Death is but crossing the world, as friends do the seas; they love in one another still."

My Grandfather & I

By Lewis Mumford, 1895 -
Urban Planner; 1964 Winner of
Presidential Medal of Freedom

Until I was eight or nine, I spent almost every afternoon in the company of my grandfather, in saunters around Central Park or along Riverside Drive. These walks furnished the esthetic background of my childhood. Along Fifth Avenue or Riverside Drive, my grandfather could tell me who lived in nearly every great mansion. Often we would sit down on a bench before the west carriage drive in Central Park to watch the regular afternoon procession of broughams, victorias, and hansome cabs in a sort of parkwide carrousel, which mingled self-display with "taking the air." (The air was yet unpoisoned.) My grandfather could identify by name, sometimes with a little personal history, almost everyone of consequence who passed by: the Astors, the Vanderbilts, the Goelets, and the rest of the Four Hundred, as well as rich outsiders, like Russell Sage, who usually drove in an unfashionable surrey with a fringed top. ("A miser," my grandfather once said of Sage. "He watches every penny; but the Old Lady is very nice.")

On Saturdays or Sundays my grandfather would take me on much farther excursions to visit friends or old cronies like the Bastians. Old Bastian, a kindly white-bearded bookbinder, with a head a little like General Grant's, was one of those gentle, idealistic Germans who came to the New World lured less by the promise of a better income than by the desire for freedom, a desire nourished mainly by Cooper's *Leatherstocking Tales*; and it was Bastian indeed who, when I was only eight, urged me to read James Fenimore Cooper. I have him to thank for my early initiation into *The Spy*, *The Pilot*, and my favorite Leatherstocking novel, *The*

Pioneers. Frank Weitenkampf, the onetime head of the Print Department of the New York Public Library, writing me only a little while before his own death, told me that he had known Bastian well, a painstaking craftsman who used to bind the Astor Library's books.

Sam Day's influence on me touched more than the outdoors: if anything, it made an even more powerful impression indoors, for the living room boasted a library of perhaps two or three hundred books, most of them far above my level of understanding or taste even at fourteen—the time of my last visit. But there was one set I remember dipping into: John Ruskin's *Modern Painters.* Sam Day had also a writing room, always known as the office, just about the size of the eight-by-nine room in which I am now working; and in the shabby little apartment that Mrs. French conveniently maintained in Bethel itself, over a shop on the main street, there were still bound copies of the *Illustrated London News,* which I used to read, to the humming of the sawmill in the gorge of the river below, on long afternoons when Herbert would go off to shoot pool with his older cronies.

How keenly I remember those pages of the *Illustrated London News!* There must have been at least ten bound volumes of them, going back through the blazing moments of Britain's imperialistic enterprise and glory, often singularly well illustrated, mainly with wood engravings. Its editors had enough esthetic sense, before photoengraving became common, to get Gustave Dore to depict with masterly vividness the awful slums of industrial London. Those wood engravings I made use of in 1938 in The *Culture of Cities.* Some of that British ichor must have seeped into my blood, though part of it may have come from the equally enigmatic pages of *Chatterbox,* a book-sized annual that was a yearly Christmas gift in my early childhood.

It was from these rural contacts that books of a higher quality first came into my life.

Edward R. Murrow &
Carl Sandburg
On Abraham Lincoln

Excerpts from a broadcast interview,
October 5, 1954

Murrow cared about many people; he reserved his affection for a few. Carl Sandburg was one of the chosen few, and Murrow interviewed him at his North Carolina goat farm for "See It Now." The broadcast was called simply "A Visit to Flat Rock—Carl Sandburg."

Murrow: And when did you really begin to be seriously interested in Mr. Lincoln?

Sandburg: Well, I have been nearly all of my life. Heard men talk about him when I was a boy—politicians and preachers—and I knew sometime I would do at least a small book on Lincoln, to be titled *The Life of Abraham Lincoln for Young People*. And as I went through the basic Lincoln research books, why, it came over me there was something else I was started on—and I ended up with six volumes and a million-and-a-half words on Lincoln. And I don't know yet what to make of it.

Murrow: A million-and-a-half words and then *Always the Young Strangers*. You sat in that chair with a pencil, a pad, and that fabulous memory of yours, and wrote it here on this rock under the trees. Is that right?

Sandburg: Trying to recollect with a memory that I think is imperfect, very—no one knows better how imperfect it is than I. But people say I have got total recall. I deny it.

Murrow: Well, let's sit in this chair where you wrote *Always the Young Strangers* and talk about Mr.

Lincoln. I have got an advance copy here of this one-volume Lincoln, and in the preface you have got some of, I think, the noblest language I ever read. Will you read a little bit of it for us?

Sandburg: Well, there are some good lines at the end of that preface. I did not write them. I chose them from thousands of commentaries on Lincoln that I have met in my life. The are among the most significant, about why Lincoln lasts:

"There is no new thing to be said about Lincoln. There is no new thing to be said of the mountains or of the sea or of the stars. The years go their way, but the same old mountains lift their granite shoulders above the drifting clouds. The same mysterious sea beats upon the shore. The same silent stars keep holy vigil above a tired world. But to the mountains and sea and stars men turn in unwearied homage. And thus with Lincoln, for he was a mountain in grandeur of soul. He was a sea in deep undervoice of mystic loneliness. He was a star in steadfast purity of purpose and service. And he abides."

Murrow: Carl, why did you spend so much time with Mr. Lincoln?

Sandburg: Oh, the straight-off simplest answer to that is because he was such good company. I have been through all the basic research material about him, and I have sort of lived with him off and on for forty years and more, and he still is good to brood about. He still has laughter and tears that are good for a fellow. Well, he was also the first humorist to occupy the White House, the first man of humor. He was pre-eminently a laughing man, and he used to say that a good story was medicine.

Phrenology

Author- Lorenzo Fowler, 1811-1896
Read by Simon Newcomb, 1835-1909
Astronomer, Member of American Hall of Fame

"Among the books which profoundly influenced my mode of life and thought during the period embraced in the foregoing were Fowler's *Phrenology* and Combe's *Constitution of Man*. It may appear strange if a system so completely exploded as that of phrenology should have any value as a mental discipline. Its real value consisted, not in what it taught about the position of the 'organs,' but in presenting a study of human nature."

"I began to study arithmetic when I was five years old, and when six, I am told, I was very fond of doing sums. At twelve I was studying algebra, and about that time I began to teach."

After the boy had grown to manhood his father wrote for him an account of his early life from which the following extract is taken:

"At fifteen you studied Euclid, and were enraptured with it. It is a little singular that all this time you never showed any self-esteem; or spoke of getting into employment at some future day, among the learned. The pleasure of intellectual exercise in demonstrating or analyzing a geometrical problem, or solving an algebraic equation, seemed to be your only object. Your almost intuitive knowledge of geography, navigation, and nautical matters in general caused me to think most ardently of writing to the Admiral at Halifax, to know if he would give you a place among the midshipmen of the navy; but my hope of seeing you a leading lawyer, and finally a judge on the bench, together with the possibility that your mother would not consent, and the possibility that you would not wish to go, deterred me."

—David Starr Jordan

Natural Religion Insufficient

Author—William Halyburton, 1674-1712
Read by John Newton, 1725-1807
English Clergyman; Hymn Writer, "Amazing Grace"

My Dear Friend,   July 14, 1775

Besides a long letter, I send you a great book. A part of it (for I do not ask you to read the whole) may perhaps explain my meaning better than I have leisure to do myself. I set a high value upon this book of Mr. Halyburton's; so that, unless I could replace it with another, I know not if I would part with it for its weight in gold. The first and longest treatise is, in my judgment, a masterpiece; but I would chiefly wish you to peruse the Essay concerning Faith, toward the close of the book, I need not beg you to read it carefully and to read it all. The importance of the subject, its immediate connection with your inquires, and the accuracy of the reasoning will render the motive of my request unnecessary. I cannot style him a very elegant writer; being a Scotsman, he abounds with the Scottish idiom. But you will prefer truth to ornament. I long to hear your opinion of it. It seems to me as much adapted to some things that have passed between us as if written on purpose.

The Inquiry concerning Regeneration and Justification, which stands last in the book I do not desire or even wish you to read; but if you should and then think that you have read a speculation more curious than useful, I shall not contradict you. I think it must appear to you in that light; but it was bound up with the rest and therefore could not stay behind; but I hope the Essay on Faith will please you.

I take great pleasure in your correspondence and still more in the thought of your friendship, which I hope to cultivate to the utmost, and to approve myself sincerely and affectionately yours.

The Last Days of Pompeii

Author- Edward Bulwer-Lytton, 1803-1873
Read by Meredith Nicholson, 1866-1947
U. S. Diplomat; Author, "A Hoosier Chronicle"

My reading at that time was of the most miscellaneous order. I read voraciously. My grandfather, who was the most indefatigable reader I have ever known, introduced me to the public library. I read all of Oliver Optic, Harry Castlemon, Mayne Reid, and Elijah Kellogg, and my lively imagination made me the hero of all these tales in succession. Then someone gave me a copy of *The Last Days of Pompeii* which led me to read others of Bulwer-Lytton's romances. They pleased me so much by their vitalization of historic times that I looked into the merits of Scott, whom I found enthralling.

The wonder is that I ever emerged from the chaos of interests in which I plunged so joyously. My heroes were so numerous and changed so constantly that it was a serious question whether I would elect to become an intrepid scout of the plain, a soldier like General Custer, whose life and writings I read, a statesman and an orator, or a writer like Mark Twain. Everything, verily, was fish to my net! If I made a mistake in taking a number from the library catalogue, I accepted the error and read the wrong book no matter what its nature. The variety of reading I did between my fifteenth and eighteenth years would shock and grieve an orderly-minded pedagogue; but, curiously enough, much that I blundered into stuck, and some of it, at least, my anemic system assimilated.

I now moved to the office of John Dye and William Fishback, who were not only lawyers of the highest standing, but students of the times—men of ideas and ideals. The cultivated thinking men of the city frequently dropped into the office, and I heard there first the names of Darwin, Huxley, John Stuart Mill, and the rest of the great Victorians.

Read Historical Biographies

By Richard Milhous Nixon, 1913-
37th President of the United States

Like many political leaders, I have long been an avid reader of historical biographies. Even during the White House years, I made time for this. Since then, I have had more time for it. For those readers who want to pursue more fully the lives of these leaders, among the books I would recommend are:

Winston S. Churchill, by Randolph Churchill and Martin Gilbert

Churchill, by Lord Moran

Winston Churchill, by Violet Bonham Carter

Churchill and De Gaulle, by Brian Crozier

The Three Lives of Charles de Gaulle, by David Schoenbrun

American Caesar, by William Manchester

Konrad Adenauer, by Terence Prittie

Konrad Adenauer, by Paul Weymar

Khrushchev, by Edward Crankshaw

Chou En-lai: China's Gray Eminence, by Kai-yu Hsu

Mao, by Ross Terrill

The Man Who Lost China, by Brian Crozier.

Collected Poems of Edgar Allan Poe

Read by Fulton Oursler, 1893-1952
Editor of "Liberty" Magazine, Novelist

Of all the books I ate alive in those five voracious years, one stands preeminent. Some kind saint must have helped it happen to me, for you may be sure that my Uncle Tom knows nothing about poetry. Perhaps it was just a book, and he thought that one was as good as another for me. He found it on the sidewalk, lying in the rain, a green bound volume with gilt tops and stamping, and he put it into the kitchen oven to dry out and then one night brought it all the way from East 23rd Street (where he continued to live half a century) to Number 715.

"I don't know what it's about," he told my father, "but I thought little Charley might like it."

He then put into my hands a book which, within two years, I committed to memory; the Collected Poems of Edgar Allen Poe. Thanks to you, old uncle, the high, clear music of pure poetry sang in my brain for the first time—the strange, chanting loveliness, its frosty remoteness. No, I did not know all that it meant, but my tongue could repeat its cadences and my soul rejoiced in its mysteries, and I fell in love with it once and for all, forever.

After my first reading of Poe, I was never the same child. For years I slept with that water-stained green book under my pillow, and surely because of it I grew to be a different kind of man—some awareness had come to me of the beauty that is in the wonder of being alive or the fearfulness of being dead; some inescapable sense of a harmony in the midst of universal confusion and discord. One could know it in the very flow of words one could not understand.

Read Good American Biographies

By William Lyon Phleps, 1865-1943

There is perhaps nothing more interesting to many minds than a good biography; it has all the charm of fiction with all the satisfaction of being real. I say *real* rather than *true*, because no man in a biography or autobiography can write the exact truth. The two or three exceptions to this only prove the rule.

For prominent men in American history, the best one-volume life of Lincoln is by the Englishman Lord Charnwood. The best two-volume life of Lincoln is by Carl Sandburg, called *The Prairie Years*. It closes with his departure to Washington, to take the Presidency. In connexion with this, one should read *Mary Lincoln*, also by Carl Sandburg.

The best one-volume life of Washington that I have seen is *George Washington Himself*, by John C. Fitzpatrick. The best two-volume life of Daniel Webster is by Claude Fuess, now Principal of Phillips Academy, at Andover. The best life of John Marshall is by the late Senator Beveridge, who surprised all those who thought he could not do it.

The best life of Lee is the one by Freeman, in four volumes. Joseph Hergesheimer wrote an admirable biography of Sheridan. I have read a number of biographies of Grant, Sherman, Jackson-but for Grant I recommend his own *Memoirs*, and for the other two I don't know which one I like the best.

The best life of our great song-writer Stephen C. Foster is by John Tasker Howard, triply qualified to write it by scholarship, by style and by musicianship. The best life of that intellectual aristocrat Henry Adams is by himself and is called *The Education of Henry Adams*. The life of Mark Twain, in three volumes, by Albert Bigelow Paine, is one of the best biographies ever written in America.

Thomas Jefferson

Read by Saul Padover, 1905-
Dean of Politics, New School for Social Research;
O.S.S. intelligence officer in WWII

A candid statement of faith becomes, for me, a concentrated spiritual autobiography. My fundamental beliefs are the products of three converging influences that have been silently at work within my personality: history, America, and Jefferson.

Thomas Jefferson's influence on my spiritual and intellectual life has been continuous and pervasive. I think I know by now every word he has ever written; I feel inside of me the very rhythm of his thought. His life and personality have been to me sources of spiritual strength and inspiration. Jefferson never failed me in any crises.

What I have learned from him, in brief, has been an abiding faith in human potentialities. I would call this the religion of democratic humanism. Following Jefferson's optimistic faith—despite examples of horror and bloodshed in recent times—I believe that man can and should be kind and just to his fellows; that man can and should strive for constant spiritual and social improvement...and keep the avenues of opportunity always open for himself and his fellow men. To state it negatively, I believe with all my heart that cruelty, injustice, and intolerance are social crimes that should be punished as severely as physical ones.

It is a cardinal article of faith with me that there is no limit to what men in society can achieve. In this context, I believe that the good, just and happy life cannot be achieved in any society where power, political or economic, is monopolized in the hands of a single person or single group. I hold, with Jefferson, that only inside a democratic society, even if it is imperfect, can human beings make a successful effort to attain happiness.

The Graphic Artists

Author- Philip Hamerton, 1834-1894
Read by Maxfield Parrish, 1870-1966
Artist

Many years later he wrote about the things at Haverford from which he received the greatest inspiration.

"I was all for becoming an architect, and once, exploring in some forgotten corner of the library, discovered a number of giant French books of engravings of classic temples; books of wonder, smelling of old mouldy leather and long years of unuse. From the astonished librarian, permission was obtained to take them one at a time to my room, where many hours were spent making tracings of capitals and things...."

"There may have been precious little art around, but there was surely a wealth of material for making it. For all there was Haverford, and the sheer beauty of the place was an influence and an education hard to equal."

Enrolling as a student at the Pennsylvania Academy of the Fine Arts in 1892, Parrish by then was preparing for a career in art rather than architecture. There he studied under Robert Vonnoh and Thomas P. Anschutz. Vonnoh, also one of the teachers of Robert Henri, originally had worked with classic artists in Paris, but eventually came under the influence of the Impressionists before returning to the United States. It is possible that Parrish used as a text at the academy *The Graphic Arts, A Treatise on the Varieties of Drawing, Painting, and Engraving,* Philip Gilbert Hamerton's comprehensive volume published in America in 1889. After he became a professional artist, Parrish frequently recommended this book to art students who sought his advice in their educational pursuits.

—Coy Ludwig

You Must Know History

By Gen. George S. Patton, Jr. 1885-1945
Commander, Third Army, World War II

Letter to his son, on D-Day, June 6, 1944

Dear George:

At 07.00 this morning the B.B.C. announced...the landing of Allied paratroopers...So that is it.

This group of unconquerable heroes, whom I command, are not yet in, but we will be soon—I wish I were there now as it is a lovely sunny day for a battle...

I have no immediate idea of being killed, but one can never tell and none of us can live forever. So if I should go don't worry, but set yourself to do better than I have.

All men are timid on entering a fight, whether it is the first fight or the last fight...Cowards are those who let their timidity get the better of their manhood. There are apparently two types of successful soldiers—those who get on by being unobtrusive and those who get on by being obtrusive. I am of the latter type and seem to be rare and unpopular, but it is my method. One has to choose a method and stick by it. People who are not themselves are nobody.

To be a successful soldier you must know history. Read it objectively—dates and even minute details of tactics are useless. What you must know is how man reacts. Weapons change, but man, who uses them, changes not at all. To win battles you do not beat weapons—you beat the soul of enemy man...

You must read biography and autobiography. If you will do that you will find that war is simple. Decide what will hurt the enemy the most within the limits of your capabilities and then do it. Take calculated risks. That is quite different from being rash. My personal belief is that if you have a 50% chance you should take it, because the superior fighting qualities of American soldiers will surely give you the extra 1% necessary...

You cannot make war safely, but no dead general has ever been criticized, so you have that way out always. I am sure that if every leader who goes into battle will promise himself that he will come out either a conqueror or a corpse, he is sure to win....Defeat is due not to losses but to the destruction of the souls of the leaders. The "live to fight another day" doctrine.

The most vital quality a soldier can possess is self-confidence, utter, complete, and bumptious. You can have doubts about your good looks, about your intelligence, about your self-control, but to win in war you must have no doubts about your ability as a soldier.

What success I have had results from the fact that I have always been certain that my military reactions were correct. Many people do not agree with me; they are wrong. The unerring jury of history, written long after both of us are dead, will prove me correct.

Soldiers, in fact all men, are natural hero worshipers; officers with a flair for command realize this and emphasize in their conduct, dress, and deportment the qualities they seek to produce in their men....The troops I have commanded have always been well dressed, been smart saluters, been prompt and bold in action, because I have personally set the example in these qualities. The influence one man can have on thousands is a never-ending source of wonder to me. You are always on parade. Officers who, through laziness or a foolish desire to be popular, fail to enforce discipline and the proper wearing of equipment, not in the presence of the enemy, will also fail in battle; and if they fail in battle they are potential murderers. There is no such thing as "a good field soldier." You are either a good soldier or a bad soldier.

Well, this has been quite a sermon; but don't get the idea that it is my swan song, because it is not. I have not finished my job yet.

Your affectionate father, George S. Patton, Jr.

De Jure Belli Ac Pacis

Author- Hugo Grotius, 1583-1645
Read by William Penn, 1644-1718
Founder of Colony of Pennsylvania

Hugo Grotius develops as one of the most significant of contemporary influences on Penn's thinking during his college days, an influence that registered only gradually as it combined with the concepts of Thomas Loe, Moses Amyraut and the whole Quaker movement, and that ultimately flowered in Penn's *An Essay Towards the Present and Future Peace of Europe.* In *No Cross, No Crown* Penn said of Grotius: "than whom these latter ages think they have not had a man of more universal knowledge (a light, say the statesmen; a light, say the churchmen, too) witness his Annals; and his book, *De Jure Belli Ac Pacis*; also his *Christian Religion*, and elaborate commentaries."

Grotius, the Latinized version of the Dutch de Groot, is considered the founder of modern international law. Hugo Grotius conceived the modern idea of an international morality. Early in his ecclesiastical-legal career he had written *Mare Liberum*; in 1625 he published his immediately popular and many times reprinted *De Jure Belli Ac Pacis*, this latter listed in Christ Church Library catalogue. In it Grotius raised the question as to whether war was ever justifiable; and even though he could conceive of some circumstances when a nation might be impelled to take up arms, he maintained that there was no justification for waging war indiscriminately. He was many, many generations ahead of his times, as he developed in his *De Jure* a list of unjust causes of war—the enfeebling of another power, raiding another country on the pretext of discovery, or subjugating another by force of arms.

—Catherine Owens

Plato to Carlyle and Ruskin

Read by J. C. Penney
Founder, J. C. Penney Company

Dr. Tapper seemed uncertain as to whether an organization like ours could provide an opportunity for the development of educational activities of the best quality. But he did not hesitate long. He has often told me that it was his wife who, by a clear perception of the vision, prompted his decision. He came, and the year immediately following I asked him to work with me in arranging a course of reading and study which I proposed to follow as a student and out of which I hoped we could ultimately deduce a study plan for adoption by our thousands of store associates. That proved to be one of the most delightful years of my whole life. I read slowly at first, then more intensively and faster. I read the masterpieces from Plato to Carlyle and Ruskin. I wrote papers on what I read, discussing with Dr. Tapper not only the structure of the written report, but the correctness of my effort at interpretation. I wondered why I had never discovered in the high school back in Hamilton how delightfully exciting the reading and appreciation of great books can be. Day after day throughout a year, I pursued this stimulating adventure. We let nothing interfere with the project. I rarely went out on the road, though store visiting was second nature with me, and no matter how important the business to be considered, I often passed up meetings of the board of directors rather than miss one of those study periods. It certainly puzzled some of my associates to witness this, but I was out for a royal adventure along one of the most delightful highways I have ever traveled. And I determined nothing should turn me back until through experiment upon myself a promising study plan had been discovered.

Pilgrim's Progress
Author- John Bunyan, 1628-1688
Read by Samuel Pennypacker, 1843-1916
Governor of Pennsylvania

There was not a novel in the house. The nearest thing to it was a copy of Bunyan's *Pilgrim's Progress*, which I devoured for the story, utterly regardless of the allegory. The *Fables* of Aesop I learned by heart.

When I was about eight years of age a young woman left a box of things in our garret. Rummaging in the box, I found a copy of *Lewis Arundel*. The book opened out vistas before me, and today I could repeat the story of the proud young man who went as a tutor, fought the poachers and remained to marry. In a geography of the world I found detailed an adventure of Audubon in the wilds of the West; in a Universal History there was a description of the assassins of India; in *Sartain's Magazine* I found an Indian story called "Hard Scrabble;" in the *Whig Review*, beside the biographies of the politicians of the day and the poems of Poe, there was told of "Jack Long, or Lynch Law and Vengeance," and along with these I satisfied my craving for romantic narrative by reading of John Smith, Hernan Cortes, Henry Hudson, Putnam's Ride at Horseneck, Marion and Sergeant Champ. Somewhere I found a copy of Montgomery Bird's *Nick of the Woods* which I still regard as the most meritorious of the tales of Indian warfare. Nothing in the shape of literature came amiss and before I was eleven I had read an elaborate natural history, Whitaker on *Arianism*, Dick's *Sidereal Heavens* and Guizot's *Washington*.

I naturally enough turned to the gathering of books, with the result that when I eventually went to Harrisburg in 1903 I left locked up in my house in Philadelphia over ten thousand volumes. In the main they were books relating to Pennsylvania and early imprints of the province and the state.

Commentaries on American Law

Author- James Kent, 1763-1847
Read by Gen. John J. Pershing, 1860-1948
Chief of Staff, U. S. Army; Author,
"My Experiences in the World War"

Some scant spare moments came now and then to teachers in remote schools, and Jack snatched his for reading the stilted, formal elegance of the legal commentaries of Blackstone and Kent. In balanced, tightly reasoned phrases, these giants of jurisprudence expounded the majesty of the common law. To a precise and questioning mind, there is a spell in the symmetry of those formidable pages with their logical arguments. And so they touched Jack Pershing. Blackstone and Kent opened his mind to rigorous thought, and the law became his great ambition. Teaching could provide money for a thorough university grounding, which might lead to a law degree, enabling him to become a prairie lawyer or even a noble and honored judge.

A chance reading of a stray advertisement in a local paper wrought the change: "Notice is hereby given that there will be a competitive examination held at Trenton, Missouri, for the purpose of selecting one Cadet for the Military Academy at West Point." It seemed somehow to jump off the page in bold type, as if, perhaps, meant especially for Jack. Never in his strangest fancyings had he considered the army as a possible career. No family tradition pointed to it, no personal inclination, nothing. However, the advertisement carried a meaning of its own to the young teacher in Kirksville, Missouri.

West Point conjured up visions of a high and stately citadel not just of martial splendor but also of polished education. Four years of hard discipline and mental preparation there, and he would be ready for the iron cadence of the law.

—Frank Vandiver

American Statesmen

By William Lyon Phelps, 1865-1943
Educator; Yale University

It is an interesting fact that the two Presidents of the United States who did the most to preserve the Union in troublous times were both born in Southern States, Lincoln in Kentucky, Jackson in South Carolina.

Whatever Jackson lacked, he did not lack courage. He loved adventurous exercises, he had the pioneeer spirit, he never hesitated to take part in a duel, and in war and in peace his life was one of continual fighting. I have always been sorry for his enemies.

When I was a schoolboy, the series of biographies called "American Statesmen" began to appear; I read every word of every one of these seventeen or eighteen volumes, and I recommend them today to all young people who wish to know something of American history. These books were never intended for young people, which makes them all the more valuable for young people.

In this series the life of Jackson was written by the distinguished Professor of Political Economy, William Graham Sumner. He cared nothing for gossip and scandal, for whatever irregularities there may have been or may have been suspected, in a statesman's life. On the title-page of this biography was

ANDREW JACKSON
As a Public Man
Who he was, What Chances
he had, and What he Did
with Them.

It was the Day of Judgment for Andrew Jackson. Although Professor Sumner belonged to the Democratic Party, that in no way obscured his vision of this hero.

Jackson was courageous and incorruptible; two excellent qualities in a politician.

Essay on Human Understanding
Author- John Locke, 1847-1889
Read by Franklin Pierce, 1804-1869
Brigadier General; United States President

After the beginning of his third year, the relative standings of the men were announced. Pierce went to scan the list and found that his was the lowest in the class. This was too much for his pride. Bitterly he decided never to attend another recitation and for several days he moped. But such conduct caused his friend Little much concern and he labored with him, aided by Caldwell, a serious fellow whose life was deeply immersed in an earnest and unflagging Methodism. Together these two prevailed upon their chum and he pitched headlong into the solution of his problem. For three months he rose at four and retired at twelve, devoting unceasing labor to repairing the inroads of idleness. Still Pierce continued with the inevitable *Graeca*; Horace sang; conic sections and mechanics were to be mastered; and in addition Locke's *Essay on the Human Understanding* and Paley's *Evidences of Christianity* were followed in the spring by Henry's *Chemistry* and Priestley's *Lectures on History*. By dint of heroic measures, Pierce achieved a mastery of Locke which left a profound impression upon his memory and modes of expression.

In this campaign for reconstruction, he had the continuous aid of Caldwell whose burning eyes and feverish earnestness considerably influenced him. In order to help in the struggle for discipline, Caldwell turned over to him his duties as chapel monitor, and thus put him on the road to regular chapel attendance. So successful was this campaign, Hawthorne could write many years later, that Pierce never again missed a class or an exercise (with two exceptions) nor went to a class unprepared.

—Roy Nichols

Economy of Human Life

Author- Robert Dodsley, 1703-1764
Read by General Zebulon Pike, 1779-1813
Western Explorer, killed in the War of 1812

Among other habits of mental discipline by which Pike was accustomed to cherish these principles and feelings, was a constant practice of inserting upon the blank pages of some favourite volume, such striking maxims of morality, or sentiments of honour, occurred in his reading, or were suggested by his own reflections. He had been in the practice of making use of a small edition of Dodsley's *Economy of Human Life*, for this purpose. Soon after his marriage, he presented this volume to his wife, who still preserves it as one of the most precious memorials of her husband's virtues. An extract from one of the manuscript pages of this volume was published in a periodical work soon after his death. It was written as a continuation of the article "Sincerity," and is strongly characteristic of the author.

"Should my country call for the sacrifice of that life which has been devoted to her service from early youth, most willingly shall she receive it. The sod which covers the brave shall be moistened by the tears of love and friendship; but if I fall far from my friends and from you, my Clara, remember that 'the choicest tears which are ever shed, are those which bedew the unburied head of a soldier,' and when these lines shall meet the eyes of our young—let the pages of this little book be impressed on his mind as the gift of a father who had nothing to bequeath but his honour, and let these maxims be ever present to his mind as he rises from youth to manhood:

1. Preserve your honour free from blemish.
2. Be always ready to die for your country."

—The Analectic Magazine, 1814

The Making of a President

James Polk, 1795-1849
11th President of the United States

He had a new ambition that, for a boy who had been accused of having none, was suddenly intense. He had a passionate desire to make up for the schooling he had lost. The books he had borrowed from Grandfather Ezekiel, in the dull days when nothing but reading had interested him, now became a doorway to that ambition.

He had a thirst for all the learning that had been denied him on the frontier because he realized that only by learning could he make himself the equal of other men.

Grandfather Ezekiel's library was only a start. Jim soon was borrowing books from any neighbor who happened to have a volume or two and would lend them. But when he spoke to his father about wanting to go to school somewhere to prepare himself for college, Sam Polk was reluctant to make any promises. College was for the very few and Jim had never shown himself to be brilliant or much of a scholar. His father told him he had better give up such ideas and learn a trade that would earn him a solid living.

If Jim was disappointed, he also was more determined than ever to impress his father. He laid out a plan of study for himself from the books available to him, spent every waking hour learning from them. He tried to enlist his mother's sympathy and even tried to get Grandfather Ezekiel to put in a word for him with his father.

Henderson soon discovered he had a prize pupil in Jim and encouraged him in every way possible. Perhaps Jim surprised even himself when he went to the head of the class. He certainly impressed his father, who was amazed to discover his son possessed such hidden ability. When the year ended, Sam Polk was so pleased by his son's progress that it was he who suggested sending him to a better school.

—Bill Severn

The Nigger of the Narcissus
Author—Joseph Conrad, 1857-1924
Read by Adam Clayton Powell, 1908-1972
U. S. Congressman

Next to the Bible, the most important book in our household of prolific readers was a huge dictionary. At dinner, the Bible was placed on the dining-room table next to my Father. He read to us from the Bible before eating from the same good book after dinner.

Just as my father had a voracious intellectual appetite that was never satiated, so had I. I read the newspapers every day. My favorite was the old New York *World*.

And from cover to cover, as soon as Daddy finished it, I read the *Literary Digest*. I also read all the Rover Boys and Horatio Alger series. Then I came across *The Nigger of the Narcissus* by Joseph Conrad. When I finished it, I laid it down with a thrill. Here was something I wanted to go into further. This was Life!

That very week in the *Literary Digest* there was an advertisement: "All Joseph Conrad's works, twenty-eight volumes, sent free to your home. If after ten days you are not satisfied, return at our expense, or otherwise pay a dollar a week." I immediately mailed in the coupon without consulting my mother and father, and the books arrived one day while I was at school. When I came home my father said, "You should have discussed this with me. If you really want the books, clean all the bathrooms in the house (there were three) and I'll pay for them." I did, and by the age of twelve I had read all of Joseph Conrad's works. These volumes still occupy a prominent place in my library.

Of course, the great standard literary works were part of the very fabric of my thinking. I read all of Mark Twain's books because everyone said my dad looked like Mark Twain...and because I liked him.

The Study of History

Author- Gabriel de Mably, 1709-1785
Read by William Prescott, 1796-1859
Historian

Prescott felt the Abbe de Mably's *De L'Etude De L'Histoire* so important for his purposes that he read it ten times. He developed a theory of style and a prescription for the writing of narrative history which by implication constituted a philosophy of history.

Prescott first applied himself to a study of the lives of great men and their exploits. He read Voltaire's *Charles XII*, Livy's account of Hannibal, and Washington Irving's *George Washington*. Prescott was in his element. Cortes was the unquestioned hero, and his dashing exploits and crushing reverses supplied enough dramatic intensity to keep even the most jaded at a high point of excitement. While reading Washington Irving's *Columbus*, he jotted down some notes revealing his method and intent. He agreed with the opinion that *Columbus* was a "beautiful composition," but found it "fatiguing as a whole." The subject of the great discovery, admittedly "full of sublimity," was a model topic for historical investigation, and Irving had performed with enviable skill. But "all after that event is made up of little details, all having the same general character. Nothing can be more monotonous, and more likely to involve the author in barren repetition." The subject of the conquest of Mexico, on the other hand, "though very inferior in the leading idea which forms its basis," was much more suited to Prescott's conceptions and devices. "The event is sufficiently grand, and, as the catastrophe is deferred, the interest is kept up through the whole. Indeed, the perilous venture and crises with which the enterprise was attended, the desperate chances and unexpected vicissitudes, all serve to keep the interest alive."

—James Bert Loewenberg

Essays

Author- Thomas Macaulay, 1800-1859
Read by Joseph Pulitzer, 1847-1911
Newspaper Publisher;
Founder of the Pulitzer Prize

The world's champion sightless reader was later said to have "read" a book every day—an exaggeration, although his own records show that his secretaries read him an average of about a hundred books a year for 21 years. Since only about one third of his reading time was devoted to books, the rest to newspapers, magazines, letters and reports, one gets an approximation of the countless millions of words that came to him by voice and a better understanding of his insistence that the voice know the book in advance so that he could summarize windy passages and get to the point—always get to the point. Dr. Hosmer was still the best reader he ever had, good at fiction or fact. Pollard read to him novels and plays in English and French. Mann, in addition to his piano-playing, read to him in German and often had the ticklish duty of reading him to sleep at night. Thwaites did little reading, but other secretaries came and went, some of them *World* men on temporary duty, and most of them spent much of their time reading to him.

Although he had long since absorbed many of the ancient classics—Plutarch, Thucydides, Herodotus, Plato, Aristotle, Tacitus—he reread stirring passages at intervals. Avoiding pure science, he enjoyed such leaders in contemporary thought as Spencer, Darwin and Huxley. He had little use for poetry, with notable exceptions such as Shakespeare and Goethe. Reading far more fiction than fact, he was familiar with scores of classics, among them the novels of Fielding, Thackeray, Sienkiewicz, the Brontes and Meredith, as well as with minor writers from Maarten Maartens to Walter Besant.

Yet his fiction reading was largely for relaxation or cultivation, and most of his favorite books were factual.

It is perhaps significant that he read many biographies of Napoleon and many accounts of the French Revolution, admiring Acton's and condemning Carlyle's. He much enjoyed Boswell's *Johnson*, Lord Hervey's memoirs, Montaigne and the memoirs of Madame Roland. In the middle of President Polk's diary he uttered an oath, pronounced Polk stupid and quit him. Since perhaps his most abiding interest was the study of greatness, and as an old orator he loved a stirring style, one of his top favorites was Macaulay's *Essays*, some of which he reread many times and could quote verbatim.

Reading, which illuminated his whole life, was so important to him that he judged his editors and secretaries to some extent by the books they had read. When a book impressed him, he would send copies of it to his editors and friends—Morley's *Gladstone*, Acton's *French Revolution*, Dasent's life of John Delane, and above all Macaulay's *Essays* and Trevelyan's *Life of Macaulay*, which he once sent to 39 people. To have failed to read a great book was to him sinful, and one of his gloomiest convictions was that most people were too lazy or uninterested to enlarge their talents by broad reading. He requested frequent reports from his children on what they were reading, and often sent them books. Constance, at least, got the inevitable Macaulay. He enjoyed having his profitable annual *World Almanac* specially bound in sumptuous leather and giving it to a score of friends with the recipient's name lettered in gold. He once ordered scores of sets of the Encyclopedia Britannica to be sent to his editors and his children.

He had saved up the reading of the *Odyssey* for his later years, looking forward particularly to enjoying the Trojan horse episode. When he found it described in seven fairly commonplace lines he said, "I was so damned mad that I could have kicked Homer!"

—W. A. Swanberg

Arrowsmith

Author- Sinclair Lewis, 1885-1951
Read by Ernie Pyle, 1900-1945
Journalist; War correspondent; Author, "Brave Men"

"The years are dealing heavily with me. No wine, no women, no song, no play....I get mail from a lot of people, but am gradually sinking into my old-time funk (from which I've been free for several months) about Jerry. I've a premonition things have gone bad again. God, if they have I don't know what to do."

He borrowed a copy of Sinclair Lewis's *Arrowsmith*. "I'm so glad I did," he wrote Jerry, "for I'm absorbed in it. When I read stories like Maugham's and Steinbeck's I think maybe I could really write some-day, but when I read such broad, meticulous things as this I know I never could." When he had finished the story of Martin and Leora Arrowsmith he told her: "I'm very moved by it. In so many ways it is so much you and so much me that it sort of haunts me. In all his faults I can see so much of myself; his one-tracked-ness, his shallow wanderings from it, his self-centered-ness, his neglects. And in her there is so much you— the seeing beyond all sham, the patience with my childishness, that acute and automatic understanding of absolutely everything that of all the people I've ever known only you and Ruth Egan possess. And maybe Cavanaugh....Somehow I knew that Lewis would have her die in the book, and the book ended there for me. I finished it, but I wasn't interested after that. Possibly because I felt it might picture my own pathet-ic and wretched flounderings if you were ever gone...." He asked Jerry to buy a few new books each month: "Maybe some day I'll have time to read them, and anyhow you know how I like to have more and more books around."

—Lee G. Miller

Serious Books Produce Serious Men

By John Randolph, 1773-1833
American Statesman, Senator

To Theodore Dudley, he wrote, "Yours is the time of life to acquire knowledge. Thereafter you must use it." Teachers might help, but reading informed by purpose was all-important: "there is a wide difference between a boy's getting his lesson from a sense of duty, or a fear of punishment, and his applying himself with real zeal, from a conviction that he is consulting his future advantage....the taste for reading, which you are now forming, will be a source of pleasure to you through life." The moral usefulness of reading is the proper source of its pleasure. Randolph's letters to Dudley and his nephews reflect a faith that properly serious books will result in properly serious men. The works in his lists of suggestions differ strikingly from those comprising his own early reading. What he urged on his "sons" connects the "dramatic immediacy" of reading to morally secure content. He discouraged imaginative literature in favor of histories and translations from the Greek and Latin. The assumption operating in his advice is that early reading impresses itself lastingly and that good, i.e., "moral," "serious" reading will have a correspondingly "good" result. He was trying to pass on the lesson of his own experience. His letters attempted to convert his own intense, literal, and imaginative reading to surer moral purpose. Here, he extended the pressure of expectation to the one place where it had functioned incompletely for him, his reading. His reiteration of the moral purpose of study to his "sons" reflects interestingly the fragmented reader he himself was. He read seriously and literally, assuming the books made the man.

—Robert Dawidoff

McGuffey's Eclectic Readers

Author- William McGuffey, 1800-1873
Read by Diane Ravitch
Historian; Author, "The Schools We Deserve"

The six McGuffey readers dominated the textbook market, and historians believe that half of all public school students used them. The fourth reader (roughly for fourth to sixth graders) included Hawthorne's fable "Hugh Idle and Mr. Toil," a selection from Louisa May Alcott's *Little Men* and another from Daniel Defoe's *Robinson Crusoe*."

The greatest literary rewards were stored up for those youngsters who reached the fifth and sixth McGuffey readers; these students were probably no more than 12 to 14 years old. They encountered not only Alcott and Hawthorne, but Shakespeare, Tennyson, Longfellow, Washington Irving, Oliver Goldsmith, Daniel Webster, Byron, Keats, Thoreau, Audubon, Thackeray and James Fenimore Cooper.

In the fifth reader, they were treated to the historian George Bancroft's account of the Boston Massacre; to Dickens's description of the schoolmaster Squeers in *Nicholas Nickleby*; to Robert Southey's antiwar poem, "The Battle of Blenheim."

McGuffey's fifth and sixth readers had an abundance of the kind of poetry that demands to be read out loud. Present-day critics may find such poems sentimental, but generations of children have loved them. I recently came across an article in a 1912 issue of *Scribner's* magazine, in which a writer fondly remembered a family ritual: "When checkers and dominoes had ceased to be exciting, some inspired member of the group suggested, 'Let's read in the Reading Book.'" Then each one selected a favorite poem from an old schoolbook and recited to the others. It is a safe bet that no one will ever turn to today's basal readers that way.

Abraham Lincoln, Theologian of American Anguish

Author- Elton Trueblood, 1900-
Read by Nancy Reagan
First Lady

Living in the White House is a very emotional experience and gives you such a sense of the continuity of history that, in the little spare time I've had, I've been reading about former occupants of the White House and especially about former First Ladies. It's been fascinating that so many of them in one way or another left their mark on the White House. They wanted it to be a beautiful, warm place with dignity and elegance and I was particularly interested to learn of the changes made by Dolley Madison, Edith Roosevelt and many others.

Just the other day I picked up a book called *Abraham Lincoln, Theologian of Anguish*, written by Elton Trueblood. The author stresses Lincoln's idea of a special destiny for America, and as I sat reading in the family sitting room, just down the corridor from the bedroom where Lincoln slept, I felt a shiver of recognition and agreement as I read the words, "Lincoln's only certainty was that God would never cease to call America to her true service, not only for her sake, but for the sake of the world."

"I must confess that I'm driven to my knees by the overwhelming conviction that I have nowhere else to go. My wisdom and that of all about me is insufficient to meet the demands of the day."
—Abraham Lincoln

That Printer of Udell's

Author- Harold Bell Wright, 1872-1944
Read by Ronald Reagan, 1911-
40th President of the United States

"I'm a sucker for hero worship," Reagan wrote in 1977, listing the books which had made a deep impression on his life as a young man. His heroes were soldiers, Presidents, athletes and achievers who started with nothing and became captains of industry or public servants. Born three years before the Great War, as Americans then knew World War I, Reagan grew up in an Illinois town where the arch on Main Street celebrated the deeds of those who had fought and died in Europe for what he was taught had been the cause of lasting peace. That arch touched older memories in a state which had given so much of its human treasure to preserve the Union. The Civil War was a living memory in Illinois when Ronald Reagan was a boy. Veterans of the Grand Army of the Republic survived in every town and hamlet. Heroes, dead and alive, were all around him.

One of his favorite books was a now forgotten novel called *That Printer of Udell's*, with a hero modeled after those in the success stories of Horatio Alger. The hero, Dick Falkner, works by days as a printer and attends night school. He marries not the boss's daughter, as would a proper Alger hero, but a beautiful socialite whom he saves from a life of prostitution. Falkner blends Christian and business principles to uplift a midwestern town, caring more for the principles than he does for either the church or the business community. At the end, he is off to Congress. "All in all, as I look back I realize that my reading left an abiding belief in the triumph of good over evil," Reagan wrote about books like these when he was sixty-six years old. "There were heroes who lived by standards of morality and fair play."

—Lou Cannon

On Reading Lenin
by Will Rogers, 1879-1935
American humorist

Now they will tell you that the worship of Leninism is their religion. Lenin preached Revolution, Blood and Murder in everything I ever read of his. Now they may dig 'em up a religion out of that, but it's too soon after his death really to tell just how great he was. History has to ramble along a good many years after a man puts some policies into effect till you can tell just how they turned out...You know, there is a lot of big men that die, but most of them are not so big that they won't be buried. Now Lenin may come through right on through the ages, but at the present time they are kinder forcing him on the people. They make the children speak of him as Uncle Lenin. Now it's always best to let the people pick out their own Hero. Don't try to force one on them; it's liable to have the opposite effect sometimes.

Mind you, you can't condemn everybody just because they started a Revolution. We grabbed what little batch of liberty we used to have through a revolution, and other Nations have revolutions to thank today. But I don't think anyone that just made a business of proposing them for a steady diet would be the one to pray to and try to live by.

We all know a lot of things that would be good for our Country, but we wouldn't want to go so far as propose that everybody start shooting each other till we got them.

There never was a nation founded without some kind of belief in something. Nobody knows what the outcome in Russia will be or how long this Government will last. But if they do get by for quite a while on everything else, they picked the only one thing I know of to suppress that is absolutely necessary to run a Country on, and that is Religion. Never mind what kind; but it's got to be something or you will fail in the end.

Misunderstood

Author- Florence Montgomery
Read By Eleanor Roosevelt, 1884-1962
First Lady, United Nations Delegate

Misunderstood was a great favorite of the Victorians; as a young girl Sara Delano also sobbed over its pages. In that book, the lad Humphrey welcomed death because it would reunite him with his mother and end an existence that had been rendered "miserable" by his father's partiality for Humphrey's little brother. She still enjoyed them, Eleanor Roosevelt wrote in 1950, but she thought them "very sentimental, foolish books to allow a rather lonely child to read." Sometimes she made a play out of the book she was reading, in which she was the principal character and her brother, six years younger, the supporting cast. *Robinson Crusoe* especially lent itself to such dramatization. The desert island was a secret place in the woods a quarter of a mile away from the main house.

She was often asked in later years to list her favorite childhood books. "I loved Dickens' *Old Curiosity Shop* and *Tale of Two Cities*; Longfellow's Poems; Kipling's *Light That Failed*; Walter Scott's *The Talisman*; *Sarah Carew*; *The Prince and the Pauper*; *The Little Lame Prince*; Ouida's *Dog of Flanders* and *Nuremberg Stove*." On another occasion she added *Oliver Twist* and *Dombey and Son* as among the books she remembered from girlhood and "with great enthusiasm a long book called *Thaddeus of Warsaw*, which was a historical novel, touching on one phase of Poland's efforts to remain a free nation." In an article for *Girl Scout Magazine*, August, 1933, she said that she had read George Eliot's *The Mill on the Floss*, *Romola*, and *Silas Marner* as she "grew a little older." Also, "a book which could not be found today in any library—*The Gad Fly*—gave me hours of pleasure."

—Joseph Lash

Rudyard Kipling, 1865-1945

Read by Franklin D. Roosevelt, 1882-1945
32nd President of the United States

The book about which Roosevelt seemed most enthusiastic as a boy was one by Anthony Hope. And there was Kipling. Someday someone may write a nice little essay on Roosevelt's lasting interest in that poet and panegyrist of empire. He pops up often in the letters. Roosevelt was shocked, as he should have been, when such a well-brought-up New England girl as Katharine Hepburn came as a movie actress to the White House and admitted she had never heard of the brushwood boy. There was something special and a little mysterious about Roosevelt's feeling for Kipling. When he was President he asked his ambassador to the court of St. James's if he happened to know the then aging English author.

"If you do, I should like to get a note to him asking him a question I have long wanted to know the answer to."

—Jonathan Daniels

"We all know that books burn—yet we have the greater knowledge that books cannot be killed by fire. People die, but books never die. . . No man and no force can put thought in a concentration camp forever. No man and no force can take from the world the books that embody men's eternal fight against tyranny of every kind. . . . In this war we know books are weapons. And it is a part of your dedication to make them weapons for man's freedom."

—Franklin D. Roosevelt, April 23, 1941, on the
anniversary of the Nazi book-burning.

Homes Without Hands

Author- John G. Wood, 1827-1889
Read by Theodore Roosevelt, 1858-1919
26th President of the United States

My own children loved Laura E. Richards's "Nursery Rhymes" dearly, and their mother and I loved them almost equally.

Even in poetry it was the relation of adventures that most appealed to me as a boy. At a pretty early age I began to read certain books of poetry, notably Longfellow's poem, "The Saga of King Olaf," which absorbed me. This introduced me to Scandinavian literature; and I have never lost my interest in and affection for it.

Among my first books was a volume of a hopelessly unscientific kind by Mayne Reid, about mammals, illustrated with pictures no more artistic than but quite as thrilling as those in the typical school geography. When my father found how deeply interested I was in this not very accurate volume, he gave me a little book by J.G. Wood, the English writer of popular books on natural history, and then a larger one of his called *Homes Without Hands*. Both of these were cherished possessions. They were studied eagerly; and they finally descended to my children. *The Homes Without Hands*, by the way, grew to have an added association in connection with a pedagogical failure on my part. In accordance with what I believed was some kind of modern theory of making education interesting and not letting it become a task, I endeavored to teach my eldest small boy one or two of his letters from the title-page. As the letter "H" appeared in the title an unusual number of times, I selected that to begin on, my effort being to keep the small boy interested, not to let him realize that he was learning a lesson, and to convince him that he was merely having a good time.

Principles of Moral Philosophy

Author- William Paley, 1743-1805
Read by Benjamin Rush, 1746-1813
Medical Pioneer & Political Leader;
Signer of the Declaration of Independence

His letters to his wife continue to be affectionate, expressive, and full of thoughts he wanted to share with her. "To a mind like mine, which so soon (perhaps from its slender size) becomes plethoric with ideas and which delights so much in communicating them, it is a new and peculiar hardship to lose at once a domestic friend, a wife, and five children, to most of whom I had been in the habits of imparting every thought as soon as it rose in my mind." He tells her that he needs people to dispute and contradict him, as this is not only "the life of conversation but steel to the flint of genius."

Even his books lose their relish without her company. Not a day goes by without his hearing and seeing many things which perish in his bosom without being communicated. He longs to put Paley's *Moral Philosophy* into her hands, since he enjoys it only by halves from not reading it with her. He wants her to become mistress of it in order to qualify her to educate their children properly.

However personal or political Rush's motives may have been in the founding of Dickinson College, there can be no doubt of his idealistic, if not Messianic, concern with the spreading of republican education.

He now began the preparation of an article published in 1785, in which he urged his fellow citizens to establish a college for the education of German youth. Two years later this campaign too was crowned with success by the establishment of Franklin College at Lancaster, later to be called Franklin and Marshall.

—Carl Binger

Historical and Critical Dictionary

Author- Pierre Bayle, 1647-1706
Read by Karl Sandberg
Prof. of Romance Languages, Univ. of Arizona

The least that can be said about the *Dictionnaire historique et critique* (1697) is that it is one of the most unique documents in French letters and certainly one of the most impressive monuments of seventeenth-century erudition. Opening its pages at random one finds each article divided into text and notes, the former apparently serving only as a springboard for the latter. In the notes, there is a vast, disparate, and unsystematic assemblage of learning, the subjects having been chosen more from the author's interest than from their historical importance. Discussions, disquisitions, and digressions turn upon such varied subjects as geography, genealogies, the souls of animals, rabbinical speculation on the origin of the world, lives of Biblical heroes, obscure scholars of the sixteenth and seventeenth centuries, real and legendary figures of antiquity, and ecclesiastical disputes between Protestants, Catholics, heretics, and libertines. But what the reader immediately notices beyond the vastness of the erudition is the eminently critical tone of the *Dictionnaire*.

Historical error, first of all, is given no quarter. In the thousands of notes which comment on and explain the hundreds of articles, there are literally tens of thousands of references to document every point upon which there might be a question. Passages are cited in Greek and Latin in case the reader has doubts about the reading given. Just as the maxims of La Rochefoucauld become screens to separate the true and supposed motivations of the people, the *Dictionnaire* becomes a crucible in which the assertions and the commonplaces of seventeenth-century learning are proved and tested.

Plutarch's Lives

Author- Plutarch, 46-120 A.D.
Read by Winfield Scott, 1786-1866
General, United States Army
Hero, War of 1812 and Mexican War

Scott spent much of his time in reading. Outside
the range of his textbook requirements, he delved
deeply in the pages of those authors whose works
then weighted the bookshelves of every gentleman
with pretensions to learning. He was especially
delighted with Plutarch, and the life stories of the
ancient heroes influenced his character and conduct
throughout his life. He was fascinated by the careers
of men like Caesar and Scipio Africanus, perceiving in
their vaulting ambition stars to which he did not hesitate to hitch his wagon. His favorite authors in youth
as in later days were Shakespeare—whose works he
studied diligently but whose philosophy he never fully
comprehended—Addison, Milton, Johnson, and
Goldsmith. His historians were Hume and Gibbon; in
poetry he read Dryden with enthusiasm; in economics, Adam Smith and John Locke. Mathematics
had but slight attraction, although he lived to regret,
like many another soldier, his early neglect of this
phase of his education.

At the head of the law department was the brilliant
Professor St. George Tucker, whose lectures were
embodied in his commentaries on Blackstone, published in 1803, the first distinctive law book to appear
in the United States. In the appendix Judge Tucker,
discussing the institution of slavery, suggested the
desirability of a gradual emancipation of the negroes.
Nearly forty years later Scott recalled the lasting
impression made on his youthful mind by these views
and expressed his complete accord with the idea.

—Charles Elliott

Teaching His Nation to Read

Sequoyah (George Guess), 1770-1843
American Indian scholar,
Inventor of the Cherokee alphabet

He had to contend with the prejudices of the Cherokees who tried to convince him that God had made a great distinction between the white and the red man by relating to him the following tradition: In the beginning God created the Indian, the real or genuine man, and the white man. The Indian was the elder and in his hands the Creator placed a book; in the hands of the other he placed a bow and arrow, with a command that they should both make good use of them. The Indian was very slow in receiving the book, and appeared so indifferent about it that the white man came and stole it from him when his attention was directed another way. He was then compelled to take the bow and arrow, and gain his subsistence by pursuing the case. He had thus forfeited the book which his Creator had placed in his hands and which now of right belonged to his white brother.

The narration of this story however, was not sufficient to convince Sequoyah, and to divert him from his great purpose. After the interview at Sauta, he went home, procured materials, and in earnest began to paint the Cherokee language on paper.

Sequoyah at first thought of no way but to make a character for each word. He pursued this plan for about a year, in which time he had put down several thousand characters. He was then convinced that the object was not to be obtained in that way. But he was not to be discouraged.

After putting down and learning all the syllables that he could think of, he would listen to speeches, and the conversation of strangers, and whenever a word occurred which had a part or a syllable in it, which he had not before thought of, he "would recollect it until he had made a character for it." In this way he soon discovered all the syllables in the language. After commencing upon the last plan, it is believed he completed his system in about a month. He adopted a number of English letters which he took from the spelling book then in his possession. "At first these symbols were very numerous; and when he got so far as to think his invention was nearly accomplished he had about 200 characters in his alphabet. By the aid of his daughter, who seemed to enter into the genius of his labors, he reduced them, at last to 86, the number he now uses."

During the time he was occupied in inventing the alphabet, he was strenuously opposed by all his friends and neighbors. He was frequently told that he was throwing away his time and labor, and that none but a delirious person or an idiot would do as he did. But this did not discourage him. He would listen to the expostulations of his friends, and then deliberately light his pipe, pull his spectacles over his eyes, and sit down to his work, without attempting to vindicate his conduct.

"After completing his system, he found much difficulty in persuading the people to learn it. Nor could he succeed until he went to the Cherokees in Arkansas and taught a few persons there, one of whom wrote a letter to some of his friends in the Cherokee Nation east of the Mississippi and sent it by Mr. Guess, who read it to his people on his return.

"This letter excited much curiosity: here was talk in the Cherokee language, which had come all the way from the Arkansas sealed up in a paper, yet it was very plain. This convinced many that Mr. Guess' mode of writing would be of some use. Several persons immediately determined to try to learn. They succeeded in a few days, and from this it spread all over the nation, and the Cherokees (who as a people had always been illiterate) were, in the course of a few months, without school, or expense of time, or money, able to read and write in their own language."

—Grant Foreman

M. Lincoln Schuster, 1897-1971
& Thomas Paine
Publisher & Co-Founder of Simon & Schuster

Benjamin Franklin declared, "Where Liberty is, there is my country." To this, Thomas Paine replied, "Where Liberty isn't, there is mine."

Paine was a born liberator, to his dying day an implacable enemy of tyranny. He carried on his inspired pamphleteering so courageously, so uncompromisingly, so brillantly, both in America and in France, that he became literally the revolutionary "hero of two worlds." He was "the North Star" of the new American republic, actually one of the Founding Fathers, and indeed the author of the phrase "The United States of America."

Born in England in 1737, he met Benjamin Franklin in London when the visiting Philadelphian was "Taken with those wonderful eyes of his." In his youth Paine had run away to sea, and in early manhood had gone bankrupt as a tobacco merchant. Franklin persuaded him to come to America, then seething with revolutionary conspiracies and aspirations.

Paine arrived in 1775, during a period he described in the immortal phrase "the times that try men's souls." A year later he was in the forefront of the fight. He wrote a classic manifesto, Common Sense, which became a truly epochal best-seller, with half a million copies distributed in short order. Jefferson, Washington, and John Adams read this pamphlet; Congress voted him $3000 for his pamphleteering services, and the state of New York awarded him three hundred acres of land. The propaganda caught fire throughout the land; the militant phrases did their work, and were reflected almost immediately in the Declaration of Independence.

Fulton J. Sheen & Books

1895-1979
Educator, Clergyman, Author

The books that all humanity has approved are the best. For those who love biography, there will be *Plutarch's Lives*. No college student should ever be given a degree unless he has read it—also, Herodotus and his description of ancient history, particularly that of Babylon. In poetry, there is Shakespeare, John Donne, and Francis Thompson; and for serious daily reading the Bible and the *Imitation of Christ* by Thomas a Kempis. The mind is like a clock that is constantly running down; it has to be wound up daily with good thoughts.

Thomas Jefferson wrote to John Adams, "I have given up newspapers in exchange for Tacitus and Thucydides, for Newton and Euclid, and I find myself much happier."

Our minds were not meant to rust in us unused. Books are readily available, and what companions they are! A good book is the same today as yesterday. It is never displeased when we put it down; it is always inspiring when we pick it up. It never fails us in times of adversity. It even makes human friends, for oftentimes a friendship develops out of a common love of a book. "Love me, love my dog" really should be "Love me, love my book." Men share a common life through common ideas.

READING books in one's youth is like looking at the moon through a crevice; reading books in middle age is like looking at the moon in one's courtyard; and reading books in old age is like looking at the moon on an open terrace. This is because depth of benefits of reading varies in proportion to the depth of one's own experience.

—Chang Chao

Plutarch's Lives

Author- Plutarch, 46-120 A.D.
Read by William L. Shirer, 1904-
Foreign correspondent; Radio commentator;
Author, "Berlin Diary"

It's rather difficult in these noisy, confusing days to achieve the peace of mind in which to pause for a moment to reflect on what you believe in. There's little time and opportunity to give it much thought—though it is the thing we live by; and without it, without beliefs, human existence today would hardly be bearable.

My own view of life, like everyone else's, is conditioned by personal experience. In my own case, there were two experiences, in particular, which helped to shape my beliefs: years of life and work under a totalitarian regime, and a glimpse of war.

Of course, there are many days when a human being feels awfully discouraged. I myself find consolation at such moments by two means: trying to develop a sense of history, and renewing the quest for an inner life.

I go back, for example, to reading Plutarch. He reminds you that even in the golden days of Greece and Rome, from which so much that is splendid in our own civilization derives, there was a great deal of what we find so loathsome in life today: war, strife, corruption, treason, double-crossing, intolerance, tyranny, rabble-rousing. Reading history thus gives you perspective. It enables you to see your troubles relatively. You don't take them so seriously then.

Finally, I find that most true happiness comes from one's inner life; from the disposition of the mind and soul. Admittedly, a good inner life is difficult to achieve, especially in these trying times. It takes reflection and contemplation. One must be honest with oneself, and that's not easy. (You have to have patience and understanding. And, when you can, seek God.)

David Gregg, Pennsylvania Cavalryman

Author- Milton Burgess
Read by Bud Shuster
Member, U. S. House of Representatives

But for little-known General David Gregg, the North probably would have lost the Battle of Gettysburg, and the South could have gone on to win the Civil War. Without this obscure cavalry officer there might not be a United States of America today. That is the inescapable conclusion of this meticulously researched book.

It is the story of a boy who was orphaned at an early age, but who graduated from the Military Academy at West Point and eventually rose to be described by his Civil War comrades as "the best all-'round cavalry officer that ever commanded a division in either army."

This book marshalls the evidence for the historical case that General Gregg, as Commanding Officer of the Union Army's 2d Cavalry Division at Gettysburg, made the daring, crucial decisions that blocked a Confederate victory in the greatest battle of the Civil War.

Gregg correctly calculated where J.E.B. Stuart's Confederate cavalry would attempt to break through, and hid his troops in the woods to meet them. Because his force was too small, Gregg countermanded his superior officer's order and commandeered a cavalry brigade led by General Custer to augment his own troops. Had he failed he could have been court-martialed. But together with Custer, Gregg led a surprise attack which stopped Stuart's cavalry from driving through the Union lines to join the Confederate infantry on Cemetery Ridge, thereby saving the Union Army from defeat.

For several reasons, General David Gregg does not rank in the pantheon of famous Civil War heros. Nevertheless, he changed the course of history at the Battle of Gettysburg.

Napoleon's Campaigns

Read by Daniel Sickles, 1825-1914
Civil War General, Hero of Gettysburg

Here was a find—a fellow with the dress, manners, speech of a Knickerbocker blueblood. And no fool! The Tiger put him in the New York State Assembly.

For the next few years Dan Sickles levied hard on his Dutch vitality. When he was not debating at Albany, his days were spent in court or at his New York office, 74 Nassau Street, working up one or other of the increasingly important cases that came to his desk. His nights, when he was not attending some turbulent Tammany meeting or convivial powwow, were about equally given to the pursuit of the feminine and to prolonged bouts of private study in his chosen fields of law, history, political theory; and—the uncanny prevision again!—in drilling with the National Guard and conning *Napoleon's Campaigns*.

When—with *Napoleon's Campaigns*, Montesquieu's *Esprit des Lois*, a battered *History of Greece*, and bound copies of the *Federalist*—Sickles arrived at Albany, the Assembly was struggling with a mass of legislation arising out of the recently revised state constitution. No few of the bills pending closely concerned Tammany interests and were of a nature to require adroit shaping in committee. Also, over and above the routine "fixing" and vote swapping, some of them required unusually skillful defense on the floor. In work of this kind, Sickles was in his element. And with one foot on the political ladder, he was not the man to miss a rung. He worked indefatigably, won from his associates a slightly startled respect, and from Governor Marcy the dictum, "As a debater he excels any man of his years in political life."

—Edgcumb Pinchon

The Meditations
Of Marcus Aurelius

Author- Marcus Aurelius Antoninus,
121-180 A.D.
Read by Captain John Smith, 1580-1631
English Adventurer; Virginia colonizer;
saved from death by Indian Princess, Pocahontas

The little book of Antoninus has been companion of some great men. Machiavelli's *Art of War* and Marcus Antoninus were the two books which were used when he was a young man by Captain John Smith, and he could not have found two writers better fitted to form the character of a soldier and a man. Smith is almost unknown and forgotten in England, his native country, but not in America where he saved the young colony of Virginia. He was great in his heroic mind and his deeds in arms, but greater still in the nobleness of his character. For a man's greatness lies not in wealth and station, as the vulgar believe, nor yet in his intellectual capacity, which is often associated with the meanest moral character, the most abject servility to those in high places and arrogance to the poor and lowly; but a man's true greatness lies in the consciousness of an honest purpose in life, founded on a just estimate of himself and everything else, on frequent self-examination, and a steady obedience to the rule which he knows to be right, without troubling himself, as the emperor says he should not, about what others may think or say, or whether they do or do not do that which he thinks and says and does.

—George Long

HISTORY makes us some amends for the shortness of life.

—Philip Skelton

The Making of a Composer

John Philip Sousa, 1854-1932
Bandmaster & Composer,
Known as "The March King"

He was blessed with an extraordinary memory and constantly astounded friends and acquaintances with his recall. He had a seemingly insatiable curiosity, partly satisfied by being an inveterate reader. His Sands Point home contained over 3,000 volumes, covering everything from light poetry to scientific subjects. Home after a tour, he could hardly be torn away from the rare book catalogues which had arrived during his absence.

Sousa was a busy man all his life. From his earliest years he was exceedingly active, making efficient use of his time. Each day was judiciously planned, including times of leisure. While a violinist in theaters, he preferred working on his compositions to relaxing with his fellow musicians during intermissions or after performances. He was of the opinion that a creative man was obliged to present all of his talent to the world and should therefore have a capacity for unlimited work.

He steadfastly proclaimed that he would never retire or give a "farewell" concert. When newspaper reporters sensed the end of his career and asked the inevitable question, his ready reply was, "When you hear of Sousa retiring you will hear of Sousa dead!" When the self-made millionaire Sousa permitted himself the luxury of relaxing, it was usually among books. He was well informed on many subjects.

Some of his happiest times were spent with his wife and children at home between tours, and among his most pleasant recollections were the times spent around the dinner table when all indulged in conversations on nearly every imaginable subject. He had the knack of drawing out their innermost thoughts, and they all cherished these moments.

—Paul Bierley

Marshall: Hero For Our Times

Author- Leonard Mosley
Read by Maj. Gen. Clyde W. Spence, Jr.
US Army-Ret.; Pres., Marion Military Institute

A criticism often leveled at educational institutions today is their failure to help young students develop value systems, such as understanding of duty, honor, country. For those institutions that do undertake this challenge, the obstacles to success are almost formidable. Young people tend to emulate those they admire—parents, athletes, political figures, and so on. And yet, they too often see deceit, corruption, drugs, and dishonor, manifested by the very people they had placed on a pedestal. Youths become cynical and question the need for and even the meaning of values.

Everyone needs a hero—a person who rises above the common level of man and stands tall in the face of disappointment and adversity. Such a hero is George Catlett Marshall, that soldier-diplomat whose integrity and honor and absolute selflessness is a model for youths of all time to follow. One of the many examples of Marshall's personal qualities portrayed in the book is a reference to his actions to insure that the bright and promising officers on his staff would receive no favors or "safe" assignments once they left. When Marshall released one such ex-aide for service in Italy, he wrote General Jake Devers:

"I want him attached to a United States Division in the line in Italy not as a liaison or observer but a member on duty with the Artillery. What I want is to give him the experience in fighting as a final step to offset his service to me here in this office. Thereafter he is on his own..."

To learn value systems in any institution, young people must "know" such leaders as Marshall. They must be surrounded by role models who live the virtues of honorable men.

Lincoln Steffens and History

Author, "The Shame of the Cities"
Editor, "McClure's Magazine;" 1866-1936

It is possible to get an education at a university. It has been done; not often, but the fact that a proportion, however small, of college students do get a start in interested, methodical study, proves my thesis, and the two personal experiences I have to offer illustrate it and show how to circumvent the faculty, the other students, and the whole college system of mind-fixing.

My method was hit on by accident and some instinct. I specialized. With several courses prescribed, I concentrated on the one or two that interested me most, and letting the others go, I worked intensively on my favorites. In my first two years, for example, I worked at English and political economy and read philosophy. At the beginning of my junior year, I had several cinches in history. Now I liked history; I had neglected it partly because I rebelled at the way it was taught, as positive knowledge unrelated to politics, art, life, or anything else. The professors gave us chapters out of a few books to read, con, and be quizzed on. Blessed as I was with a "bad memory," I could not commit to it anything that I did not understand and intellectually need. The bare record of the story of man, with names, dates, and irrelative events, bored me. But I had discovered in my readings of literature, philosophy, and political economy that history had light to throw upon unhistorical questions. So I proposed in my junior and senior years to specialize in history, taking all the courses required and those also that I had flunked in. With this in mind I listened attentively to the first introductory talk of Professor William Cary Jones on American constitutional history. He was a dull lecturer, but I noticed that, after telling us what pages of what books we must be prepared in, he mumbled off some other references "for those that may care to dig deeper."

When the rest of the class rushed out into the sunshine, I went up to the professor and, to his surprise, asked for this memorandum. He gave it to me. Up in the library I ran through the required chapters in the two different books, and they differed on several points. Turning to the other authorities, I saw that they disagreed on the same facts and also on others. The librarian, appealed to, helped me search the bookshelves till the library closed, and then I called on Professor Jones for more references. He was astonished, invited me in, and began to approve my industry, which astonished me. I was a curious boy. He lent me a couple of his books, and I went off to my club to read them. They only deepened the mystery, clearing up the historical question, but leaving the answer to be dug for and written.

The historians did not know! History was not a science, but a field for research, a field for me, for any young man, to explore, to make discoveries in and write a scientific report about. I was fascinated. As I went on from chapter to chapter, day after day, finding frequently essential differences of opinion and of fact, I saw more and more work to do. In this course, American constitutional history, I hunted far enough to suspect that the Fathers of the Republic who wrote our sacred Constitution of the United States not only did not, but did not want to, establish a democratic government, and I dreamed for a while—as I used to as a child to play I was Napoleon or a trapper—I promised myself to write a true history of the making of the American Constitution.

Of course I did well in my classes. The history professors soon knew me as a student and seldom put a question to me except when the class had flunked it. Then Professor Jones would say, "Well, Steffens, tell them about it."

The Journal of the Pilgrims at Plymouth in New England, in 1620

Edited by George Cheever, D. D.
Read by Richard Storrs, Jr., 1787-1873
Pastor; Anti-slavery Leader;
Co-editor, The Independent

It was a happy thought of our respected friend Dr. Cheever, to commemorate the anniversary of the Landing of the Pilgrims by the re-publication of their original *Journal*. The orthography, etc., of the original are strictly preserved; and as much of its total appearance as will allow. We apprehend, however, that Mr. Bellarmie would hardly recognize in this gilt-edged representative the dingy and obscure pages of what was doubtless reckoned in its day a wondrous trophy of his typographical skill. The difference is a suggestive one. And it will be well for us as a people, if in our sumptuous and ornate civilization, which is so rapidly throwing into the shadow the simpler manners of the Fathers, we retain as much in practice, as does this volume in record of that which gave them power and life.

Of the interest which attaches to the *Journal*, we need not speak. It is already familiar to many of our readers, through Dr. Young's *Chronicle of the Pilgrims*, and its simplicity and true pathos, as well as its pervading spirit of trust and thoughtfulness, opening to us a clear view of the feedings and the events of more than two centuries since, would give it much attractiveness, aside from its associations with those whom it recalls. The illustrations show an earnest and reverent regard for the godly farseeing and fearless men of whom they treat, and a discriminating and comprehensive view of the work which they did, and the influences they have exerted. The volume is full of interest and instruction.

Declaration of Independence

Read by Harriet Beecher Stowe, 1811-1896
Author, "Uncle Tom's Cabin"

Before she was eight, she proved to Lyman Beecher's satisfaction that she could master the content of adult books, so he granted her permission to use his library, which contained hundreds of volumes.

She was allowed to remain in the study while Lyman Beecher wrote his sermons, and one day he read the Declaration of Independence to her. Years later she wrote:

"I had never heard of it before, and even now had but a vague idea of what was meant by some parts of it. Still I gathered enough from the recital of abuses and injuries that had driven my nation to this course to feel myself swelling with indignation, and ready with all my little mind and strength to applaud the concluding passage...I was ready as any of them to pledge my life, fortune and sacred honor for such a cause. The heroic element was strong in me, having come down by ordinary generation from a long line of Puritan ancestry, and just now it made me long to do something, I knew not what: to fight for my country, or to make some declaration on my own account.''

The extent to which that yearning remained prominent in her mind is impossible to determine but can be exaggerated if common sense is not applied. Countless thousands of children have felt the ambition to perform great deeds, and it would be absurd to repeat the claim of her early biographers that Harriet Beecher Stowe pursued her goal with single-minded ambition. It may not be accidental that her pen later produced a document that, though far less concise than the Declaration of Independence, was almost equally influential in shaping the destiny of her country and the world.

—Noel Gerson

The History of the Decline and Fall of the Roman Empire

Author- Edward Gibbon, 1737-1794
Read by Charles Sumner, 1811-1874
U.S. Senator, Anti-slavery Leader

He was a thoughtful, studious youth, always fond of reading. His mother, in later life, often spoke of this trait of his boyhood. He enjoyed history most of all, reading it not in an easy, careless way, but with earnest attention, sitting on a low seat, and with maps spread out before him. When fourteen years of age, he wrote a compendium of English history, from Caesar's conquest to 1801, which filled a manuscript-book of eighty-six pages. The penmanship is elaborate in the early part, but less careful towards the end. The events are succinctly narrated, in good English, and dates are given, with the year and often with the month and day. With a boy's humor he begins with this title: "A Chronological Compendium of English History, by Charles Sumner, Copyright secured. Boston, 1825." This abstract, probably begun at his father's suggestion, was a discipline in composition and study, which prepared the way for larger acquisitions. In 1826, when fifteen years old, he read Gibbon's *History*, copying at the same time the extracts which pleased him. Some of these he re-copied into a commonplace-book, which he began in his Senior year in college. His inquisitive mind sought knowledge as well in conversation as in books; and he plied with many questions travelled persons, and his father's friends who had served as army officers in the unsettled territory of the West. This trait survived boyhood, and he always listened well to those who could tell him aught worthy of note that they had seen or heard.

—Edward Pierce

Harper's Weekly

Read by William Howard Taft, 1857-1930
U. S. Supreme Court Chief Justice;
27th President of the United States

After district school they all attended the Woodward High School, named for its notable founder, William Woodward, a formidable schoolmaster whose reputation was nation-wide. It was a grim-looking building, terra-cotta in tone, with an iron fence suggestive of the Bastille. Woodward was vigorous in imposing high standards of education and his school had considerable reputation in its day. He thought nothing of dropping forty percent of the class if they did not meet his stiff standards. It was a free school and the students were expected to work or leave. Five boys in Horace's class went on to Yale and four were Phi Beta Kappa. The school was particularly strong in mathematics. The boys pored over historical books and the young Tafts went in strongly for Scott, Dickens, Thackeray, Cooper, and, in lighter moments, the Oliver Optic books, adventure stories with patriotic undertones. Will spent hours reading *Harper's Weekly* at the home of his friend, Rufus B. Smith.

—Ishbel Ross

HISTORY is a record of human progress, a record of the struggle of the advancement of the human mind, of the human spirit, toward some known or unknown objective.

—Nehru

Pilgrim's Progress

Author- John Bunyan, 1628-1688
Read by A. J. P. Taylor, 1906-
Military Historian; Author,
"The Origins of the Second World War"

On social evenings my father could not follow the general conversation and sat at the back of the room with a book, usually Dickens. He read the other nineteenth-century novelists as well, but Dickens was his favourite—not the Dickens we take so seriously nowadays, but the Dickens who created a world of fantasy characters much like my father himself. As I recollect, my parents were almost totally unaware of contemporary literature. Meredith and Arnold Bennett had reached them, but not Hardy or Wells.

I could read before I was four. *Pilgrim's Progress* was my favourite from the start. I read it again and again and knew it almost by heart except that I skipped the theological conversations. I rightly equated Vanity Fair with Lord Street arcade. I had a favorite fairy-tale book about Tufflongbow, which I have never managed to trace, and *The Adventures of Prince Kebole*, with sectional illustrations of his castle which started my interest in architecture. I have never managed to draw sections, only ground plans, which perhaps also applies to my writings. I read of course the two Alice books and also *Peter and Wendy*, a narrative version of *Peter Pan*. I don't seem to have read much poetry except for nursery rhymes, certainly no Lear or Belloc—lamentable omissions that I remedied when I read to my own children.

Boswell's *Life of Johnson* was my favourite book and has so remained. I went on from it to *The Lives of the Poets*, the book I should most like to have written. I do not mean that it is the greatest book I know or even the most admirable. I mean only that, if I had greater gifts, it would be within my range.

Bayard Taylor Memorial Poem

Editor, New York Tribune, 1825-1878
By Henry Wadsworth Longfellow,
1807-1882

Dead he lay among his books!
The peace of God was in his looks
As the statues in the gloom
Watch o'er Maximilian's tomb,
So these volumes from their shelves
Watched him, silent as themselves.
Ah, his hand will never more
Turn their storied pages o'er.
Never more his lips repeat
Songs of theirs, however sweet.
Let the lifeless body rest!
He is gone who was its guests.
Gone as travelers haste to leave
An inn, nor tarry until eve.
Traveler! in what realms afar,
In what planet, in what star,
In what gardens of delight
Rest thy weary feet tonight.
Poet, thou whose latest verse
Was a garland on thy hearse.

Except a living man there is nothing more wonderful
than a book!—a message to us from the dead—from
human souls we never saw, and who lived perhaps
thousands of miles away; and yet these words on
those little sheets of paper speak to us, amuse us, and
comfort us.

—Kingsley

The Heroic Books

Read by Henry David Thoreau,
1817-1862
Philosopher; Essayist;
Author, "Walden"

"How admirably the artist is made to accomplish his self-culture by devotion to his art!"

Thoreau's art was literature; and it was one of which he had conceived most ambitiously. He loved and believed in good books. He said well, "Life is not habitually seen from any common platform so truly and unexaggerated as in the light of literature." But the literature he loved was of the heroic order. "Books, not which afford us a cowering enjoyment, but in which each thought is of unusual daring; such as an idle man cannot read, and a timid one would not be entertained by—which even make us dangerous to existing institutions—such I call good books." He did not think them easy to read. "The heroic books," he says, "even if printed in the character of our mother-tongue, will always be in a language dead to degenerate times; and we must laboriously seek the meaning of each word and line, conjecturing a larger sense than common use permits out of what wisdom and valor and generosity we have." Nor does he suppose that such books are easily written. "Great prose, of equal elevation, commands our respect more that great verse," says he, "since it implies a more permanent and level height, a life more pervaded with the grandeur of the thought. The poet often only makes an irruption, like the Parthian, and is off again, shooting while he retreats; but the prose writer has conquered like a Roman and settled colonies."

—Robert Louis Stevenson

.Pendennis.

Author- William Thackeray, 1811-1863
Read by John Toland, 1912-
War Historian; Author,
"The Battle of the Bulge"

It was not one book that influenced my life but the combined novels of Dostoevski, Dickens, Thackeray and Trollope. From these men of the 19th Century, I learned the way things really are. I discovered reality and the pitfalls that lay ahead of me. Since all of these authors were not only fascinating to read but instructive, I was able to experience second-hand many of the tragedies resulting from the vagaries of human nature and the temptations of life. Dostoevski taught me the danger of gambling, Dickens the futility of great expectations, and Trollope the corruption of wealth and liquor. Perhaps the most cautionary book of all was *Pendennis* by Thackeray whose hero's follies and foibles exposed my own flaws.

THACKERAY:
"Next to excellence is the appreciation of it."

DOSTOEVSKI:
"So long as man remains free he strives for nothing so incessantly and so painfully as to find someone to worship."

DICKENS:
"There is a wisdom of the head, and...a wisdom of the heart."

TROLLOPE:
"Of all the needs a book has, the chief need is that it be readable."

Robert E. Lee

Author- Douglas Freeman, 1886-1953
Read by Harry S. Truman, 1884-1972
33rd President of the United States

from correspondence with his wife Bess:

July 9, 1935

Well I've been reading the Bank Bill, the Social Security Bill, Water Carrier Bill, and Freeman's *Lee* at night as well as the *New York Times*. I am to have dinner with the assistant manager of the Pennsylvania Railroad tonight and that's all I have on for this week. So I guess I'll finish Freeman's volume one. You sort of gave me a blue feeling again. I'll be glad when this damned session is over. I think maybe we better get a flat and stay here summer and winter.

Washington, D.C., 1939

I usually read myself to sleep every night. Have found another book on the Civil War, by Colonel A. H. Burne, an Englishman. He makes a comparison of the leadership of Lee, Grant, and Sherman in the last year of the war. Looks like he's going to rate them in that order.

Roanoke, Va., November 10, 1941

You know a great man can take a defeat and still be great. Lee is one of the few in history who took it and was still great in after life. I think Washington could have done it. Maybe Lincoln could. Alexander couldn't, neither could dozens of others who fill pages of history. We are in the midst of one of the periods of history—and that is what sometimes gives your old man the headache and the pain in the middle. If I could only use the historical background to see what's to be expected—then there'd be no headache. What we do is of vital importance to our daughter's generation and the next one.

...Kiss Margie, love to you, Harry

Kim

Author-Rudyard Kipling, 1865-1936
Read by Mark Twain, 1835-1910
American Writer

About a year after Kipling's visit in Elmira, George Warner came into our library one morning in Hartford with a small book in his hand and asked me if I had ever heard of Rudyard Kipling. I said, "No."

He said I would hear of him very soon and that the noise he was going to make would be loud and continuous. The little book was the *Plain Tales* and he left it for me to read, saying it was charged with a new and inspiring fragrance and would blow a refreshing breath around the world that would revive the nations. A day or two later he brought a copy of the *London World*, which had a sketch of Kipling in it and a mention of the fact that he had traveled in the United States. According to this sketch he had passed through Elmira. This remark, added to the additional fact that he hailed from India, attracted my attention— also Susy's. She went to her room and brought his card from its place in the frame of her mirror, and the Quarry Farmer visitor stood identified.

I am not acquainted with my own books but I know Kipling's—at any rate I know them better than I know anybody else's books. They never grow pale to me; they keep their color; they are always fresh. Certain of the ballads have a peculiar and satisfying charm for me. To my mind, the incomparable *Jungle Books* must remain unfellowed permanently. I think it was worth the journey to India to qualify myself to read Kim understandingly and to realize how great a book it is. The deep and subtle fascinating charm of India pervades no other book as it pervades *Kim*; *Kim* is pervaded by it as by an atmosphere. I read the book every year.

Wealth of Nations

Author- Adam Smith, 1723-1790
Read by John Tyler, 1790-1862
10th President of the United States

In 1802 John Tyler traveled to Williamsburg to enter the secondary division of the College of William and Mary. The twelve-year-old boy boarded in town with his brother-in-law, Judge James Semple. In 1806 his name first appeared on the roll of the collegiate students, although it is probable he began college-level studies a year earlier. The curriculum at the time was a narrow one, but in his undergraduate years Tyler was introduced to history and political economy. The text used in the economics course was Adam Smith's recently published *Wealth of Nations*, and Tyler seems to have committed its concepts and leading arguments to memory. His subsequent speeches on the tariff and free trade were drawn almost verbatim from this influential work. Indeed, Smith's persuasive arguments for government noninterference in the sphere of individual enterprise neatly complemented emerging states' rights arguments in the field of economic policy, and Tyler was quick to enlist them in the South's struggle against all latitudinal constructions of the Constitution on tariff and trade questions.

The most important single fact that can be derived from John Tyler's formative years is that he absorbed *in toto* the political, social, and economic views of his distinguished father, John Tyler, Sr., Revolutionary War patriot, governor of Virginia, and judge of the United States Circuit Court. Judge Tyler was a congenital rebel and individualist, an intellectual child of the French Enlightenment, devoted in person, idea, and political loyalty to his friend and contemporary, Thomas Jefferson. These qualities and attitudes he passed undiluted to his son, and the William and Mary faculty saw that they stuck.

—Robert Seager II

Dissertation on the Progress of Ethical Philosophy

Author- James Mackintosh, 1765-1832
Read by Jones Very, 1813-1880
Author, "Essays and Poems"

Very developed the habit of keeping a record of books read and admired, copying into notebooks the passages he felt to be important, and adding comments whenever appropriate, or whenever he felt the entries needed clarification or qualification. He filled three notebooks during the next fourteen years. Most of his "Journal for 1833" was devoted to studies undertaken for the classes he conducted at the academy, and to studies intended to be the equivalent of a college course. The "Journal" therefore offers much evidence of Very's involvement with Greek and Latin authors: Homer, the classical dramatists, Plato, Aristotle, Plutarch, Virgil, Cicero, Sallust, Persius, Ovid, Horace, and a number of scholarly commentators.

The first of these corrective influences which Oliver made available to Very was James Mackintosh, the Scottish moral philosopher, from whose *Dissertation on the Progress of Ethical Philosophy* Very frequently quoted. Intentionally eclectic, the work drew heavily upon David Hume, Joseph Butler, and David Hartley. Of the three, the views borrowed from Bishop Butler had special impact on Mackintosh, and through him (as Oliver intended) on Very.

Such views, appropriated by Mackintosh, were transmitted to young Very. But when the time came for Very to build upon his groundwork inherited from eighteenth-century moral philosophy, he left the plodding Mackintosh far behind, although he never quite obliterated the traces.

—Edward Gittleman

Paradise Lost

Author- John Milton, 1608-1674
Read by John H. Vincent, 1832-1920
Episcopal Bishop; originator of
The Chautauqua Movement

John Vincent says that he mastered his grammar to the extent of having all the rules and definitions at tongue's end and was able to parse glibly. "I spent months in thus dissecting Milton's *Paradise Lost*, and I nevertheless still revere the poem and its author."

They were a reading family. Here is a list of the books to which the boys had access in their father's library; the catalogue, if small, is by no means contemptible. On the shelves might be found the *Encyclopedia Americana;* Pitkin's *History of the United States*; Rollin, Gibbon, and Plutarch; Shakespeare, Milton, Bunyan, and *The Spectator;* the poems of Thomson and Pollock; Hervey's *Meditations,* and some book by Lardner, but whether by Dionysius or Nathaniel is not manifest. Himrod Vincent owned as a matter of course certain of Wesley's writings, and it is to be hoped that the *Journal* was among them; also Clark's *Commentaries* and a fair collection of religious biography. Doubtless the usual amount of current (and ephemeral) denominational literature found its way to the house.

It will be observed that the above list contains no fiction. One would hardly expect to find the works of the Eighteenth-century novelists and Wesley's *Sermons* cheek by jowl. Scott and Cooper would not have been out of place. One can picture the entire household as absorbed in *The Spy and Old Mortality.* I have never heard that Himrod Vincent frowned on books of this nature; he merely regarded them as unprofitable. The boys read *Robinson Crusoe, The Swiss Family Robinson,* and *The Pilgrim's Progress;* the last of the three was not considered fiction.

Plutarch's Lives

Author- Plutarch, 46-120 A.D.
Read by Lew Wallace, 1827-1905
Civil War General; Novelist, "Ben Hur"

In the State House library he made the acquaintance of Irving and Cooper, whose vistas succeeded those of Olney's *Geography* and *The Life of Daniel Boone*. "My name was Idleness," he testified fifty years later, "except that I read—every moment that I was still I was reading." The book that stayed with him longest was *Plutarch's Lives*; here were military heroes far enough removed from the turgid Hoosier scene, but he had the magic ability to see them and hear them and forget that he was turning pages.

But he was not a recluse. He took part in one of the Indianapolis Thespian Corps' performances of *Pocahontas*, a vigorous blank-verse play by Robert Dale Owen; William Wallace was the heroine, and Lewis, her sister "Numony." Here was first manifested a lifelong sympathy with the theater. Henceforth Wallace often thought and acted dramatically, even melodramatically.

In 1843, he took down from David Wallace's shelves, still accessible, a new three-volume work by the great Prescott: the *253*.

253. In this the apprentice hewer of tales saw his block of marble: "As a history, how delightful it was!" he rhapsodized in 1896, "as a tale, how rich in attractive elements!— adventure, exploration, combat, heroisms, oppositions of fate and fortune, characters for sympathy, characters for detestation, civilization and religion in mortal issue." And, not having heard of two forgotten novels by Robert Montgomery Bird, he believed that the field was "absolutely untouched" in fiction.

—Irving McKee

Abraham Lincoln

Read by John Wanamaker, 1838-1922
Postmaster General, 1889-1893,
President Harrison's Cabinet, Founder
Wanamakers in Philadelphia, 1876

Lincoln is the great American example of the boy developing into the full-rounded man.

From his humble birth to his tragic death, as you read his life story, you will realize that everything he did he did—With all his Strength, With all his Mind, With all his Heart, With all his Will.

Lincoln was a boy among boys. He was full of animal spirits. He delighted in childish pranks. He liked to play. He had his favorite swimming hole, like other boys. He had his boyish tragedies and his boyish comedies. He was intensely human.

From the time his father Thomas Lincoln put an ax into Abe's hands and together they built their first log cabin in their new home in Indiana, to the very day of his death, Lincoln was a man of great physical strength, energy and endurance.

Abe's neighbors said he was lazy. Abe himself once said that "his father taught him to work, but he never learned him to love it." Often while working on a neighbor's farm he would gather the men about the stump which he was trying to uproot, and in his droll manner tell them a story. This story-telling habit Lincoln never lost, and later in his life, when he was plunged in the depths of his country's misery and despair, he himself said that it was his one safety valve which prevented him from going insane.

But there was something going on in the MIND of this tall, gaunt boy which made a neighbor once stop when he passed Abe sitting on a rail fence, and say to his son: "Mark my word, John, that boy will make a great man of himself some day."

The Mary Gloster

Author- Rudyard Kipling, 1865-1936
Read by Earl Warren, 1891-1974
U. S. Supreme Court Chief Justice

Warren's books, by and large, were those of a serious, thoughtful man. On shelves nestled books about and by U. S. Supreme Court Justices. These included biographies of Holmes and Cardozo; books by Hughes, and Brandeis, and Douglas' *Almanac of Liberty* and, interestingly, a small old volume entitled *Early Days in California: Attempted Assassination of Justice Field.*

In the center of the room on a round mahogany table next to his twin bed rested a new large-size, color-illustrated Bible given to the Chief Justice by his youngest son, Bobby. Following a lifetime habit, Warren tried to make it a practice of reading the Bible a few minutes daily, when rising and retiring.

In addition, these books also were neatly piled up on his night table: Sandburg's *Abraham Lincoln: The Prairie Years,* lawyer Lloyd Paul Stryker's *The Art of Advocacy,* Alan Barth's *Government by Investigation,* sports autobiographer Grantland Rice's *The Tumult and The Shouting* and *Our Spiritual Recovery* by Edward Elston, President Eisenhower's pastor. Sandwiched in between were *Conservatism in America, The Faulkner Reader, Constitutional Law Principles, A Long Line of Ships, The Supreme Court in U.S. History, The Nuremberg Case, The Olympics, Legal Aid in the U. S., Everyday Life in Ancient Times* and various nature books about fish and wildlife. One can only guess how many he actually read or merely skimmed.

—Jack Pollack

Webster's Spelling Book

Author- Noah Webster, 1758-1843
Read by Booker T. Washington, 1856-1915
Educator; Orator; Author, "Up From Slavery";
Member, American Hall of Fame

From the time that I can remember having any thoughts about anything, I recall that I had an intense longing to learn to read. I determined when quite a small child, that, if I accomplished nothing else in life, I would in some way get enough education to enable me to read common books and newspapers. Soon after we got settled in some manner in our new cabin in West Virginia, I induced my mother to get hold of a book for me. How or where she got it I do not know, but in some way she procured an old copy of Webster's "blue-black" spelling book, which contained the alphabet, followed by such meaningless words as "ab," "ba," "ca," "da." I began at once to devour this book, and I think that it was the first one I ever had in my hands. I had learned from somebody that the way to begin to read was to learn the alphabet, so I tried in all the ways I could think of to learn it—all of course without a teacher, for I could find no one to teach me. At that time there was not a single member of my race anywhere near us who could read, and I was too timid to approach any of the white people. In some way, within a few weeks, I mastered the greater portion of the alphabet. In all my efforts to learn to read, my mother shared fully my ambition and sympathized with me and aided me in every way that she could.

WHEN you read the best books, you will have as the guests of your mind the best thoughts of the best men.

—Grenville Kleiser

Contemplations, Moral and Divine

Author- Sir Matthew Hale, 1609-1676
Read by George Washington, 1732-1799
1st President of the United States

The instruction of Washington at home was good and pure. He was early taught the rudiments of learning, in what was then called a "field school," by a village schoolmaster who rejoiced in the name of Hobby. This man was one of his father's tenants, and joined the profession of schoolmaster with the more melancholy business of sexton. It is not probable that George learned very much in that school, as the old schoolmaster had a habit of getting drunk whenever one of his pupils had a birthday. But the teaching at home was of a better sort. In addition to the scriptures, in which he was daily taught, he read and pondered Sir Matthew Hale's *Contemplations, Moral and Divine*—a great book which told the secret of a great man's worth and success. This very volume, out of which Washington was taught by his mother, is still preserved at Mount Vernon.

He was next entrusted to a Mr. Williams, whose school he attended from the home of his brother, and from whom he learned a knowledge of accounts, in which he was always skillful. He also studied under Williams geometry, trigonometry, and surveying, in which he became adept, writing out his examples in the neatest and most careful manner. All the school instruction which Washington ever received was thus completed before he was sixteen.

—Louis Albert Bank

The Library and Thomas A. Watson

1854-1934
Associate of Alexander Graham Bell

I spent days in the Public Library in search of some suggestion that would lift us out of the slough. One day in a fit of desperation, remembering my experience with the "spirits" and being still of the belief that it really was spirits that did the table tipping and slate writing, I decided to consult a medium (without Bell's knowledge) and see if there was any help to be got from that source. I read the advertisements of mediums in newspapers, which were numerous at the time, and selected one by a woman whose announcement seemed convincing, and arranged with her a seance. But she gave me such rubbish I never afterwards tried to get the spirits to give the telephone a boost.

I went back to the books of the Public Library as a more certain source of inspiration. One dreary day in November, when Bell was away and my depression at its deepest, I ran across something there in a book on the telegraph that started our experimental machinery going again. It was a description of a quick-acting magnet used in the Hughes Printing Telegraph, quite similar in principle to some we had already used but more delicately constructed. The word—quick acting—struck me at once for that was the first essential for a telephone magnet. It wasn't many minutes before I was back at the laboratory rummaging in a big box of scraps for the materials to construct a magnet like the one of which I had been reading. I found part of what I wanted there and then rushed down to Williams' for the rest of the stuff I needed. In an hour or two, I had the new magnet ready. From that moment all telephones requiring electromagnets and batteries went into the discard.

America's First Traveling Book Salesman

Parson Mason Weems, 1759-1825
Physician; Author, "The Life of
George Washington," the book that
became the role model for Lincoln

Obituary of Parson Weems appearing in the Raleigh, North Carolina, *Register*, July 23, 1825:

In Beaufort, S.C. on the 23rd of May last, after a long and painful indisposition, the Rev. Mason L. Weems, of Dumfries, Va. well known as the author of the Life of Washington, and various other popular works, which have passed through numerous editions, and have had a most extensive circulation. He was a man of very considerable attainments both as a scholar, a physician and divine. His philanthrophy and benevolence were unbounded. Early in life he liberated his patrimonial slaves, from conscientious motives, and voluntarily commenced a career of incessant bodily toil, to disseminate moral and religious books in various remote and destitute portions of the country. From Pennsylvania to the frontiers of Georgia was the principal theatre of his indefatigable labors, and it is supposed on good authority, in the course of his life he has been instrumental in circulating nearly a million copies of the scriptures and other valuable works. That in this laborious calling he was principally actuated by an expanded philanthropy, is proved by his entire neglect of the means of accumulating a large fortune and dying in comparative poverty. His very eccentricities, for failings they could not be called, were the eccentricities of genius and benevolence. He finally fell a martyr to his arduous exertions to do good, and died in the full enjoyment of faith, and blessed hope of immortality.

The Spectator

Author- Joseph Addison, 1672-1719
Read by Isaac Watts, 1674-1748
Theologian; Hymn Writer,
"O God, Our Help in Ages Past",
"When I Survey the Wondrous Cross"

There is so much virtue in eight volumes of *Spectator,* such a reverence of things sacred, so many valuable remarks for our conduct in life, that they are not improper to lie in parlours or summer-houses, to entertain our thoughts in any moments of leisure.

"If I can any way contribute to the diversion or improvement of the country in which I live, I shall leave it, when I am summoned out of it, with the secret satisfaction of thinking that I have not lived in vain."

The *Spectator,* no. l (March 1, 1711)

"The spacious firmament on high,
With all the blue ethereal sky,
And spangled heavens, a shining frame,
Their great Original proclaim."

The *Spectator,* no. 465 (August 23, 1712)

"For wheresoe'er I turn my ravished eyes,
Gay gilded scenes and shining prospects rise,
Poetic fields encompass me around,
And still I seem to tread on classic ground."

A Letter from Italy (1703)

Commentaries

Author- Julius Caesar, 100-44 B.C.
Read by "Mad Anthony" Wayne, 1745-1796
Revolutionary War General

Anthony Wayne's self-directed military education was the outgrowth of his times and his boyhood drilling, his father's sporadic soldiering, and a strong Wayne family tradition in arms.

His first reading of military history was Caesar's *Commentaries*, a good and bad beginning. As exciting as were the triumphs of the legions, the author's self-esteem so pervaded the text that Wayne must have caught a store of it to add to the goodly quantity gained from his own family heritage. Marshal Saxe's memoirs, *Mes Reveries*, a military classic, stirred his fervor as well. Carlyle might say the Saxe memoirs were "a strange military farrago" and that they must have been composed under the influence of opium, but they did have a place in the self-education of one of America's leading combat generals.

As a result, by the time he had become an important officer in the Continental Army, Wayne was perhaps better versed in the history and methods of warfare than any of his brother generals, even the bookstore keeper, Henry Knox. He discovered in early years what William Cobbett described as the "joy of reading," though Caesar must have been a bit more dull for Wayne than Jonathan Swift's was for Cobbett. Unfortunately for Wayne, books were not readily obtainable when he needed them later in the Georgia and Ohio forests. Although the quantity of one's "common sense" is presumed to be innate, there can be no doubt that the capacity to judge soundly in military matters quite as much as in lay affairs often is nourished and brought into fuller flowering by the extent of one's reading.

—Glenn Tucker

Don Quixote

Author- Miguel de Cervantes, 1547-1616
Read by Daniel Webster, 1782-1852
U. S. Senator, Secretary of State

Daniel seemed to have been born knowing how to read. And whatever he read he learned. He memorized Watts's Psalms and recited them to the teamsters as he took care of their horses.

The first school Daniel attended was held in a log cabin. There he found that he was at least the equal of his first teachers and that most of his early education would have to come from his own reading. Books were hard to come by in the village, but he read everything he found, discovering Addison in a tiny circulating library, committing Pope's *Essay on Man* to memory from a pamphlet edition brought home by his father, mastering a Latin grammar that fell into his hands by chance.

Dr. Samuel Wood was one in a long line of older men who recognized the special talents of Daniel Webster and volunteered to push him forward. A Dartmouth graduate, himself, and one of the leading clergymen in the Merrimack valley, Wood prepared more than a hundred young men for college, many of them at his own expense. Under Wood's tutelage, Webster began to study Greek and to read the Latin classics. He also discovered the Boscawen Social Library with about two hundred volumes, including works by Milton, Pope, Thomson, and Cowper. It was here that he first encountered *Don Quixote*, a book which so fired his imagination that he devoured it in a single sitting. In August, the boy returned to Salisbury, only three miles distance, and prepared for the more momentous journey to Dartmouth. He made the trip on horseback, his head crammed with new knowledge, and a feather bed tied to his saddle. He was fifteen years old.

—Irving H. Bartlett

The Real Origin of Methodism: The Mother of John Wesley

Mrs. Wesley's education in the splendid religious environment of her father's house, and her diligent self-improvement during her married life, gave superior qualifications for the training of the school in the home.

"I insist," she says. "in conquering the will of children betimes, because this is the only strong and rational foundation of a religious education, without which both precept and example will be ineffectual, but when this is thoroughly done then is a child capable of being governed by the reason and piety of its parents, till its own understanding comes to maturity, and the principles of religion have taken root in the mind."

To begin the child's education was better than a banquet, and the first effort must, if possible, be a decided success. In the school hours of the learner's first day the alphabet was acquired. The second day spelling and reading began in the Holy Scriptures, with the Book of Genesis. Much stress was laid on good reading and writing. Then came the multiplication table, elementary mathematics, grammar, history, and geography. The drill which John acquired in grammar flowered out into his later authorship of short grammars for the study of English, French, Latin, Greek, and Hebrew. Reading aloud became a specialty with the older children, from such authors as Milton and Shakespeare. John Wesley declared that his sister Emilia was the best reader of poetry he had ever heard. The wise mother drilled the mental faculties, the "memory drill" being another specialty.

"Why do you go over the same thing with that child the twentieth time?" said the rector impatiently to his wife.

"Because," said she, "nineteen times were not sufficient. If I had stopped after telling him nineteen times, all my labor would have been lost."

A Bridge Too Far

Author- Cornelius Ryan, 1896-
Read by Theodore White, 1915-1986
Journalist; Author, "The Making
of the President" series

Cornelius Ryan's *A Bridge Too Far* sweeps you off to adventure. The story begins softly with the sound of horses' hooves, church bells, village clatter in occupied Holland, on the banks of the Rhine. Then the Dublin violinist tunes up. The theme comes in now, hard. It is only sixty-four miles from the Allied bridgehead on the Dutch border to the Rhine crossing at the great bridge of Arnhem. A swoop, a dash, an ultimate act can grab that road, seize that bridge, and once across the Rhine at Arnhem—the Ruhr lies naked, Germany can be gutted, the war closed. The air fills then with the sound of planes as the greatest airborne army in history prepare for the swoop. Then you are in battle: the Irish Guards, pressing the snouts of their single-file tank column into ambuscade as they spearhead the push to reach the paratroops; Gavin's 82nd Division Americans crossing the river in canvas landing craft to seize the bridge at Nijmegan; and the doomed handful of Frost's 2nd Battalion holding the bridgehead of Arnhem, promised relief in forty-eight hours, waiting and dying for seven days, spending their last ammunition as gallant misers.

The story of *A Bridge Too Far* is all story—but is also stunning history. His merciless treatment of Field Marshal Montgomery is accompanied by Eisenhower's excoriating recollection of Montgomery's personality and generalship; Ryan's treatment of the command confusion in the leaderless First British Airborne Division is based on contemporary logs and direct interviews with the participants. His reconstruction of the German response comes not only from the German battle archives but their field commander.

Leaves of Grass

Author- Walt Whitman, 1819-1892
Read by William Allen White, 1868-1944
Kansas Newspaper Editor,
"The Sage of Emporia"

In the spring of 1891, I bought *Leaves of Grass* and became for the time inebriated with Walt Whitman's philosophy. I don't know how I came to buy that book. I had known of Whitman casually as a student of American literature knows a poet. Professor Canfield who was a beacon of light and leading in my life, may have turned my mind to Whitman. I don't remember. But the amazing thing about my madness was that I did not in any way connect the Whitman democracy with the Farmer's Alliance. For here, parading down Main Street, was a barbaric yawp if ever there was one—a pure Whitmanesque picture! I was ten years making it all out! In those ten years two poets, entirely different, almost antagonistic, held me enthralled—Walt Whitman and Rudyard Kipling. I fear that Kipling's philosophy, rather than Whitman's, colored my mind in its practical attitudes toward life. But the two must have jangled and left me disturbed and uncertain. Later I tried to imitate Kipling, but in the early nineties what I wrote still was a pale moonlit shadow of Riley and Eugene Field. My mother, who loved Tennyson and Whittier, exposed me to her favorites, left them in my room, sometimes read them. I liked them. I was polite to them. Often I sat alone browsing in them, sometimes reading a page or a poem; but I was bound to my idols—Whitman, the great democrat, and Kipling, the imperialist. These I took under my arm when I went girling under the spring moon, which was often. What a pest I must have been to three or four girls in that town, who had something else on their minds as they should have had!

Novels of Sir Walter Scott, 1771-1832

Read by Walt Whitman, 1819-1892
Poet; Author, "Leaves of Grass"

"If you could reduce the leaves to their elements," he was to tell Traubel, "you would see Scott unmistakably active at the roots." He read Cooper's *The Spy*, *The Last of the Mohicans* and *Red Rover*, a tale of insurgency and ocean adventure that stirred him up "clarionlike: I read it many times." He became and remained "a most omnivorous novel-reader."

At eleven, all the formal schooling he was to have behind him, Walt worked as an office boy for a firm of lawyers, James B. Clarke and his son Edward, on lower Fulton Street. They gave him a window nook to himself, and he remembered gratefully.

"Edward C. help'd me at my handwriting and composition, and, (the signal event of my life up to that time,) subscribed for me to a big circulating library. For a time I now revel'd in romance-reading of all kinds—first, the 'Arabian Nights,' all the volumes, an amazing treat. Then, sorties in very many other directions, took in Walter Scott's novels, one after the other, and his poetry."

—Justin Kaplin

SIR WALTER SCOTT:
"True love's the gift which God has given
To man alone beneath the heaven:
It is not fantasy's hot fire,
Whose wishes, soon as granted, fly;
It liveth not in fierce desire,
With dead desire it doth not die;
It is the secret sympathy,
The silver link, the silken tie,
Which heart to heart and mind to mind
In body and in soul can bind."

A Catalogue of Books

Read by Eli Whitney, 1765-1825
Inventor of the Cotton Gin;
Member, American Hall of Fame

To Whitney the library and the museum were banquet tables spread with new and nourishing foods on which his special talents fed. One of the items he always treasured was the catalogue of books in the Library of Yale-College in which is inscribed, "The Authority of the College induced by the esteem and regard which they have for Mr. Eli Whitney, Junior Sophister, present this valuable pamphlet for the trifling consideration of nine pence lawful money."

The library had about 2,700 volumes—about the size of John Adams' private collection—but almost a third of the books were obsolete, having been given by Dean Berkeley in 1733; the rest were in deplorable condition. But the library could boast that its copy of the *Principia* had been presented by Sir Isaac Newton himself. The charge for use of the books varied from nine cents a month for a folio to a penny for a pamphlet; it was double for all books which were "recited."

"Libraries are the shrines where all the relics of the ancient saints, full of true virtue, and that without delusion or imposture, are preserved and reposed."
—Francis Bacon

Great Women and Books

EMMA HART WILLARD, 1787-1870
Pioneer in Education

She was the 16th of her father's 17 children, and the 9th of the 10 children borne by the second Mrs. Hart to her husband. The Hart household provided a good deal of intellectual nourishment—Mr. Hart discoursed to the children on American history and on the philosophies of John Locke and George Berkeley, while Mrs. Hart enthralled them with readings from Chaucer, Shakespeare, and Milton. A Jeffersonian liberal, Mr. Hart encouraged his daughters, especially the inquisitive Emma, to develop their minds.

—Joan Marlow

MERCY WARREN, 1728-1814
Poet, Historian

Mercy Warren was born in Barnstable, Massachusetts, in 1728. When she was eleven, her brother James went off to Harvard; Mercy remained at home reading Sir Walter Raleigh's history. But Mercy Warren not only read history, she lived and recorded it. A woman of her temperament and ability would doubtless have found ways to participate in the great events of life. Mrs. Warren had other reasons. Her husband, her brother, and all her male acquaintances were playing exciting and meaningful roles, and Mercy Warren was not one to hide behind her femininity. "At a period when every manly arm was occupied," she wrote in the preface of her history, "and every trait of talent or activity engaged...I have been induced to improve the leisure Providence has lent, to record as they passed...new and unexperienced events..."

—Bert Loewenberg

Frederick Douglass

Author- Booker T. Washington, 1856-1915
Read by Talcott Williams, 1849-1928
1st director, Columbia School of Journalism

The life of the most distinguished man of African descent in the last generation by the most distinguished man of the race in this generation, *Frederick Douglass*, by Dr. Booker T. Washington, has as much interest for the author as its subject. Out of a narrative, already told, so that no new facts are added, Dr. Washington, consciously or unconsciously, weaves a defense of his own policy and position. In the initiative, the eloquence, the energy, the opportunism, the pleas for industrial education, the liberal religious views and the emancipation from the prejudices of his own race, the head of Tuskegee plainly sees the justification of his own course. He is attacked by his own race, charged with taking a position too moderate on the rights of his fellows, criticized for his alliance with the more moderate friends of his people, and widely assailed for his compromises—all this was also true of Frederick Douglass. To the familiar record of Douglass' life, slavery, his escape, his share in the early abolition agitation, and his conspicuous leadership in the decade before the Civil War, his new biographer gives a vivid and pithy description. Every page is alive with sympathy, with comprehension, with insight of the special position of Douglass. The story of this struggle has not before been told with such intelligent vigor and clear perspective. A fresh admiration must be felt by every reader for both men and the mingled blood and common experience which has created both. Our American system has done much that will be remembered: but one achievement history will not forget is that it has given the negro his first national career, and begun the practical communion of humanity.

War As I Knew It

**Author- Gen. George S. Patton, Jr.,
1885-1945
Read by Porter Williamson
Served with Patton in World War II;
Author, "Patton's Principles"**

In his own book, Gen. Patton gives the full text of his Letter of Instruction to his Commanders on Discipline. Gen. Patton states, "There is only one sort of discipline—PERFECT DISCIPLINE." (caps used in his letter!)

I heard Gen. Patton explain perfect discipline as instant discipline. He often stated, "No one can avoid discipline! To delay punishment for breaking discipline increases the punishment! The child who is not disciplined by his parents will be disciplined by school, police, jail or by self. Self-discipline may be as severe as death." Gen. Patton made such statements in 1941. This basic principle of discipline is evident today as we battle cocaine, and our athletes break discipline and die from drugs. Discipline is a law of Nature.

Perfect discipline gives instant punishment. The finger that touches a hot stove will never touch a hot stove again!

In the preface to the great historian, Douglas S. Freeman, writes, "Gen. Patton wrote in a tone so unmistakable and so clearly patriotic that it will not be misunderstood by historians." *War As I Knew* It is an accurate report of the campaign in Africa and Europe.

from Patton's cavalry journal, 1933:

"Wars may be fought with weapons, but they are won by men. It is the spirit of the men who follow and of the man who leads that gains the victory."

Varieties of Religious Experience

Author- William James, 1842-1910
Read by Bill Wilson, 1895-1971
Co-Founder of Alcoholics Anonymous

At Stewart's they were never more than a small handful but Bill knew immediately and instinctively that these were his people. He could say anything to them, they anything to him, and it would be all right.

It was with them that Bill learned that even his experience at Towns was not unique. He could never recollect if it had been Ebby or Roland who gave him a copy of William James's *Varieties of Religious Experience*, but he remembered the impact of the book. It was James's theory that spiritual experiences could have a very definite objective reality and might totally transform a man's life. Some of these experiences, James believed, arrived with a sudden burst of light, while others developed more gradually; some, but by no means all, came through religious channels—there were indeed many varieties. All, however, appeared to have one common denominator and that was their source in pain and utter hopelessness. Complete deflation at depth was the one requirement to prepare the recipient and make him ready for a transforming experience.

"Deflation at depth." These words leaped from the page as Bill read them. For what else was hitting bottom except deflation? Wasn't this what had happened to him when Silkworth had condemned him to insanity or death? Wasn't it the story of every ex-drunk he knew?

Powerlessness. Deflation at depth. Then, only then, was an alcoholic made ready. As he read William James, as he reviewed Roland's story, his own story, Bill's mind raced ahead. He saw what had happened: one drunk taking the word to another.

—Robert Thomsen

History of the Second World War

Author- Winston Churchill, 1874-1965
Read by Pete Wilson
U.S. Senator; Governor of California

My favorite historical book is *History of the Second World War* by Winston Churchill. It is an eloquent account of how freedom-loving peoples, through muddled thinking and profound self-deception, permitted dictators to endanger liberty and destroy millions of lives. It should be required reading for every public servant and anyone else who would understand our turbulent century:

"You have no doubt noticed in your reading of British history—and I hope you will take pains to read it, for it is only from the past that one can judge the future, and it is only from reading the story of the British nation, of the British Empire, that you can feel a well-grounded sense of pride to dwell in these islands—you have sometimes noticed in your reading of British history that we have had to hold out from time to time all alone, or to be the mainspring of coalitions, against a Continental tyrant or dictator, and we have had to hold out for quite a long time: against the Spanish Armada, against the might of Louis XIV, when we led Europe for nearly twenty-five years under William III and Marlborough, and a hundred and fifty years ago, when Nelson, Pitt, and Wellington broke Napoleon, not without assistance from the heroic Russians of 1812. In all these world wars our Island kept the lead of Europe or else held out alone.

"And if you hold out alone long enough there always comes a time when the tyrant makes some ghastly mistake which alters the whole balance of the struggle...never since the United States entered the war have I had the slightest doubt that we should be saved, and that we only had to do our duty in order to win."

Life of Lincoln

Read by Woodrow Wilson, 1856-1924
28th President of the United States

Lincoln owed nothing to his birth, everything to his growth; had not training save what he gave himself; no nurture, but only a wild and native strength. His life was schooling, and every day of it gave to his character a new touch of development. His manhood not only, but his perception also, expanded with his life. His eyes, as they looked more and more abroad, beheld the national life, and comprehended it; and the lad who had been so rough-cut a provincial became, when grown to manhood, the one leader in all the nation who held the whole people singly in his heart; held even the Southern people there, and would have won them back. The most valuable thing about Mr. Lincoln was that in the midst of the strain of war, in the midst of the crash of arms, he could sit quietly in his room and enjoy a book that led his thoughts off from everything American, could wander in fields of dreams, while every other man was hot with immediate contest. Always set your faith in a man who can withdraw himself, because only the man who can withdraw himself can see affairs as they are.

We should not be Americans deserving to call ourselves the fellow countrymen of Lincoln if we did not feel the compulsion that his example lays upon us— the compulsion, not to heed him merely but to look to our own duty, to live every day as if that were the day upon which America was to be reborn and remade; to attack every task as if we had something here that was new and virginal and original, out of which we could make the very stuff of life, by integrity, faith in our fellow-men.

Human Understanding

Author- John Locke, 1632-1704
Read by William Wirt, 1772-1834,
Attorney General of the United States,
1817-1829

When I was about fourteen years old, a friend intimated if I would read Locke through twice, and produce a certificate from a gentleman whom he named, that I was master of his meaning. I recollect, when I received this letter; I instantly took to the book. I was soon heels over head among "innate ideas," subjects which I had never before heard of, and on which I had not a single idea of any kind. I stuck to him however intelligently, till I got to his chapter on "Identity and Diversity," and there I stuck fast, in the most hopeless despair; nor did I ever get out of that mire, until I again met with the book in Albemarle, when I was about twenty-three years of age. Even then, as I approached the chapter on Identity and Diversity, I felt as shy as the Scotch parson's horse did, when repassing, in summer, part of a road in which he had stuck fast the preceding winter. Locke is certainly a frigid writer to a young man of high fancy. But whoever wishes to train himself to address the human judgment successfully, ought to make Locke his bosom friend and constant companion. He introduces his reader to a most intimate acquaintance with the structure and constitution of the mind; unfolds every property which belongs to it; shows how alone the judgment can be approached and acted on; through what avenues, and with what degrees of proof, a man may calculate with certainty on its different degrees of assent. Besides this, Locke's book is auxiliary to the same process for which I have been so earnestly recommending the mathematics; that is, giving to the mind a fixed and rooted habit of clear, close, cogent and irresistible reasoning.

Presidents of the United States

Life of Francis Marion
Author- Parson Weems, 1759-1825
Read by James A. Garfield, 1831-1881
20th President of the United States

At night stories are told, the scanty library over-hauled and its precious information repeated without end. There is one book which is a source of never-ending comfort, the Holy Bible.

Among the books were two of great interest to young James, Weem's *Life of Marion*, and Grimshaw's *Napoleon*. "Mother read to me about that great soldier," he says almost every night, and as the martial deeds of the first man of France are recited the boy's eyes dilate, his breast swells, and once he exclaims, enthusiastically, "Mother when I get to be a man, I am going to be a soldier."

—Gen. James S. Brisbin, 1880

Washington and his Generals
Author- George Lippard, 1822-1854
Read by Calvin Coolidge, 1872-1933
30th President of the United States

My grandmother Coolidge liked books and besides a daily Chapter in the Bible read aloud to me *The Rangers or the Tory's Daughter* and *The Green Mountain Boys*, which were both stories of the early settlers of Vermont during the Revolutionary period. She also had two volumes entitled *Washington and His Generals*, and other biographies which I read myself at an early age with a great deal of interest.

At home there were numerous law books. In this way I grew up with a working knowledge of the foundations of my state and nation and a taste for history.

Nickel Library

Read by Frank Lloyd Wright, 1869-1959, American Architect

Books read together: *Hans Brinker*, Ruskin's *Seven Lamps of Architecture*, Jules Verne's *Michael Strogoff, Hector Servadac*, Goethe's *Wilhelm Meister, The Arabian Nights*, as always *Aladdin and his Lamp*—and many tales. Whittier, Longfellow, Bryant. If they were not poets, they were at least, poetic.

A seductive touch upon dreaming life were the enchanting pages of the *Arabian Nights!*

Enchantment, no less, the tattered illiterature of thrills—the Nickel Library—secretly read. Hidden at the reading for hours. The culprit appearing at meal-time—still elsewhere—would fail to answer in time.

Was the Nickel Library really bad? Why would Mother or Father or teacher take the blood-and-thunder tales away and burn them if they caught us with them? Greasy, worn and torn like old bank-notes they would secretly circulate in exchange for a glassie or an aggie or two. One would go from pocket to pocket until it would have to be patched together to be read, fragments maddeningly missing at critical moments. Stark, they were, with the horror of masks and corpses—dripping with gang-gore—but cool with bravery in the constant crash of catastrophe. The bravery thrilled. The daring hero, usually some lad like ourselves, triumphant all the time. Going down, only to come right-side up through scrambled Indians and half-caste cut-throats, carcasses, bowie knives, and cutlasses.

The movie requires no imagination. The Nickel Library did. And all was utterly arranged in every detail to the perfect satisfaction of the girlish heroine whose virtue, meantime, was tested and retested from every possible angle—she too, at the critical moment emerging manhandled but unspotted—with style all the while!

The love of reading enables a man to exchange the wearisome hours of life, which come to every one, for hours of delight.

—Montesquieu

GREAT THOUGHTS
ON READING

It is the books we read before middle life that do most to mold our characters and influence our lives.

—Robert Pitman

How to Read

By Noah Porter, 1811-1892
President, Yale University

The first rule which we prescribe is: read with attention. This is the rule that takes precedence of all others. It stands instead of a score of minor directions. Indeed it comprehends them all, and is the golden rule. To gain the power and habit of attention is the great difficulty to be overcome by young readers when they begin. The one reason why reading is so dull to multitudes of active, eager minds is that they have not acquired the habit of attending to books. The eye may be fastened upon the page, and the mind may follow the lines, and yet the mind not be half awake to the thought of the author, or the best half of its energies may be abroad on some wandering errand. The one evil that comes from omnivorous and indiscriminate reading is that the attention is wearied and overborne by the multitude of the objects that pass before it; that the miserable habit is formed and strengthened of seeming to follow the author when he is half comprehended, of vacantly gazing upon the page that serves just to occupy and excite the fancy without leaving distinct and lasting impressions.

It was said of Edmund Burke, who was a great reader and a great thinker also, that he read every book as if he were never to see it a second time and thus make it his own, a possession for life.

...Rely on your own strength of body and soul. Take for your star self-reliance, faith, honesty and industry. Don't take too much advice—keep at the helm and steer your own ship, and remember that the great art of commanding is to take a fair share of the work. Fire above the mark you intend to hit. Energy, invincible determination with the right motive, are the levers that move the world.

Self Education from Books

By Burton Rascoe, 1891-1957
Critic; Literary Editor of the New York Tribune

M. Lincoln Schuster wrote a paper in which he voiced a truth more general than obvious. He began:

"College graduates who do not know how to read constitute a major indictment of American educational methods and a constant challenge to the country's publishers and booksellers.

"Large numbers of college graduates do know how to read, in the fullest sense, but there are far too many whose acute apathy might be described as an occupational disease. To observant teachers and candid publishers, this statement is a commonplace of the day's work."

For myself I must confess that, culturally, I got very little out of high school and almost nothing out of college; but out of the books I read in the public library when I was in high school and in the college when I was in university I got a great deal. I have often said I quit college before taking my degree because I found that college was interfering too much with my education. That may sound facetious, but it is the solemn truth. Cut-and-dried class routine and "disciplinary" homework cut seriously into the time I was able to put in at the library to satisfy my consuming desire for an education, my curiosity about life, men and emotions, the things of the heart and intellect that are expressed in the art of the written word.

The best-educated men and women I have known have been self-educated. This is true even of those who have been to college; for they did not go to college with an attitude, so often prevailing among students, of "I dare you to educate me!" but with an eagerness to learn, an eagerness that sent them to good books even when they found their classroom work dull, stale and unprofitable.

Original Thinkers Read

By William Mathews, L.L.D., 1818-1909
Editor, Founder, "The Yankee Blade"

The most original thinkers have been most ready to acknowledge their obligations to other minds, whose wisdom has been lived in books. Gibbon acquired from his aunt "an early and invincible love of reading, which," he declared, "he would not exchange for the treasures of India." Doctor Franklin traced his entire career to Cotton Mathers' *Essays to Do Good*, which fell into his hands when he was a boy. The current of Jeremy Bentham's thoughts was directed for life by a single phrase, "The greatest good for the greatest number," caught as the end of a pamphlet. Cobbett, at eleven, bought Swift's *Tale of a Tub*, and it proved what he considered a sort of "birth of intellect." The genius of Faraday was fired by the volumes which he perused while serving as an apprentice to an English bookseller. One of the most distinguished personages in Europe, showing his library to a visitor, observed that not only this collection, but all his social successes in life, he traced back to "the first franc he saved from the cake shop to spend at a bookstall." Lord Macaulay, having asked an eminent soldier and diplomatist, who enjoyed the confidence of the first generals and statesmen of the age, to what he owed his accomplishments, was informed that he ascribed it to the fact that he was quartered, in his young days, in the neighborhood of an excellent library, to which he had access. The French historian Michelet attributed his mental inspiration to a single book, a Virgil, he lived with for some years; and he tells us an odd volume of Racine, picked up at a stall on the quay, made the poet of Toulon.

Novels and Novel-Reading

By Martin Ballou, 1820-1895
Publisher; Founder, "Boston Globe"

Gray thought it the height of earthly felicity to lie on a sofa all day long and read French novels, and there are few persons who can plead not guilty to having, at some time in their lives, devoured novels with more eagerness than any other works of literature. We are afraid to guess how many mathematicians have been beguiled from the problems of Euclid by the romances of Scott; and as for enumerating the boarding-school misses who have wept themselves blind over the *Sorrows of the Werther,* it would be like attempting to count the sands on the seashore. Presses have groaned, pulpits have fulminated against this passion for fiction; all to no purpose: novelists have found twenty times as many readers as historians or essayists. The love of fictitious tales is not a local or temporary passion; the oldest nations had their fables and parables, and centuries ago the bearded Oriental listened with grave delight to the romance of the itinerant storyteller. The troubador amused the illiterate knights of the age of chivalry, as Scott delighted their descendants. But it is only of late that sound moralists, instead of uselessly arguing against a popular taste, have wisely turned it to account.

It is somewhat curious to remark the changes of style and character that novels have undergone in modern days. Some very excellent stories—among them Miss Edgeworth's—had been written, when the genius of Scott flashed upon the literary world like an Aurora Borealis. The popularity he attained induced writers of all opinions and classes to adopt the novel as the best means of securing the popular ear, and we have had novels historical, philosophical, polemical, didactic, military, nautical; in a word, every theme that human intellect pursues has been treated in a novel form.

What to Read

By Bruce Barton, 1886-1967
U.S. Congressman; Business Executive;
Author, "The Man Nobody Knows"

A mother asked me recently to recommend a list of books for her boy to read.

I answered:

Start him with a "Life of Lincoln"; then a "Life of Washington"; then a "Life of Cromwell"; and Franklin's autobiography. When he was read these, I will recommend some more.

Do not buy these books for him. Take him to a bookstore and let him buy them for himself. Let his library be his own library. The love of books is an intoxicating habit, like the love of liquor. If more boys were taught to haunt bookstores, fewer of them would haunt saloons.

Then I went on to say:

And don't forget that the best and biggest and wisest book lies all around him and costs nothing. Do not let your boy grow up without some knowledge of the miracle of creation as it is exhibited in the growth of a garden of flowers.

These books that I have recommended are the biographies of mighty men. Nature is the autobiography of Almighty God.

No matter where you live or how busy you are, help your boy to make a garden. Perhaps you are penned up in an apartment. Never mind. Let him plant something, if it be only a packet of seeds in a window-box.

By all means, teach your boy the love of good books. But do not let him hold his books so close to his eyes that he fails to read the greatest mystery serial story in the world—the serial story of which God writes a new and more wonderful installment every spring.

As a Nation Reads

By Richard Sill Holmes 1842-1912
Registrar, Chautauqua Movement 1887

The shops of booksellers have shelves filled with the treasures of the ages, but in the windows given to advertising are novels, novels, novels. Melodrama long ago drove the essay to the last place in the corner by the rear wall of the bookshop. Look over the shoulder of the pretty girl in the chair next you in the parlor car. You will find her reading "The Prodigal Judge." Who ever saw even a college girl reading "Sartor Resartus" or "The Diamond Necklace" on a railway train? Perhaps the title of "Diamond Necklace" might captivate her, but the reading of two pages of Carlyle's masterly vigor would condemn humor and satire and history to the limbo of the ash barrel. If the boy and girl readers of to-day become the fathers and mothers of to-morrow, what will their children read? Will they follow in the path of "Lydia Languish" and hide their books from the vigilant scrutiny of the Argus-eyed aunt when she appears? Abraham Lincoln was made on the dirt floor of a log cabin by three great books— the Bible, Shakespere, and Blackstone. Are America's future Lincolns being so made today?

The hour has struck for a new renaissance—a reading renaissance. Will the bell stroke be heard by America's reading millions?

We heard the question asked recently: "Why was there no 'dark horse' run in the race for the presidential nominations?" The answer came without hesitation: "There are no 'dark horses.'" Is it true? Have our "simple great ones gone forever and ever by?" What has produced the dearth? We have given the answer already. As a nation reads, so are its deeds, and we have become a people whose only reading is "words, words, words."

How and What to Read

By Mary Haskett
Author, "A Noble Life," 1919-

One's reading is usually a fair index of one's character. Abstain from those books which, while thy have some good things about them, have also an admixture of evil. You can not afford to read a bad book however good you are. "The influence is insignificant," do you say? I reply that the scratch of a pin has sometimes produced lockjaw.

Inferior books are to be rejected in an age when we are courted by whole libraries and when no man's life is long enough to compass even those which are good and great and famous. Why should we bow down at puddles, when we can approach freely to the crystal spring head? To read with profit, the book must be of a kind calculated to inform the mind, correct the head, and better the heart. These books should be read with attention, understood, remembered and their precepts put in practice.

To those who plead the want of time to read, we would say, Be as frugal of your hours as you are your dollars, and you can create time in the busiest day. The time you devote to reading good books is time well spent.

Of all the books ever written, not one contains such instructive and such sublime reading and so great a variety of it as the Bible. Resolve to read it. You will find realities there more wonderful than any picture of fiction drawn by the finest pencilings of the master-hand of the most practised novelist that has shone in the dazzling galaxy of ancient or modern writers.

We should read slowly and try to remember what we read. Reading is good pastime for young and old. We should not neglect so important a duty as reading. It is a duty we owe to ourselves and our families.

McGuffey's Reader
By E.R. Eastman
Author, "Journey To The Day Before Yesterday"

Aside from the Bible, there are few books which have had as much influence in molding the lives of young people growing up Day Before Yesterday as the *McGuffey's Readers*. McGuffey was born in 1800. He became a teacher and educator, and in 1836 he was elected president of Cincinnati College. In that same year, the first two volumes in the series of Readers were published. The worth and popularity of these Readers (which finally covered every school grade) are proven by the fact that over 122 million copies were sold between 1836 and 1920. Not only the children but the entire family read them, and no one could read them without getting a fairly good knowledge of the classics and of literature in general. One has only to glance at the list of authors to be impressed...there were John Greenleaf Whittier, Charles Kingsley, Oliver Goldsmith, Leigh Hunt, Henry Wadsworth Longfellow, Nathaniel Hawthorne, William Cullen Bryant, Washington Irving, William Cowper, Daniel Webster, Amy Lowell, George Bancroft, Alfred Lord Tennyson, Thomas More, William M. Thackeray, William Shakespeare, Charles Lamb, Samuel Johnson, and many, many more.

When they were first published, rural papers and similar publications had no pictures in them; and I often wonder how our grandfathers, with their poorly fitted glasses, managed to read the fine print. But the publications of those days had little or no competition. Even at the time when I was a boy, at the turn of this century, reading material was so scarce—at least in rural homes—that anything and everything was eagerly pounced upon and thoroughly read.   Remember the stories of the difficulties Abraham Lincoln had to get something to read? His case was fairly typical of the scarcity of reading matter in his time and for many years afterwards.

The best of a book is not the thought which it contains but the thought which it suggests; just as the charm of music dwells not in the tones but in the echoes of our hearts.

—O.W. Holmes

When you sell a man a book you don't sell him just twelve ounces of paper and ink and glue—you sell him a whole new life.   Love and friendship and humor and ships at sea by night—there's all heaven and earth in a book, a real book I mean.

—Christopher Morley

I hate to read new books.   There are twenty or thirty volumes that I have read over and over again, and these are the only ones that I have any desire to read at all.

—Hazlitt

The first necessity of a book is that it shall be entertaining.   If it is not entertaining, it might almost as well be printed with blue ink on blue paper.   If therefore, the book does not interest me, I consider that I have, prima facie, a right to put it on one side, before it puts me to sleep.

—Edward E. Hale

The man who adds the life of books to the actual life of everyday, lives the life of his whole race.   The man without books lives the life of one individual.

—Jesse Lee Bennett

There is history in all men's lives.

—Shakespeare